Wh

To
Julia

Mineral Analysis	
Typical Values	mg/l
Calcium	44.36
Magnesium	6.41
Potassium	2.23
Sodium	48.19
Bicarbonates	176.81
Chloride	37.11
Sulphate	37.95
Nitrate	1.28
Fluoride	0.20
Dry Residue at 180°C	274.06
pH (at source)	7.79

♲ BOTTLE - PLASTIC
widely recycled

Origin

Bottled at source in Churchstoke, Montgomery, Powys for Co-operative Group Ltd., Manchester M60 0AG
www.coop.co.uk/food

Contact Us

📞 Freephone
0800 0686 727
7 days a week

@ customer.careline
@coop.co.uk

Quoting 'TSB222', the Barcode Number and the Date Code

Advice Best served chilled.
Storage - Once opened keep in fridge and consume within 3 days.

For every litre of this water sold by us and drunk by you we donate 3 pence to The One Foundation. What's so special about 3 pence? Over the past decade those 3 pennies have added up to over 7 million pounds in donations, which has been invested in clean water, sanitation and hygiene projects for those in desperate need.

Photograph ©b-photos.co.uk

Together we've helped over 1.5 million people.

People like Veronica in Malawi who was seriously ill because she had to use contaminated ground water. See how your donations have transformed hers and so many others' lives www.co-operativefood.co.uk/food-matters/fairbournesprings

Mineral Analysis	
Typical Values	mg/l
Calcium	44.36
Magnesium	6.41
Potassium	2.23
Sodium	48.19
Bicarbonates	176.81
Chloride	37.11
Sulphate	37.95
Nitrate	1.28
Fluoride	0.20
Dry Residue at 180°C	274.06
pH (at source)	7.79

♲ BOTTLE - PLASTIC
widely recycled

Origin

Bottled at source in Churchstoke, Montgomery, Powys for Co-operative Group Ltd., Manchester M60 0AG
www.coop.co.uk/food

Contact Us

📞 Freephone
0800 0686 727
7 days a week

@ customer.careline
@coop.co.uk

Quoting 'TSB222', the Barcode Number and the Date Code

Advice Best served chilled.
Storage - Once opened keep in fridge and consume within 3 days.

For every litre of this water sold by us and drunk by you we donate 3 pence to The One Foundation. What's so special about 3 pence? Over the past decade those 3 pennies have added up to over 7 million pounds in donations, which has been invested in clean water, sanitation and hygiene projects for those in desperate need.

Photograph ©b-photos.co.uk

Together we've helped over 1.5 million people.

People like Veronica in Malawi who was seriously ill because she had to use contaminated ground water. See how your donations have transformed hers and so many others' lives at:
www.co-operativefood.co.uk/food-matters/fairbournesprings

For all those who love Lourdes
or who are searching
for a little Lourdes in their lives

Where Echoes Meet

Nine Lives
Changed by Lourdes

Catherine Simon

INTRODUCED BY
ABIGAIL WITCHALLS

P³P

Published in Great Britain 2008
THREE PEAKS PRESS
9 Croesonen Road
Abergavenny
Monmouthshire NP7 6AE
mail@p3p.org   http://p3p.org

Designed & set in Fournier at Three Peaks Press
Book cover illustration by Creative Leap
www.creativeleap.com

With thanks to Marie-Bernarde Soubirous

Printed in Wales at Gwasg Dinefwr, Llandybie

A catalogue record for this publication
is available from the British Library

Contents

Introduction

Abigail Witchalls

I FIRST VISITED LOURDES as a healthy energetic nineteen year old, on my day off from a demanding summer job. I was living and working as a helper in a nearby community for people with learning disabilities. I had come to try and help those I considered to be needy and less fortunate than myself.

Over the course of the summer I discovered that I was receiving far more than I was giving. The people I had come to help became my friends and my teachers, revealing to me my own weaknesses and showing me how to live truthfully. I walked into the sanctuary of Lourdes seeking direction and peace. I found there an atmosphere of joy and was touched by the smiling faces of the pilgrims I passed, particularly those in wheelchairs. And yet I was sceptical and questioning. I wanted to understand their faith, to know the source of their joy; I wanted to experience Lourdes from the 'inside', as a pilgrim not a spectator.

Eight years later I returned (on the 2006 Arundel & Brighton Pilgrimage), now married with two healthy energetic young children, and as a wheelchair user myself. I found myself living the mystery of Lourdes from the 'inside', but it was not as I had expected.

Since my spinal injury the previous year, I had prayed for healing. And now in Lourdes I asked God to 'heal me in the way I need most, according to Your will.' He did heal me – not physically – but He freed me to love life and to know daily the joy I had longed for. To my surprise, I find that I have more to give now that I'm paralysed than I did when I was able-bodied. This is one of God's little miracles.

There are many miracles to witness in this book. Catherine Simon takes us on a journey into the lives of ordinary people who have something extraordinary to teach us about pain and healing. Reading their stories is a pilgrimage in itself. Like a pilgrim in Lourdes, we can find ourselves challenged, moved and strengthened by the testimony of those we encounter. We learn most from the people who are weakest and are changed by the people we were hoping to change. We find healing where we didn't even know we were wounded.

Such is the surprising and transforming work of God. Such is the paradox of the Cross:

> For it is in giving that we receive;
> It is in pardoning that we are pardoned;
> It is in dying that we are born to eternal life.

St Francis of Assisi

You will receive much from the people in this book. They offer you the opportunity to accompany them to the Cross and to find there a place of blessings.

On behalf of the reader, the Arundel & Brighton pilgrims and Pilgrimage Office, and the hundreds of people who share her love for Lourdes, I would like to thank Catherine for her dedication and generosity in writing this book. She has listened to her interviewees with courage and compassion and portrays their stories with honesty and insight. In her humility she says of the experience: 'Now…I know the beginnings of what faith truly tastes like, what pain resembles and what wonders God can achieve.'

With wisdom beyond her years Catherine has captured the spirit of Lourdes and the essence of what it is to be a pilgrim.

Acknowledgements

THIS BOOK has been inspired by a 'beautiful lady' who appeared one hundred and fifty years ago in a little Pyrenean town, whom I could never thank enough.

It has also been a collective effort from so many individuals whom I wish to thank. Firstly, thank you to the Arundel and Brighton Lourdes Committee, and particularly Sarah, who agreed to the project and who has encouraged me all along the way. I am very grateful to all those who have sponsored this project, amongst whom numerous parishes from the Arundel and Brighton diocese. I would like to thank Fr Tom Treherne and Christ the Prince of Peace parish in Weybridge who provided me with a quiet place to write.

My sincerest thanks are in order to Marie, Marilyn, and Dad, who faithfully transcribed many hours of interviews. I would like to thank my family, my sister, Lizzie, my brother, Joe, who have supported me on my personal journey and whose love has been a flowing source that I will always draw on in times of difficulty. Thank you Nanna and Grandad for being so faithful in your prayers, and Granny and Grandpa, my angels from heaven. I will never forget how my mother was unfailingly supportive and loving and how my father was so faithful and constant in editing the chapters, advising me and sharing in my journey. Moreover, it is with joy that I thank my publisher, Mike Woodward, who arrived unexpectedly as a gift and who has inspired trust from the beginning, and a great thank you to Mervyn Caldwell for the beautiful book cover design. Thank you, Abigail, for writing the introduction. You are such an inspiration to us all.

Finally, eternal thanks are due to all those whom I interviewed, who were courageous and honest in talking about those people whose stories have been recounted, and who have led the readers and myself to the essence of Lourdes.

CHAPTER 1

A Journey through Lourdes

A little girl

A LITTLE GIRL IS FACED WITH A BURDEN AND GREAT JOY. Her eyes are opened and she sees. A key is freely handed to her, one which unlocks the beginnings of an outer and inner world, an invisible and visible presence, the kingdom of God.

Why was an infant entrusted with such a precious key? The blissful ignorance and happy thoughtlessness of her age would certainly make her prone to drop it somewhere; leave it unguarded, unattended. Why did the lady in white not place her sacred trust in the wise parish priest, whose brow is furrowed with study and worry, who knows the value of caution and could explain many a term or phrase from his pulpit? In a sense, that little girl hides within us all. She is us and we are her. We are all small before God. We are all freely given His trust, without having earned it or even desired it. A divine key hides within all of us, trembling to fulfil its sole purpose of creation: to unlock the door to heaven.

One such girl was a young teenager called Bernadette Soubirous. Born on 7th January 1844, she lived in the little Pyrenean village of Lourdes with her family. They dwelt in poverty in an old prison cell, scrounging for every morsel of food which touched their lips, fighting winter's cruel bite.

One ordinary day, Bernadette, her sister, Toinette, and a friend, Baloume, hurried along to the Grotto of Massabielle to collect firewood. Whilst Toinette and Baloume spiritedly crossed the freezing waters of the mill stream by the River Gave, Bernadette found herself alone in front of the Grotto, unable to cross because of her asthma. As she bent down to take her shoes off and prepare for the excruciating cold, she heard a noise like a gust of wind. The same noise re-emerged. Looking up at the Grotto, she saw that the bush of thorns was moving. A soft light began to fill the dark hole inside the Grotto and out of it appeared a smile, a girl in white with open arms. Bernadette rubbed her eyes vigorously, only to find the same, smiling girl. Instinctively, Bernadette reached to her apron and found her rosary. As she tried to make the sign of the cross, her hand fell. She became scared. Instead, the apparition made a reverent gesture. Unblocked, Bernadette's arm made a large sign of the cross. All fear disappeared. Only joy remained. She knelt. This day, 11th February 1858, became known as the first Apparition of Our Lady of Lourdes. There were to be seventeen others, which awoke increasing interest and attracted growing numbers of onlookers.

Many bore witness to Bernadette's indescribable, illuminated smile, her 'undignified' though obedient consumption of the earth by the Grotto, which revealed a stream, and her messages from this beautiful lady. The apparition requested that a church be built and that people come in procession. 'I am the Immaculate Conception,' she told a confused Bernadette, four years after this 'dogma' had been announced by the Church.

A poor peasant girl who did not even know the meaning of the Trinity was seeing Our Blessed Mother? Bernadette was interrogated, accused, forbidden, acknowledged and admired. None were indifferent. Many converted.

The apparitions ended on Friday 16th July 1858. Our Lady told Bernadette: 'I will not make you happy in this life but in the next.' She became a nun and suffered extremely from illness until her death on 16th April 1879. One of the most famous phrases which emerged from Bernadette's silence and discretion was: 'My duty is to tell, not to make you believe.'

Aftermath

On 18th January 1862, the Church pronounced its verdict on the extraordinary events of the Grotto of Massabielle. Bishop Laurence declared, 'We judge that the Immaculate Mother of God truly appeared to Bernadette.'

The judgement was partly based on the number of cures which were occurring. When Bernadette ate the dirt and grass as the apparition had asked her to, and she revealed a stream, she was not aware that this water would still be flowing one hundred and fifty years later, nor that it would cure thousands of people of supposedly 'incurable' diseases and disabilities. The water was tested by scientists who looked for any healing properties, but it was declared normal. Lourdes soon became known by believers and unbelievers alike for its 'miracles', 'medically inexplicable' cures or 'signs from God'.

Above and beyond the sixty-seven recognised miracles, uncountable unrecognised cures and never-ending healing have sprung out of Lourdes. Fr Dominic O'Hara, a priest from Arundel and Brighton, muses, 'If you've got six hundred medically inexplicable cures and sixty-seven miracles, then how many tens of thousands of people have come back from Lourdes better, whatever better might mean?'

Canon Seamus Hester, former Director of the Pilgrimage, tells us, 'People ask, "Have you ever seen a miracle?" And I say, "All the time!" People become alarmed and say, "Tell us about them!" I say, "The spiritual healings. We mustn't overlook the spiritual healing that takes place."'

One pilgrim comments, 'One of my favourite statues was in the old hospital: the child Jesus is with Our Lady and is holding up his finger and wants our Lady to heal it. I think we are all like that. We all have a little finger which needs healing.'

Dr Patrick Theillier, Resident Doctor and Doctor-in-Chief of the Lourdes Medical Bureau, which was established in 1880 in order to study the cures, says: 'The Church has always been very prudent and did not want faith to repose on miracles. The miracle necessitates both the rational and the spiritual. Perhaps in Lourdes we have put too much emphasis on the rational. It is the tradition in Lourdes because it started in a very rationalist period and very much subject to the media, but there are risks in that as well.'

Our Lady's request that people come and process was listened to. Pilgrimages come to Lourdes from all around the world, making it a hive of universality. Pilgrimage calls to mind community and journey. One pilgrim remembers that her first time in Lourdes as a spectator left her 'with no desire to return': 'I arrived there, hated the commercialism, and then when I got to the Domain, everyone was going round looking very happy, and I thought they were under a spell like a religious cult. And I just thought, "What is going on here?" With the benefit of hindsight, I realise that those who were going around looking happy were the carers working with the sick.' Joanna Tobiasiewicz, another pilgrim, voices a feeling suffered by many: 'It is weird if you go as a spectator. It's not a place to gawp at. Lourdes is a place to love and you can't love if you just go and watch.' Pilgrimage brings Lourdes alive.

What of Bernadette, whose 'yes' allowed the place of Lourdes to be born to the world? After her death, her body was exhumed three times from the grave. It was found incorrupt each time. It now lies in a glass coffin in

Nevers. On 14th June 1925 she was beatified and on 8th December 1933, the feast of the Immaculate Conception, she was canonised by Pope Pius XI.

Bernadette is very dear to Dr Theillier, who follows in her footsteps in his mission to tell the truth with respect for people's freedom. He admires 'her smallness, her simplicity, her humility, her purity, her transparency. At the same time, she was not a weak person. She was a strong woman, who had a strong character and was upright. She is an example of the strong women from the Gospel, who knows what she wants, who is kind, who is self-assured, who has character and suppleness. She was at the service of the message of Lourdes.'

Discovering Lourdes

'Although we speak of Lourdes as not being concerned with image,' suggests the Bishop of Arundel and Brighton, Kieran Conry, 'so much of Lourdes is visual.' From being a modest, hidden village, Lourdes has become a peopled, commercialised area, the second tourist destination in the whole of France. Though the quiet and prayerful atmosphere of Lourdes is almost untouchable, the makeup of the town has changed with time, divided between a commercialised area, consisting of hotels, shops and cafes, and the Sanctuary, the centre point and soul of the town.

I enter St Joseph's gate. The hustle and bustle of the outside fade into silence. A hush takes over my body and soul. I walk down the sloping path, careful not to tread on the red-painted wheelchair lane, worn with the number of users. Soon I am faced with a glorious sight: a tall, crowned statue of Our Lady, smiling down on her children. Around her feet is a bed of flowers, many of which have been brought as offerings. To my right, I can see the entrance of the vast Underground Basilica, St Pius X, built to accommodate thousands of people.

As I arrive at the Crowned Statue, where it is customary to say three Hail Marys to ensure one's return to Lourdes, I look out on a vast space, with tarmac running down both sides, a grassy area in the middle, and St Michael's gate at the end. It is on the left that can be found, amongst other buildings, the Medical Bureau where cures are pondered over and doctors from far afield gather together. Turning my back to the Crowned Statue, I perceive the Rosary Basilica in the distance, with a ramp on either side leading to the top, 'Jesus' arms surrounding you,' remarks one pilgrim. I make my way towards it, noticing an altar on the left side and an arch on the right, through which pilgrims pass frequently. As I make my way through,

I see a bridge stretching over the musical waters of the Gave river, which reinforce the overwhelming sense of peace.

One nun, a Daughter of the Cross, called Sister Rose Mary Cush muses, 'It sounds like a choir of monks singing in the distance. It's as though the whole singing is reflected into the water and is coming back with you again.' Over the other side of the river is a vast prairie, where people promenade in a happy aura. To the right, I can see a church, St Bernadette's, and a hospital, known as the *Accueil*, the French word for welcome, which preserves the beating heart of Lourdes. As I continue my walk, I notice hundreds of candles for sale and a line of taps, from which pilgrims extract water and bless themselves, thirsty for every drop.

Suddenly, the granite comes into view, then the arch shape, and, finally, the statue of Our Lady, nestled in the rock, visible for all to see. This is the Grotto. As I process through it, the rock feels smooth from the touch of pilgrims. Deep in the bowels of the rock lies the singing stream that Bernadette dug out many years ago. A box where petitions are placed, safe with Mary, appears. An altar, that timeless table, sits in the centre of the Grotto. Some pray the rosary or sing softly. Others kneel in silence.

Past the Grotto emerge the rows of candles, lights of desire, and the Baths, filled with the water from the spring where people bathe themselves to be free. A pilgrim wrote

> It's here, in this place of great humility, that one can saunter freely around...touch...feel...reflect or just pass the time absorbing the great spiritual aura encapsulated there.

In speaking of the Grotto, a woman recalls, 'One priest said to me, "Look how it is shaped like the womb. Our Lady is there and Jesus came from that. When you pray there, Our Lady helps you to be and to get to know Jesus."'

Lights, camera, action

It is in this atmosphere that special events are lived. The first event is the journey itself.

Cardinal Cormac Murphy O'Connor, Archbisop of Westminster, believes: 'It's a reminder of our journey of life. We journey, we come in this world, we're born, and we're going back to God. When you go on a pilgrimage, when you go to Lourdes, the journey helps people to belong together, because you've got to help one another on a journey. You don't know exactly what's happening next. You meet new friends and also you're able, walking together, to talk about things you don't normally talk about at your office and even in your immediate family. All that there is on a pilgrimage, is you, the other people, and God. On a pilgrimage, God speaks through us.'

The Torchlight Procession, a regular, nightly gathering of international pilgrims, allows everyone to walk in unison to the Rosary Basilica. The processors gently enter a state of complete peace with the echoes of other-worldly music and the intensely soft candlelight, formed by the hundreds of torches, which are lifted into the fading daylight upon sound of the verse, *Ave Maria*. It is also possible to process in a different way through the Blessed Sacrament Procession and the Stations of the Cross, which remind pilgrims of the central meaning of Lourdes and of their faith.

Cardinal Cormac talks of the gift of the Sacrament of Reconciliation in view of the 'terrible culture of blame' in our society: 'One part of Lourdes which I think is important for all people, but particularly young people, is Reconciliation. A lot of them haven't been to Confession for a very long time and there's a great difference between forgiveness and feeling guilty. A lot of people today have guilt because they have done things wrong but they don't experience the forgiveness of God.'

Amidst such a large gathering of sick and disabled people, the Sacrament of the Anointing of the Sick is celebrated. This is a highpoint for many pilgrims. For Bishop Kieran, 'The intimacy of Lourdes is most profoundly experienced there.' Our Pilgrimage celebrates this together in the immense Underground Basilica. For the moment of the Anointing of the Sick, all the hotel groups form circles, as the music softly prepares everyone for the coming of the Holy Spirit.

One pilgrim states, 'It's a time when you get so close to the sick on a different level. You've been out with them, you come to the Anointing, and the sacrament reminds you that Jesus is there in a special way.' Though the service is focused on the sick, those around them almost feel their buried, inner suffering on the tips of their fingers. Canon Seamus is touched by 'the way that the people put out their hands and reach out to God. See the tears flow, the faith of the people.'

Chris Xerri, a Lourdes pilgrim, comments, 'I think, for me, it's probably the most beautiful moment in Lourdes.' Finally, the pilgrim Nick Harvey recounts, 'My father died when I was twenty-one in 1983 and I was the eldest boy in the family. I tried to give the persona of being the strong, stable one. In 1987, I went to Lourdes and I hadn't really cried. And, then:

the Anointing service. I had no idea what I was letting myself in for and it was like a tap had been opened. I came out of that feeling clean. I felt like something had been washed out of me.'

'What do you do with a fractious exhausted child at the end of a hot summer's day? You give him a cool bath,' affirms Julia Renouf, a pilgrim who works in the Lourdes Baths once a year. Hundreds of pilgrims queue up in the women's and men's sections, sometimes for hours, always amidst sung or spoken prayers, to feel the cold water of the spring touch their bodies, as an offering for Our Lady. 'We have a spiritual bath: we feel refreshed and our cares have been taken away. I have a bath and it all goes. In each cubicle, we're putting about two hundred people through in a two-hour session. There's another dimension.' For Julia, the Baths are 'a huge act of faith.' Charlotte Burnell has also worked in the Baths. She testifies, 'When people come in, some of them beg from the bottom of their souls. The moment you open the curtain and they come in behind, you just hold them and hug them because they are burdened. Sometimes you can't understand the language. One woman begged once for her depression to be lifted. She was only there for a few minutes but it was so powerful and I did pray. When she went into that water, I just thought, 'God, please help her.' When you are stripped down of your clothes – one leg or two legs, one breast or two breasts – we're all the same. It's raw emotion. You're not bringing any gifts with you, no money. You're not bringing any of the trappings of life. I think it is an opportunity to be human in front of Our Lady, to stand there with your white shroud round you and nothing else.'

A journey through the unknown

I felt that something was missing in books about Lourdes in terms of capturing the real message and had been thinking that we should write a book about the sick who had come with the Pilgrimage. At a meeting about Lourdes, people said that we needed to raise money. The inspiration came to me on holiday in August 2006. I woke up, and thought to myself, 'Why don't we see if Catherine would like to write the book? She loves writing and she could do it in her gap year...'

Adam Simon

A sixteen year old at the time, I accepted my father's challenge. I agreed to a project of which I knew no implications, no challenges or difficulties, and thought that we would simply raise money for our Lourdes Sick Fund as we would through a car boot sale. 'I will be fine,' I said to myself. 'I have always loved to write. It's my dream to be a writer.'

Also I loved Lourdes with a passion which was beyond me yet so deep within me that I hardly recognised it. It was the place where I had grown up, which had accompanied me along my path from childhood, when life had been so simple and joyous, to teenage years, where questions bit at me like frostbite.

Two years later, I had already accomplished the first of sixty interviews in total. Producing this book has taken me on an uneven path from interviewing; a far subtler art than I could have imagined, and transcribing; which required patient listening, to selecting and assembling. Over the five month period, I experienced intense human interaction and quiet solitude, understanding and misunderstanding, smiles of delight and tears of misery.

In the beginning, I searched out the people who vividly remember or know the nine people. Each interview is so memorable and flavoured according to the interviewee. The objective was then to shape the testimonies according to the aspects of each person's life. Therefore, each interview became scattered across a chapter and, in some cases, the whole book. The result is that the recollections, observations and expressions of belief are not formal or literary. They are living voices that you hear, echoing and resounding throughout the chapters and weaving a thread which feeds the essence of the book. I was pulling the strings of a multi-coloured tapestry which was and will forever be far greater than me.

I became immersed in a world of listening and talking. As a young girl of eighteen, I had enjoyed a protected childhood, divided between England and France, always armed against adversity with a stable family and supportive friends. My only knowledge of suffering had originated from the media, art and my own searching through life as a young adult. To hear from the victims themselves of cases of murder, abuse, illness, and suicide, amongst many other tragedies, was all too much. I spent a few nights at home crying in my parents' arms, one of the few places where I felt safe. I would go to mass in deep emotion, my eyes glued on the large, wooden cross above the altar. Can the cross – God in suffering – be the key to our human condition? Shall we never be satisfied until we meet our Maker? There I was, always having profoundly disliked horror films or depictions of evil, writing my own!

Yet, with Lourdes came healing, with healing came hope, with hope came love, and with love came God. This was the deepest meeting I have ever had with God and perhaps ever will. I was seeing Him in action amongst pits of gloom that no-one would consciously enter into, total darkness that seems to anticipate nothing but itself, and blood-red pain which would scorch anyone touched by it. Lourdes had transformed these people's lives and, in doing so, changed my own forever. My prayer is: 'Thank you Our Lady for this privileged time with you.' Now that I know the beginnings of what faith truly tastes like, what pain resembles and what wonders God can achieve, I can walk through the gates of Lourdes with an understanding that here, in this valley of song and tears, a 'big bang' is in operation, scattering sin and sorrow to distant lands, where people are entering as dark and weary souls, and exiting, clothed with robes of luminous white.

INVITATION TO THE READER

The nine people, deceased or alive, who have been chosen for this book as instruments of the message of Lourdes, are ordinary individuals whose lives have been touched by the extraordinary.

Their stories have left an indelible mark on the minds and hearts of pilgrims through suffering and powerful healing. Deceased or alive, they are an invitation to come and see, to visit Lourdes from the inside out. Their stories are messages from which we can learn and reflect, watch and believe.

As Dr Theillier simply invites us:

Lourdes is a place of blessings.

Come and see.

You have to see it.

CHAPTER 2

Love in Action

TIM MARTIN

Three words

'WE WERE TALKING IN A GROUP, ON ONE OCCASION,' RECALLS JOHN Sexton, photographer and one of the Pilgrimage leaders, 'on how you would describe the Pilgrimage and people were describing it in all sorts of ways.

'When it came to Tim, he just spelt out on his board, "Love in Action", and that was it, as simple as that, those three words. And we discussed it afterwards. We talked about the whole concept of love and he said that love doesn't exist on its own. It's not simply an idea. Love has to do something: the action of people serving one another in Lourdes is an act of love and it's different from somebody who might have a vocation through the medical profession, for example, or through social care. They might do it very lovingly but they've entered it as a profession, whereas Tim was seeing that this was given freely and lovingly by the helpers. People who were being physically served and cared for were giving so much back.'

Canon Seamus Hester recalls, 'I'll never forget when he said at a celebration one night that Lourdes was just all about L-O-V-E. I'll never forget the standing ovation he got for that.'

Beyond his death, Tim is remembered by pilgrims for this sparkling expression and continues to impact on them just as he did when he was alive. 'Love in action' soon became the Pilgrimage's vision statement, which sums up in three clear words what Lourdes is about.

John reveals, 'I used that expression when I was doing appeals to raise funds and promote the Pilgrimage and I would talk about Tim.' His story encapsulates the Lourdes spirit. In Tim's case, love was the here and now, the acted out and the alive: love was God's presence amongst us.

How does that simple phrase speak to the pilgrims who knew him? Libby Sexton, John's wife, feels, 'I just thought it was beautiful because the whole of life and everything we do should revolve around love and Lourdes is a place where people forget themselves and try to love others, even if they don't like them or are a little bit put off by whatever's wrong with them. That's what we're called to do. Tim actually just put it into words.'

John reflects on his friend's expression: 'I think love, in a way, is one of the most abused words in the English language. I suppose, if we are looking for a definition of love, it is when you put the other person's needs first, when, automatically in your mind, in your words and above all in your actions, you're putting your own desires to one side. I used to struggle with the phrase when Jesus said, "No greater love can a man have than to lay down his life for his friends." That's what we do in Lourdes: we lay our life to one side. Without a helper the other person would not be able to experience pilgrimage. I think Tim witnessed that. Wasn't it Mother Teresa who said, "It's not how much you do that matters; it's how much loving you put into the doing"? That is what our Pilgrimage is about. Tim observed that and described it in his typical way. He genuinely reached out to others and whilst he coined the phrase, "Love in Action", he, in many respects, was the one who put it into action more than others.'

Accident

Tim's mother recalls the reason for her son's lifelong disability: 'He was at boarding school and, one Sunday night, they all went into the gym at St Philip Howard, a Catholic high school in Barnham. They were doing acrobatics. It was Tim's fault because, of course, he shouldn't have been doing it, as they were told not to. He was trying to kick the ceiling with his feet on the parallel bars. Anyway, he slipped off onto the floor and fell on the back of his head.

As the person who was watching over them left the room for a minute, Tim got up from the floor. He told me he went up to the chapel to do the Stations of the Cross. He knew he'd hurt himself. He must have come out of the chapel and he fell eventually on the stairs and became unconscious.

Getting up, he only had a little fracture in the head but it cut an important artery. He was sent to the doctor and the doctor had him sent to Chichester where he had an operation straight away.

We were living in Bath at the time, because the Navy had been moved to Bath out of London. It was dreadful, of course. He was unconscious for about two and a half months and it was a nightmare. They took him into Great Ormond Street, a children's hospital in London. And they said, "You know we don't do miracles here," because he was quite off. I think he was just making a noise.' He was twelve years old.

Tim was born in 1944 and became the eldest of four boys. Andrew came two years after Tim, followed a year later by Nigel, and then Jonathan, who was born eleven years after Nigel.

Aged nine when his brother fell, Nigel tells us: 'He had brain damage because of the blood on the brain. There were very new techniques coming out for brain damage operations and they managed to save his life by using these new techniques. If it had been a few years earlier, he probably wouldn't have survived.'

Furthermore, John recounts: 'During that time, his parents visited him daily. They were told that, if he simply lay still, his muscles would deteriorate, so they exercised him. While he was in a coma, his parents were moving his arms and legs so that he could retain some muscle tone.'

His mother confesses, 'I was heartbroken really. I was going up the stairs in Bath, and a voice spoke to me – I might have been saying prayers and I'd been going to Mass every morning – "Pray to St Joseph." I didn't know then that St Joseph was the saint for dying people and the hospital had said that Tim wasn't so well and was already on the danger list. After that prayer to St Joseph, he seemed slightly better in himself: no change, but I used to ring up every day. I said to my husband, "You go now; I really haven't got the courage." Michael came back and said, "I'm sure he knew me." Then I went up the following day, and I knew he knew me at once because he sort of waved and called out! He couldn't speak at all then and his speech never came back. And from then on, it was just one joy bubble because he was happy.'

Nigel recounts, 'We, the brothers, didn't see him for about six months or so after his accident.' After being cared for in Great Ormond Street, Tim was moved to the Lord Mayor Trelaw hospital in Alton. By that time, he was starting to walk again.

The accident affected some more than others: 'His grandfather loved him dearly and his grandmother said that it killed him,' reveals his mother. However, faith was what kept her sane. She tells us: 'My mother wrote a letter when Tim was very ill and said, "Do your best every day." Peace came to me in church.' She recounts that, through the trauma, she was brought closer to God: 'Not only that, but my husband came into the Church.'

Inability and ability

Such a severe fall left Tim disabled for life. His mother recalls, 'He could laugh and smile. He couldn't talk at all.' After being cared for in Alton, Tim was brought home by his father, who was dissatisfied with the way in which his son was being treated. Instead, the family paid for a Welsh nurse to look after him who was 'wonderful', according to Tim's mother.

John recalls visiting Tim at home: 'In their bungalow Tim had his own room and also his own entrance to his room from outside so that he had some degree of independence.'

Tim rose from a state of bleak unconsciousness. He soon left his wheel-chair and became able to walk using a stick. His mother suggests, 'I think he knew that he'd been called or that it was a miracle.' His twenties were marked with achievements. 'He started to ride a bicycle around the garden wearing a crash helmet,' says his brother Nigel.

'And he was actually climbing trees!' adds his mother. Nigel recalls, 'In his twenties, he used to drive around in invalid cars: he managed to pass his test but his concentration used to go a bit when he was driving. He was hardly up to it really. The police used to phone up when they had found him in the ditch.' John affirms, 'Most of the time from then on he was wheel-chair bound. He could get out of the wheelchair with support and stand. If he got up out of his wheelchair and tried to walk, he would fall over. He would constantly pull you in one direction because he was losing balance.' Nigel signals, 'Growing up into his early twenties, he got to his peak and then, later on, from when he was about forty onwards, he started slowing down and started to deteriorate.'

A quick system of communication was created by Tim's father when he realised that Tim was intellectually alert. John states, 'He had no speech but his father recognised that Tim was attempting to communicate just by facial expression and the movement of his eyes. So he made him an alphabet board, simply a piece of board with letters of the alphabet painted on the board. Tim was able to point to letters on the board to spell out a word. That's how he communicated and he became very skilled at it, and would spell out words very quickly, more quickly than most people could follow because he was so skilled. He would also take short cuts.'

Nick Brown, a friend who cared for Tim in Lourdes, says, 'He refused to have anything more complicated, and he just used to point at this board. We worked out in the end how his family did it. They didn't look at the letters that he was making. They'd got used to looking to the shape that the hand made in the air. And after a week we were starting to do that. You got to know facial expressions when he was saying something positive or negative. And when he said something that he wanted you to agree with, it was usually a wide open grin, eyes narrowed, a great big smile on his face and, "Aaaah!"'

John recalls the shock he received one morning in Lourdes when sharing a tent with Tim at the camp site: 'When we woke up he spoke to me. He said "John" and "Good morning". For a moment, in my naivety, I thought that it was a miracle: "Tim's got his voice back!" And I said to him, "Tim, you spoke!" And then it just went and he spelt out on the board, "It sometimes happens in the morning after I've had a good rest." He could just come out with two or three words, and that was all. I felt so privileged because he said, "You are one of the very few to have heard this."'

Tim could not feel satisfied with basic communication. He went beyond what many able people are capable of. Nick recalls, 'You thought you knew him in your mind because he didn't speak. And how wrong I was! As the week went on, what came out from his board was just amazing.'

John Burnett, who also met Tim in Lourdes, reveals, 'He was very well read and you could have conversations with him over a wide range of subjects.' John Sexton testifies: 'One time, he was spelling out a word, and I said that I couldn't get the word and asked him to repeat the word. He did it again a few times. He had broken into French! When Tim met people of other nationalities in Lourdes, he would often greet them in their own language: French, Italian, Spanish, Polish... He had picked up bits of language as his hearing was terrific and he was highly intelligent.'

One experience which particularly left an impact on John Sexton was when Tim was a helper's best man: 'I had to give Tim's best man speech on his behalf and Paul, the bridegroom, had spent some time working as a teacher in some Pacific islands called 'Kiribati.' In his speech, Tim referred to Kiribati. I said, "Let me read through the speech to make sure I've got it all right." And when I got to Kiribati he stopped me and on his board he spelt out phonetically, "It is pronounced Kiribash." Tim wasn't just highly intelligent. He had tremendous general knowledge.'

Tim's disability brought unexpected gifts with it. The first was that it brought him closer to several members of the family. According to his mother, 'His grandmother and he used to do the *Telegraph* crossword puzzle together and they got on very well indeed.' As for her own relationship with 'Timmy' she hints, 'It brought us perhaps a little nearer together.'

Nigel states, 'I had to take him to the toilet and that sort of thing because he really couldn't do that on his own, so I had to be a sort of carer. I got on really quite well with Tim.' Although Jonathan's relationship was hindered by the significant age gap and the resulting communication problems, their mother reveals: 'Jon didn't ignore him because he still played with him.'

His mother adds, 'You learn to be patient and be quite happy with the more ordinary things. On a day to day basis, it makes you content maybe with lesser ambitions.' Did any of them pray for a miracle for their severely disabled loved one? Nigel, who questioned God at times, admits, 'I think I probably did for him to recover.' Despite this, he concludes: 'I learnt to accept it.' He remembers how comforting the Mass was to several of the family members.

The family's eventual acceptance was mirrored in Tim's disposition. His mother affirms that Tim did not seriously struggle with his disability. She muses, 'He accepted it—not only that. He rather enjoyed it, I think.' John Burnett adds, 'He could have easily just lapsed into a "why has this happened to me?" type syndrome, and "look at me: I can't do this and I can't do that". Not a bit of it! He turned the coin around the other way and said, "What can I do?" He was one of the doers of this world, not a follower.'

John Sexton confirms, 'At home, for example, he had his jobs to do. One of them was to do the washing. They had a front-loading washing machine and Tim would shuffle around the house on his hands and knees to collect his Mum and Dad's washing and go to the laundry room and he would do the washing. That was his job, and his contribution to the family. Many years ago, when he was younger, he was involved in the parish delivering football pools and Tim was a regular sight around the area.'

Contagious laughter rang in the air wherever Tim happened to be. John Sexton tells us, 'He had a wicked sense of humour... he put his head back and roared! Although he didn't speak, he made noises and when he laughed, everyone could hear Tim!' Fr Stephen Ortiger, who knew Tim through Lourdes, marvels: 'He had multiple disabilities but he was so cheerful, full of beans, going like Concorde: the human spirit just forging ahead despite all.'

John Sexton testifies that it was not just Tim's acceptance of his situation that was incredible: 'He accepted people caring for him in whatever way they did. Because Tim couldn't talk, people would automatically assume he was deaf and when speaking to him would speak loudly or shout at him. Most people would react to that but Tim didn't. I did and I would sometimes say, "He's not deaf!" I'd get angry and irritated by this person: "Just speak normally to Tim!" Tim never ever reproached people for that sort of thing. He just accepted people as they were.'

Such a startling man did not perceive himself as disabled in any way. John Sexton remembers, 'He once said to me in Lourdes, "People think I'm handicapped," and I was quite taken aback by this because there was Tim in a wheelchair, unable to speak, unable to walk unattended, needing things doing for him. I remember having a deeply personal conversation with him when we were talking about the joy of Lourdes and the fact that it was a place of healing, and I asked, "Should we be expecting physical healing? Should we be praying and asking everyone to pray very hard that you would be physically healed, that this disability that you've got which ties you to a chair be removed, and that you'll be able to speak again?" And he just spelt on the board, "But then I wouldn't be me."'

The fulfilment of Tim

'Somebody left us a little money and I had a great urge to take Tim to Lourdes,' claims Tim's mother. At that time, Tim was still a teenager. After considering different alternatives, all the family set off to Lourdes, independent of a pilgrimage.

The mother declares, 'I was absolutely thrilled.' She also testifies, 'I thought it was lovely, not only that but the children could run about, the traffic was very slow: everything seemed to be safe.' Nigel reveals: 'It did feel like another world.' His mother had helped to plant a seed that year. Year on year, Tim faithfully returned to the place that touched him deep inside and fulfilled his every need. Nigel affirms, 'It was the holiday of the year for him because he didn't go on any other holidays.' Cardinal Cormac Murphy O'Connor, reflecting on his years as Bishop of Arundel and

Brighton, could make a similar observation: 'He just loved Lourdes. He enlivened the whole of the community he was in. He felt so strongly that he had a contribution to make even though he was so disabled.'

The most basic wonder of Lourdes for Tim was the community. He often alternated his visits to Lourdes with different pilgrimages, whether it was his diocesan one or the pilgrimages he had come with as a teenager: HCPT [The Pilgrimage Trust] for children and then Jet Set later on.

John Sexton marvels, 'He was very well known in Lourdes and he was greeted by so many different people. Tim just knew absolutely everyone and everyone knew Tim. It was almost like bees round a honey pot.' Nick Harvey, who became friendly with Tim in Lourdes, adds, 'The attention Tim used to get! He was never lonely.' Why? Libby says, 'I think he probably felt loved. He loved being one of the boys. Tim was out half the night with the boys, if he could get away with it! His Mum would often say, "When Tim comes back from Lourdes, he sleeps for a week. He's absolutely exhausted!"'

Tim was known by many for his boundless sense of fun. Libby confirms, 'Although he was absolutely sound and devout, he was also tremendous fun to be with.' Cardinal Cormac reveals, 'He always had some fun remark: "How are you? You're looking tired this morning. You're doing too much or you're drinking too much!" Everybody just loved him.'

John Sexton had the privilege of spending a week with Tim in Lourdes one year when they shared a tent at the 'Camp des Jeunes,' the international youth camp, which is just outside Lourdes and where most of the helpers stayed at the time. Tim chose this over staying in the hospital. John recalls: 'He'd spilt soup down his shirt. So I went to get him a clean shirt. When I went through his case for the shirt, I noticed a glass medicine bottle with his prescription label on the front with "Tim Martin". I went back to him and said that I'd noticed a bottle of medicine in his case and whether he should be taking this. And he signalled, "Yes," and I said, "When do you need to take it?", and he replied, "Tonight would be good but I need to take it with plenty of water." So I said, "Tim, should you have been taking it before?" and he said, "Perhaps." This went on and on and on and then I said, "Tim, what is it?" and he said, "Shampoo." His mother had put shampoo in this medicine bottle and he was teasing me. He knew I was wound up in case I hadn't been caring for him properly!'

Tim was just as easily teased as he never took himself seriously. John Sexton tells us, 'We always teased him because he loved to have the girls around him and they'd see him and come up and say, 'Hi Tim!', and put their arms around him and give him a kiss on the cheek!' John recounts, 'When I first met Tim, he would wrap his lips round the straw instantly and drink through it. In the latter years of his life, he would have to have the straw rested on his lower lip and you'd wait whilst he was struggling to close his mouth on the straw. We were really quite wicked with Tim because he had such a wonderful sense of humour. Sometimes, he would be struggling to get a grip of the straw and just at the moment he was about to grip onto it, somebody would crack a joke and he would put his head back and roar with laughter. And he'd have to go through the whole procedure again; which was an awful thing for us to do, but Tim loved it. Libby said to him on one occasion, "Can you pucker your lips Tim and give me a kiss?", and she was puckering her lips and he was struggling to do the same. Somebody said something funny and he put his head back and absolutely roared with laughter, and I just happened to be in the right place and got that photograph, and that, to me, epitomises Tim.'

The relationships that Tim made in Lourdes spanned the year. John Burnett, who often attended the same Mass as Tim, testifies, 'Tim used to have visitors very regularly from the Pilgrimage. He lived at home with his parents and this gave him another family, the Lourdes family.'

Besides the people, Lourdes was a truly spiritual experience for a very prayerful man. John Burnett believes, 'It truly was another home. I think Our Blessed Lady played a great part in his life and he really felt that he was truly visiting her when he went to Lourdes.'

John Sexton recalls one striking example of Tim's spirituality: 'We did the Stations of the Cross together and he insisted on walking. This was the High Stations in Lourdes which are very hilly, rocky, steep coming down, and well over a mile long. Tim and I walked together and, because of the shape of his legs, following the accident, one leg crossed over the other as he took a step. I held his arm so that he was upright but it was really disconcerting walking with him: you really felt he was going to have a heart attack, because he was puffing so much. His breathing was laboured and loud: "Are you all right, Tim?" "I'm fine, stop fussing!"'

Not many have been able to experience Jesus' excruciating labour under the burden of the cross. Tim was carrying his own cross, helped as Jesus was helped, and above all, determined to reach the end.

John Sexton concludes, 'I suppose Tim was experiencing a bit of heaven when he was in Lourdes.' It was part of his life but I think the difference with Tim was that he carried Lourdes with him for the rest of the year, which most of us try to do but fall down every now and again. The spirit of Lourdes remained with Tim.'

Messenger

Tim became a messenger of joy to others, determined to fulfil the new mission that he had been given though his disability.

A large number of people have called Tim an 'inspiration'. What immediately struck others was Tim's joyful disposition. Lady Sarah Clutton, the Arundel & Brighton Pilgrimage co-ordinator and organiser for the last thirty-two years, recalls, 'I remember Tim Martin because he used to come to Mass at Arundel, and he used to give me the thumbs up. He used to scream when he saw me!' John Burnett comments, 'Tim had his serious moments like we all do but he was a smiler and, whenever we saw each other, there was always that beam. I told him about this nickname that I had as a young fellow – "Smiler"– and somehow we just connected.' He adds, 'It was a joy to be with him because he was so full of life: to work with somebody for a week who totally pulls you out of yourself and makes you forget those problems, those issues.'

Nick recalls with fondness his week in Lourdes when he shared a room with Tim and was put in charge of all of Tim's care. He reveals, 'It was the most special week in Lourdes ever. Out of the twenty-four I've done now, that was by far the most amazing. It was just so humbling to spend all my time with him and look after him and see how he lived his life. There I was, at the time, high up in a Japanese company, and this guy, who has lost everything in life that most people would hold dear to them, has a full and wonderful life... and the patience of a saint, because it would take us forever to figure out what he was trying to tell us sometimes and he would just smile and carry on trying and trying until you got it.'

One incident which occurred during the week and which is vividly remembered by Nick is a perfect example of Tim's happiness and ability not to take himself or life too seriously: 'Tim's bowels weren't the greatest! Adrian Burnett, who was the nurse, said, "Bowels are irregular but we need to make sure he goes before the end of the holiday because otherwise the journey on the train could be a complete disaster." After a couple of days, Tim had stopped going. Adrian gave him some powder. Adrian came in next morning, "Any sign?" No. So he gave him some laxative. We had two mornings left. Next morning, Adrian came in: "Any success?" No. So we had to try a suppository, and that didn't have any success, so on the last day

Adrian walked in, big smile, and said to Tim, "Now you know what's happening today!" and Tim went, "Mmmmm…" It was the phosphate enema. The phosphate enema will make anyone go! It only takes about ten minutes! We were really starting to laugh at this point. It could be quite a horrible situation and Tim just turned it around completely. He made it into a joke and he was smiling. Adrian, of course, had done it before with Tim. So we were sitting on the bed and waiting for things to start rumbling. Adrian said, "Anything happening, Tim?" No.

"Anything happening Tim?" No.

After about ten minutes, Tim went, "Mmmm! Mmmm!"

"Is it working Tim?"

"Mmmm!"

"Do we need to go to the bathroom now?"

"Mmmm!"

We grabbed him. We got half way across the room and that was it! Adrian said, "Keep going! Keep going!" We ran into the shower. And the three of us collapsed in the corner of the shower, absolutely wetting ourselves. It was one of the funniest moments of my life. We were crying with laughter. It couldn't have happened with anybody but Tim. It was just a fantastic moment! You wouldn't have thought so, would you? That was the defining moment with Tim. That was Tim through and through.'

Through his courage in accepting his disability, Tim was an example to many able and sick or disabled people. Nick reveals, 'He humbled me completely. He taught me not to make assumptions about people. And to take what I found about people and then probably add another 50% or 100% to that person as to what they were capable of. He taught me that what people would think is a crippling disability doesn't have to be at all. You are just as much a part of society and the social makeup of a group as anybody is.' For Nick, one of the messages in Tim's life is, 'Never give up.'

Libby adds, 'If anybody else who was disabled had become depressed with their disability, he often used to get himself next to them and he talked to them. Apparently, whatever he said to them was like waving a magic wand but I never did actually hear what he said to them.'

John Sexton recounts a story in which Tim clearly reached out and touched a pilgrim's heart: 'Deirdre Leach had Tim in her group and they were sitting in prayer. Deirdre's husband, Tony, had died some years ago and their wedding anniversary is around the time of the Pilgrimage. So it is always a very difficult time for Deirdre and she was probably remembering in a group prayer session her memories of Tony. She was crying gently. She looked up and saw Tim catch her eye from the other side of the room and he just did this action to show the tear running from the eye down the cheek. Then, he blew her a kiss. It was a deeply moving moment for Deirdre, a deeply emotional moment, and she said she received so much more from that little action from Tim than from anything words could have said.' Deirdre realised at that point that she was the one in need of help and that Tim was the helper.

Tim preached through example from the heart of the Gospel messages. He taught people about love. Libby believes that for non-believers and believers alike, 'His message was: love one another, be nice to people, be kind. Tim had this charisma that poured out of him and, like something gathers dust, Tim gathered people round him. Strangely, I can't remember Tim saying a lot about his faith to me but he didn't need to. He didn't have to. There was obviously something much more to Tim: deep, deep faith and the joy of his heart.'

Indeed, John Burnett could only assume from Tim's quiet actions that this man was extremely spiritual: 'I used to notice Tim in the Lady Chapel where we have a life size statue of Our Lady of Sorrows with the swords piercing her heart. I used to see him from a distance at Mass and he was always in a concentrated mood, certainly not fiddling around. He was a permanent and regular attender at church. I only mention that because it would have been easy for someone who was as disabled as Tim to turn over on a Sunday morning, and yet he was always there.' John Sexton, who spent many a moment with Tim, adds, 'He had a devotion to Jesus. He would pray out loud by using his board and occasionally he would sometimes spell out a prayer which was always brief but profound: "Jesus is pleased with us today."' Libby finally recalls, 'Tim always used to start laughing at the Anointing when everybody else started crying and I said to him afterwards, "Tim, why are you so happy when everybody's in tears?" He said "I've just been anointed. Why should I be sad? I've just received the Anointing of the Sick and it's wonderful and it makes me feel happy."

Many people's faiths were influenced by this quiet example, firstly his mother's: 'Tim affected my faith enormously. Now I don't like to say "No" to anything and I don't. I try to say the rosary every day.' John Burnett comments, 'Before meeting him and meeting those very special people that come to Lourdes, I had practised my faith. I think it made my faith deeper when I met Tim and others through Lourdes. Perhaps at times I took my faith for granted. I knew it was there and that's fine. I think they made you think about it more, about what it should really mean, what you should be doing with your life.' John Sexton adds, 'Tim cemented my faith without any doubt. What I believed, I witnessed being lived through Tim.'

The light of transformation

If there is one element which will be forever intertwined with the person of Tim, it is the light of transformation which shone out from his life. Cardinal Cormac leaves us wondering at 'his interior life of prayer' and at 'how his face would light up.' His face and life became enactments of mystery, queries with no answers to the infinite possibilities and power which lie with God.

The Mass was perhaps more important for Tim than he ever realised. His mother recalls, 'I did take him to Mass at Bognor one day and took him to Holy Communion: just for a minute or two, his face became quite beautiful, and he never had the look again but it was beautiful. It's difficult to explain. Just the once I saw it. Only for a second and it never came again.' She shares her thoughts on such a facial change: 'I think there was a little bit of a get together between God and Tim.' Libby equally testifies, 'When he received Communion, his whole demeanour changed and I can't really describe it. All I can say is he was completely transfixed on receiving Jesus and it had to be seen to be believed. His face lit up and his eyes twinkled and he was happy.'

The Baths in Lourdes are said to have been Tim's favourite place, according to John Sexton: 'Tim used to do what he described as a Novena at the Baths. Tim would sometimes go twice in a day in order to get nine Baths in during the Pilgrimage and he always did it for other people. It wasn't for himself. He'd be offering it for particular people, people he'd met: a couple were desperately trying to have a baby and nothing was happening and he would be moved by that. I had the great privilege of not just caring for Tim but going into the Baths with him where they would have preferred to put him on a stretcher but it was his preference to walk in and so they respected that.' Libby recalls, 'He used to ask to be plunged under the water.' John adds, 'The expression on his face: you just couldn't describe it. You had to witness it. There was something about it which made it almost unreal.'

At the Grotto, Tim entered into deep reflection on what was before him. John Sexton again recalls one very moving experience: 'There was one night when we went to the Grotto and I asked, "Do you want to stay for a short moment, Tim, or a long time?", and he replied, "Fairly long I think." I said "Well, I'll give you some space so you can be at prayer but I'll be nearby. Just turn and signal to me when you are ready." I was just slightly behind him, giving him space and he suddenly started moving forward out of the wheelchair. I was concerned at what he was doing. He struggled out of the wheelchair, onto his knees and spent time in prayer on his knees. It's one of the most humbling experiences I've ever known. To see this man with such a disability do that. And to see his face: it's something I will never forget. They say that when Bernadette experienced the apparitions, she had the most beautiful expression you can ever imagine and Tim was exactly like that. Just the slightest hint of a smile but he looked absolutely serene kneeling there. It brings tears to my eyes just thinking about it.'

The final transformation of all came on 12th February 2003. Aged fifty-eight, Tim passed away at St Bridget's Cheshire Home in Littlehampton from 'an apnoeic episode and spastic quadriplegia,' in other words, from failure in breathing due to the brain damage.

His mother reveals, 'Sometimes he would come here and after getting up the stairs into his room, he would be near collapse.' Nigel states, 'He was cheerful to the end.'

The funeral was in Arundel Cathedral, where the Martins sometimes attended Mass. Nigel states, 'A lot of parishioners were there and people from Lourdes. One of the priests at Arundel was surprised at how many people were there.' John adds, 'It was a great reunion of Tim's friends.'

In what state of mind did the Tim-shaped hole leave his loved ones? Nigel admits, 'If he'd gone downhill more for the next eight more years, it would have been too difficult for him. It was almost a release to a certain extent.' Above and beyond the grief, John Sexton recalls, 'There was a sense of great joy that he'd gone home because, without a doubt, he has, and it's part of Tim's faith and his deep love of Jesus and Mary that he will be there with them.'

His mother concludes: 'I didn't feel any great sadness. I do pray for him. The thing about Tim is I feel he is safe and sound. In other words, I think he is in heaven.'

CHAPTER 3

Knocking on Heaven's Door

GREGORY TOBIASIEWICZ

A frail body stares out at a sea of expectant faces. A hush spreads from the rows of wheelchairs to the waves of benches and to those standing, dotted around the exterior, wanting to be a part of the flock. All eyes are fixed on one pair. All hearts rest on one heart. All breaths are held. Slowly and silently, he rises out of his chair, against the fire of the midsummer heat, the momentary unsteadiness, the usual nausea, the pulsating veins that only he can hear. He takes one step then another. All walk with him, like a mother absorbed in her infant's first steps. He stands tall and erect. A gasp – many see through watery eyes – the love of God floods on everyone and all are blessed.

Gregory's Confirmation day

The ordinary and the extraordinary

WHEN CRIES AND SONGS OF JOY ECHOED AROUND THE WORLD IN celebration of the greatest victory for God and mankind, a child let out its first scream as it was brought out of the wound of creation. Somewhere in a small hospital room, a tired but elated mother and father lay nurturing their vulnerable child. This gift would accomplish his mission in sixteen short years, at the end of which his cancer would return him to God.

Born on Easter Sunday, 19th April 1987, into a Catholic Polish family, bred in England, Gregory Tobiasiewicz 'just had something special that most people don't have,' reveals his girlfriend, Jenny. She adds, 'There was something that made people want to know or listen to him.' Gregory's headmaster spoke about him at the annual parents' evening and claimed that in all his years as a head, he had never come across such a young man who had so much presence, who was always so charming, who always reached out to other children, and who was so clever.

'The thing that struck you was his intellectual ability,' his mother declares. 'What Luke brought home from school, Gregory, aged three, would already be looking at and understanding. His mind was like a sponge: it just soaked everything up. Nobody taught him to read.'

There's an incident which Gregory's father likes to recall: 'Once, my friend noticed that Gregory's shoelace had come undone. Gregory must have been eighteen months. Until then, we only spoke Polish to Gregory. My friend said in English, "Your son's shoelace is undone", and Gregory stooped down to tie it up. That's the first time that I realised he could understand English.'

Aged nine, Gregory went from year three to his sister Weronika's year five class. In year six, he came top of the class. Aged fifteen, Gregory sat his eleven GCSEs as he gradually became more ill; he achieved A* in all of them. He was at the height of academic excellence for his age. He had an 'insatiable spirit', according to his elder brother Luke. 'He wasn't a boy who would sit at the back of the class. If he was interested, he would sit at the front,' confirms Joanna.

This surprising young boy was blessed with the gift of all-roundedness. 'He seemed to excel in anything he tried his hand at,' marvels Luke. As well as playing the piano and the violin, he was an accomplished linguist, fluent in Polish and English as well as a lover of French and Japanese, the latter of which 'stretched him' as an artist. He became the youngest contributor to see his painting exhibited at the Institute of Contemporary Art. In the life of the school, 'he was everywhere,' testify his parents. As well as acting out main parts in dramatic productions, he also played chess, a game of careful planning and fast thinking. Where he excelled, he explored his ability, and where he was not naturally gifted, he pushed himself to improve. Although he 'wasn't well-coordinated', he played sports enthusiastically.

One of the reasons why he was very popular was his brilliant sense of humour, which stayed with him throughout his sickness. His family all agree that, as the 'joker' of the family, 'he had a wicked sense of humour'. Weronika recalls that 'he always used to crack the best and the worst jokes at the most appropriate and inappropriate moments.' She sighs, 'It's what we all miss at home. It's definitely much quieter.' His mother comments 'He was an actor on stage, but he wasn't an actor in every day life.' His good humour stemmed from deep happiness and contentment. It was this which lit up his features and made him so photogenic. Luke explains that 'he was very happy', full of the joys of life and the hopes that so many young people live by.

Jenny suggests that Gregory's happiness was an active and engaging one: 'He made a difference to so many people's lives because he was so happy.' Gregory's quiet self-confidence was an inspiration. Incredibly for a teenager, Luke tells us, 'I think he believed in himself.' His sister, Weronika, laughs as she recalls that Gregory liked to pay attention to his image more than the other members of the family. Perhaps this was another way in which he strove to be better.

Being brought up with Christian values and the spirituality of the Focolare movement, Gregory knew how important it was to think of others. His illness allowed his thoughtfulness to shine through. Fr Emmanuel Agius, a family friend, remembers, 'Each time I visited him in the hospital, he always used to say, "Thank you for coming, Father, thank you."'

Despite his talent and intellect, according to his mother, 'he would never dominate'. Jenny reveals, 'It didn't matter who you were. If you had something to say, he'd listen to you.' For his parents' 20th wedding anniversary, Gregory decided to organise a raffle in the hospital of all the gifts he had received. He used a portion of the money raised to contribute towards a new dinner set from the children, which he chose on a special shopping trip with his aunt Zosia. Two young men distracted Zosia, and she discovered her purse had been stolen: 'When I realised, I was so angry. I said, "If it wasn't for the fact that I was a Christian, I would curse!" Gregory replied, "I will for you!" However, he stopped himself and said, "We mustn't. We've got to pray for them."'

Gregory became the centre of a web of relationships during his illness. There were the five children – Luke, Weronika, Gregory, Bernadette, and Maks – who were respectively eighteen, seventeen, fifteen, eleven and nine when illness struck Gregory and their parents—Joanna and Richard.

Swelling this bond of love were wider family members, old friends and angels sent by God, each at the right time. Though relationships never measured up to perfection, as people would often wish for after a death, each person prized their individual relationship with him. All were bound to Gregory with an everlasting thread.

Illness' grasp

'When told he had leukaemia at that first meeting, he must have known, but he didn't say, "Am I going to die?"' recalls his mother. 'The doctors said:

"80% chance of recovery." Nobody used the words "death" or "die." We were all very happy because it had been diagnosed immediately.'

Gregory fell ill at the beginning of June 2002. His father recalls, 'He used to go to bed early and we thought, "He's doing his GCSEs, so that's very sensible." He started turning a little bit yellow. I took a photo of him and said, "Greg, you look really awful in this photo." I had a closer look at him and he looked really awful.' Weronika remembers, 'He just got really tired and really pale. I don't think we thought it was anything serious.'

On 13th June, Gregory was diagnosed with leukaemia. After developing more symptoms and much painful testing, Gregory was diagnosed on 4th July with Acute Myeloid Leukaemia (AML) of the monocytic type. It was very unusual for a boy of fifteen to suffer from this type of AML, as it is more usual in children of under two years of age.

Understanding the treatment and its unavoidable consequences was crucial to its potential success. Chemotherapy treatment commenced on Sunday 7th July 2002. It was given in four one-week bursts with recuperative periods, finally ending in October. Richard clarifies, 'When you have chemotherapy, you hit rock bottom and then slowly improve. When you are better again, they hit you with the next lot of chemo. Somehow, you have to keep your spirits up, because when you feel grotty, it really is very bad. Your hair falls out and your gums hurt. It's a very nasty treatment.' By the end, according to his parents, 'it was only his nose tube that kept him physically going. He had no sense of taste. He would only drink if his mouth was dry. He was never thirsty.' However, 'the beauty of his treatment and his care,' says his mother, 'was that as he was able to adjust the morphine dose, he was able to be both active, but generally out of pain.' Bernadette still has the mask moulded to the exact shape of Gregory's head, which secured his head when he was having his radiotherapy treatment, as any movement at all could have caused him brain damage. She remembers that his feet hung off the end of the bed because he was six foot one.

In November, Gregory was allowed to go back to school, which he attended until Christmas. The family thought that they were able to turn a page on a traumatic chapter of their lives. Gregory even managed to score top marks in the half-term exams, to his friends' disbelief, despite having missed the first few months of school. Gregory became his normal self.

In the Christmas holidays, the family decided to go skiing to France for a well-earned break. Gregory was admitted to hospital: he had suffered a relapse. When Gregory arrived at the hospital in Grenoble, he had emergency chemotherapy into his spine, after which he felt much better and was able to travel back to England with his mother in an air ambulance. Bernadette states, 'I think that was the hardest Christmas because it was without Greg and without Mum. I don't like Christmas any more.' Luke confirms, 'Although he was still weak, things were on the up. It was very frustrating. The mood became a lot quieter, more sombre.' Weronika confesses that there were moments in those dramatic few days when she thought that she would perhaps never see him again.

Back at the Royal Marsden, just ten minutes away from home, Gregory was reinstated into hospital life. His mother says, 'The problem with Gregory was that he did not react according to the protocol and the problem for the medical profession was that they didn't have a contingency plan.' His bones became so weak that when his younger brother, Maks, accidentally sat on his arm, it snapped. Maks recalls that moment with a tinge of pain although Gregory accepted it with no anger or complaint: 'I didn't know if he was slightly angry at me. I could never bring myself to go up to him and talk about it. I just found it too hard.'

By Easter 2003, the treatment was not working for Gregory. It was immediately arranged that he would have a bone marrow transplant. In simple terms, it consisted of total body radiation in which Gregory's bone marrow would be wiped out and replaced by donor marrow, which should start producing non-cancerous white blood cells. After testing all of Gregory's brothers and sisters, it emerged that Luke was the best suited bone marrow donor. Luke states, 'He was sick and he needed something and I was more than happy to do so. I didn't feel like it was any trouble on my part.'

The transplant was carried out and Gregory was placed in isolation. Only his parents and one other (his aunt Zosia), were allowed into his room, to reduce his exposure to germs. Weronika recalls celebrating his 16th birthday with friends and family on either side of a glass door. Zosia remembers the regular visits from Gregory's girlfriends, and humorously passing on kisses between them.

At the time, the doctors had not discovered the cancerous tumour in Gregory's shoulder. Nevertheless, the transplant allowed Gregory to live longer than he would have done, Jenny believes: 'He wouldn't have gone to Lourdes. He wouldn't have affected all those people.'

Gregory lost his hair and struggled with not being able to eat the food that he wanted so he lost weight. He became weaker, his feet swelled until no shoes fitted; he even called himself 'elephant feet'. Jenny recalls that his freedom was also curtailed by his illness: 'When he'd been taken out of isolation, he could go home, but he wasn't allowed to be around small children, and he wasn't meant to be anywhere where there was air conditioning or large groups of people. We took him to the pub and he loved it. There's no reason why he shouldn't have lived for a couple of hours doing what he wanted to do.'

Soon after the bone marrow transplant, and without warning, the doctors made a terminal diagnosis. He was moved from the cancer treatment team to palliative care. His parents were asked to keep Gregory away from the hospital, his temporary home for the past year. Thereafter, he stayed at home and only went back to the Royal Marsden for blood, which became his only source of life. He needed a blood transfusion every week and then it became progressively more often. His mother reveals, 'Once he had become so sick, death was the only answer for him.'

Inner change

'The first few weeks, when he was doing his GCSEs, Gregory denied that he was ill,' Joanna testifies. 'School was his thing. He enjoyed school. He liked learning. We brought him up to ignore his aches and pains. The fact that he might die was not part of his life plan.' Weronika recalls that during the first treatment, Gregory had chosen his four AS levels – Japanese, History, Maths and Chemistry – and was hoping to return to school as soon as possible. She declares, 'he was always talking about what he would do after hospital.'

There then came a marked loss of interest, provoked by one seemingly innocent suggestion: 'When the doctor said, "Don't do any more work" that had an especially negative influence on the way he approached his treatment because it took his particular life skills away. Gregory's life at the age of sixteen was going to school, learning, taking exams, and taking a full part in the life of the school. The doctors understood the illness but they didn't understand the patient. He had the stuffing knocked out of him by being told not to study and he didn't know what to do with himself. He developed a passive mental attitude. He was not actively engaged in fighting his disease mentally. He was happy for the medical profession to do what they thought should be done.'

Despite denial and determination, there came a time when Gregory began to assimilate his illness and openly acknowledge its possible outcome. Jenny reveals, 'Before he went in for his transplant, he said, "You probably don't want to hear it. I may not come out of this."'

Joanna recalls a moment in the hospital not long after Gregory's bone marrow transplant when Gregory cried. He had found out that a young boy in the ward called Matthew had just died after a similar transplant: 'That was when he realised that having all the treatment and having the bone marrow transplant might not save the day. He said, "I might not live. This might not cure me." What could I say? I agreed, "We don't know if this will cure you."'

Gregory developed a desire to seize the day and live life to the full. Weronika says, 'I don't remember him ever refusing to see his friends.' After being told by his parents that his transfusions were going to be stopped, he simply asked to organise a small party with his friends. On the Thursday before he died, he had a game of billiards, the cue in one hand and his morphine pump in the other. On Friday, the day before he died, he was planning to go and see a football game with his GP, in which his favourite team was playing but unfortunately was too sick to make it. His aunt Zosia claims, 'He just got on with living.'

Gregory's greatest example to others was a total acceptance of his fate. Bernadette believes that, if he had fought it, the situation 'would have been even harder' for his family. Bishop Kieran says that he touched so many people in Lourdes 'because he was so courageous.' He adds: 'There was no anger within him, no resentment. A lot of people admired him for probably what they thought they couldn't do. He was outstanding in that sense and a marvellous example to many people of a faith that allowed him to face the challenge and inevitability of death with such calm and acceptance.'

A point of strong disagreement between Gregory and the consultant was on the subject of sperm-banking. Knowing that future sperm would be sterile after the total body irradiation, the consultant asked Gregory to put the sperm in a sperm bank for future in vitro fertilisation. Gregory's reply was, 'There are thousands of children in the world who need parents. I'll have some of those.' By this time, Gregory had let go. He was not hanging on to the stuff of dreams, but had acknowledged a sense of irrelevance in the matter. The control was no longer in his hands. It was in God's.

The fire of faith

'I'm sure that it was his faith that sustained him and that brought him to Lourdes. He just seemed so confident and calm and I'm sure that must have been the result of a deep faith that everything would be all right,' believes Bishop Kieran.

Fr Emmanuel Agius, a family friend, recounts: 'Once, we had a Mass at his aunt's and they brought Gregory. He wanted to rest because he was so weak. He went upstairs and used the room that I had used the previous night. By the bed, there was a table, and on it, there was a small crucifix. When I went to pick up my luggage to go, I found that the crucifix was not in the position I had left it. He had turned it towards him.' Fr Emmanuel personally believes that 'the strength he got was his love for Jesus... he had Christ in his life, not Christ because of the sickness.' Zosia speculates, 'How can you come to terms with the fact that you're going to die at such a young age without a faith?'

From birth, Gregory had been immersed in a very strong faith. This became priceless for the whole family as well as for Gregory. Jenny remarks, 'I can see how their religion got them through... their faith is what gave them strength.' Through the experience, Bernadette is able to say, 'I really understand why we have Mary and why she's so special. She had to accept everything. The strength of Mary is the strength we're given if we lose someone, because Mary lost Jesus. I feel that the only reason throughout the past four years that I did not turn away from the Church completely was that with God there is heaven and with heaven there is a chance of reuniting with my father figure, closest family member and best friend.' Heaven is the ultimate and most important source of comfort. Maks pictures his brother 'sitting in a grassy field with tall trees and playing one kind of sport or another.'

Part of what sustained Gregory's faith was his and the family's efforts to live it. Before Gregory's bone marrow transplant, Fr Emmanuel said a Mass for Gregory and his family and anointed him in his room in the Royal Marsden. Zosia described the sight of Gregory attached to tubes as the Mass was said as 'very powerful.' Fr Emmanuel gave a homily on suffering. Zosia recalls, 'He emphasised the fact that suffering is an unwanted blessing. We mustn't waste it. God doesn't want us to suffer. If He permits it, by offering it up, it's so powerful because we offer it up united with Christ, and it brings down many graces not only on the person who's suffering but also on the people that he's praying for or offering it up for. For Gregory, it was an opportunity for him to let God know how much he loves Him by being able to offer it up.'

Gregory also went to a parish healing Mass on the Friday before he died and often received Holy Communion from Fr Emmanuel: 'There was one occasion where he was completely quarantined and I passed the host through to Zosia.' For Gregory's parents, 'Mass is an expression of the way you live. Mass is a time when you can be a bit quieter and in those quiet moments God can speak to you or you can sort out some of your jumbled up thoughts. You listen to the readings. Whatever the readings were, we were able to slot them into our lives. We used to pray quite regularly as a family. If you go to Mass every week, week in, week out, it's this constant reminder of the ideals that you want to live by.'

The Focolare movement, a Catholic lay community carrying on a lively dialogue with Christians of various churches as well as faithful of the major religions, and working together for unity in the world, had a great spiritual influence on Gregory. This young boy once said to Fr Emmanuel how, in his sickness, the spirituality of the Focolare had helped him and how the idea of 'Christ forsaken on the cross' had inspired him. According to Zosia, the Focolare movement taught him how much happier he would be by caring for others: 'That was very powerful in Gregory. He never excluded others. That was his faith. He lived his faith.'

Gregory found God in a silent place. Richard wonders: 'To a certain extent, that's what Gregory found when he was taken out of the teenage environment and put into a world which was a little bit quieter... he had to find what his relationship was with God because he understood that that was where he was going.'

Journey to Lourdes

Joanna and Richard's immediate response to the terminal diagnosis was a request to take Gregory to Lourdes. They shared this plan with the consultant, who agreed with reluctance. Jenny recalls: 'I was only told I was going five days beforehand. I was nervous: I had to learn the Hail Mary.' At the airport on Friday, the little group of travellers assembled ready for departure. To Gregory's astonishment, more people started arriving: Fr Emmanuel, Gregory's aunt Zosia and two of her children, Andrzej and Victoria, all turned up as a surprise!' The joy had begun.

What expectations hid behind their sparkling eyes? What hope fed them through the struggle of the preparations? Jenny recalls, 'I did think that it would all be about miracles, which it isn't. They didn't go there for a miracle for Greg. They just went there for some peace.' As well as peace for themselves, Bernadette says, 'They just went to Lourdes to give him peace.'

Healthwise, Gregory was not the patient that he had been in England. His parents remember: 'He had a huge up! When he went to Lourdes, he suddenly didn't need blood, which amazed the doctors. He had blood laid on in Lourdes. It was all organised from here. They did his blood typing. They sent an order to France. The Lourdes hospital said that they had the blood in stock and Gregory could come and get it whenever he needed it. They thought that the flight would finish him off. So the first thing they did, when he landed, was to go to the clinic to have his blood taken. They said, "Nothing wrong with this boy's blood. Everything looks fine," and he didn't need blood all the time he was in Lourdes.'

Gregory knew, however, that death was always near. On the return flight, the ground crew wanted to place him on a metal chair to allow him to be carried up the steep staircase, but this would have badly damaged his now very frail body. The stewardess initially refused to allow him to fly home as the chair could cause an uncontrollable haemorrhage due to his low platelet count. Jenny recalls Joanna clearly explaining, 'He's got four brothers and sisters at home that he's not going to say goodbye to unless you let him get on the flight!'

On the night that they arrived, they all went to the top of the Basilica to watch the Torchlight Procession from above. For Jenny, 'It was so sad! Whenever they sang songs… and because he looked so ill and because I knew he was dying.'

Zosia recalls, 'Gregory was being held up because he couldn't see over the parapet from his wheelchair. The candlelight was reflected on his face and he really looked quite angelic.' Moments later, an Italian man came up to them and 'just wanted to touch Gregory and shake his hand', remembers Zosia. 'We told this man it was going to be his Confirmation. He came and searched Gregory out. He was there for his Confirmation. At the end of it, he came up and said, "Do you mind if my wife and I have our photograph taken with you?" That was a complete stranger whose heart was touched by Gregory.'

The patron saint of lost causes

Whereas many are prepared for Confirmation in the comfort of a home or a church hall, Gregory learnt about God in a place of suffering, often amidst hurried nurses and doctors, uncomfortable or agonising patients and bare white walls and floors.

Fr Emmanuel taught him with great enthusiasm, arriving by Gregory's bedside at all hours to set this young man's mind whirring about the infinite, divine mysteries within or beyond our reach. Fr Emmanuel recalls, 'He was very thoughtful.' Gregory wrote a thank you note to Fr Emmanuel at the end of their sessions which said:

> Dear Fr Emmanuel,
>
> Thank you very much for doing such a great deal to help organise my pilgrimage to Lourdes, and for encouraging so many people to pray for me while I am sick. Thanks also for all your prayers and blessings, for sitting with me, and helping to explain and discuss all and everything about God.
>
> All my love,
>
> Gregory

This young patient was unusually aware of the magnitude and commitment tied to the Sacrament of Confirmation. Fr Emmanuel recounts, 'When we were speaking with the Bishop, Gregory said, "I know that I am going to receive the seven gifts when I am confirmed, but in my life I am going to have to unlock them."'

Gregory's final preparation for Confirmation occurred minutes before the service. Fr Emmanuel recounts: 'As I went to dress up, he sent a message for me: "Tell Father I want to speak to him before the celebration."' When Fr Emmanuel found Gregory, this young boy said, as Fr Emmanuel recalls it, 'What I want Father is for you to hear my confession as the last preparation for my Confirmation.'

The evening before was a very eventful one for the choir. One member recalls the wonder which poured into the group when its conductor arrived at the rehearsal and said, 'Throw the programmes away! We've got a sixteen year old boy with cancer who is being confirmed and he has chosen all the hymns!' This choir member affirms, 'What a difference it made to the choir!'

The actual service is remembered by Jenny as a 'blur.' It was performed at St Bernadette's altar, outside the Rosary Basilica, thus exposed to the sweltering heat of a July day. The hymns were all chosen or approved by Gregory. One of the bidding prayers, written by Zosia, read:

> May all who suffer pain, illness or disease know that they are joined to Christ in his suffering through his salvation of the world. Teach us the virtue of patience in human illness.

This is exactly what was being acted out in front of the congregation's very eyes. The Confirmation name that Gregory asked to be given was appropriate and moving. His parents recall, 'It was only after he had that terminal diagnosis that he chose Jude, the patron saint of lost causes, because he appreciated that on earth his case was hopeless.'

Sarah Clutton will never forget the effort it took Gregory to stand up out of his wheelchair and walk forward a few steps to be confirmed. This visible effort touched the hundreds of people watching beyond words. Only one person, however, felt exactly what it had cost Gregory to stand up. Victoria, his cousin and sponsor, had her hand on his shoulder as he was being confirmed. To feel him shaking so noticeably in his effort gave her sharp stomach pain. She was touching what so many others could see: a determined spirit fighting its corporal enemy. At the end of the service, Gregory accomplished his last great action by reading out a prayer that his aunt had kept in her bag, unused for many years, just waiting for the right moment. Eyes welled up and hearts opened as he read the following words:

O Spirit of truth, enlighten me with your truth
That I may first live the truth of love, peace and
Righteousness.
Help me that I may be able, with my words and deeds,
To proclaim every day the Word of the Father
In its full light, to everybody.

Pour out the gift of love into my life
That from now on, I may love God in you above all,
And my neighbour as myself.

Pour out on me the gift of wisdom
That in everything I do, think, feel and decide
I may always think, decide and act in your light.

O Spirit of Counsel, descend on me
That I may, with my knowledge and the Word of Love
Help those who ask me for counsel.
Let my every word be a light to others.

Spirit of Jesus, grant me the gift of your Strength
That I may stand every trial and do the Father's will,
Especially in the times of hardship.
Spirit of fortitude, strengthen me in the hours of frailty.
I ask this through Christ our Lord.
Amen.

At the end of the Confirmation Mass, everyone clapped and cheered. 'It wasn't just Gregory receiving the Holy Spirit at his Confirmation,' remarks Zosia. 'God used him as an instrument because when he read that prayer, we were so touched, we were so overwhelmed that our hearts opened and we were all filled with the Holy Spirit. A lady standing at the back was proof of this to me. Her husband had died the previous year and she stopped going to church but she still went to Lourdes. She was so angry with God for having taken her husband. When Gregory was reading out that prayer, she was so filled with pain looking at him as he was so young that she screamed and she said, "Why God? Why?"

'Later on, when we came to the reunion, she came up to me and I said, "How are you? Have you forgiven God yet?" She said, "How could I not?"'

'The best days of my life'

During their time in Lourdes, the group of people accompanying Gregory filled just a few days with many rich experiences.

Joanna states, 'He wanted to go to the Grotto. He wanted to look around. He wanted to touch the stones and feel the water. He didn't just go to Lourdes to watch. He wanted to participate in everything.'

After his Confirmation, Gregory decided to go to the Lourdes Baths accompanied by his father and his cousin, Andrzej. Zosia remembers, 'We were very concerned... I was terrified.' Richard remembers waiting in the queue for the Baths: 'Gregory and I looked around and we didn't say anything but he knew and I knew that the people around him were in a worse state than he. At the end of the day, his illness only lasted fourteen months, which is a long time, but not compared to some of these people... We must have waited for an hour and a half.' Andrzej was terrified too. How were they going to get this poor, broken body into the freezing water? Richard recalls arriving in the cubicle: 'It took longer than for three or four other people to have a bath... Undressing him with his broken arm wasn't too bad, but you can imagine getting undressed and shivering from cold. He had no body fat. Poor old Greg, he was freezing. He had to be lifted in. He let out a cry as they lowered him into the water...'

Andrzej told his mother afterwards how moved he was by Gregory's determination to be immersed in the waters and how the helpers had held Gregory with such delicacy. Richard recounts, 'Once he'd stopped shaking and they managed to get his clothes back on him, he said, "I'm coming again next year!"'

Lourdes opened the door to love. Gregory was overwhelmed by the community that he had let himself become a part of. Bishop Kieran comments, 'He wasn't withdrawn from the rest and he didn't go to Lourdes as a private person just to share his grief and illness and suffering with his family and small group of friends. He went to be part of a larger pilgrimage. I think he found a home with the diocese in those few days.'

Gregory was greeted upon arrival and waved off for his departure. As they left on the Sunday, they were surrounded by people. Jenny declares, 'I just felt so welcomed. Everyone was interested in me or Greg... everyone wanted to come and meet him.' She adds, 'He was treated so well everywhere he went.' Gregory was able to go to the Little Flower bar and enjoy the sense of community there. He even had half a beer, which he had not been able to do for months. That sense of togetherness projected itself into Gregory's encounters. Jenny recalls, 'He got to hold a baby! There's a photo of his massive hand and her tiny one. He was about to die and she was only just born.'

There was no sense of inhibition or social status, to the extent that the Bishop held the coffee mug for Gregory to drink out of, and went late night shopping with him. Kay Longbottom, who was not planning to travel to Lourdes that year, stayed up all night with Gregory, watching over him as he slept. Kay said afterwards, 'I was meant to come'.

Gregory's parents conclude, 'For him, it was an understanding of what total love means because that was what he experienced. That for me is the beauty of Lourdes. You just love your neighbour. We were loved to bits. Love was all around. If this isn't the presence of God, then there is no other presence of God.'

When Gregory arrived, he met Ollie Johnson who was sitting in her wheelchair. Feeling nervous about the experience that lay ahead, he told her that the worst aspect of being in a wheelchair is people staring at you. To this, Ollie replied, 'Don't worry. Lourdes is different.' Twenty-four hours later, he came back to Ollie and said, 'You're right. In Lourdes, they look at you with love.'

After confessing to Fr Emmanuel before his Confirmation, Gregory admitted, 'Father, I know my days are counted but I will try and live them to the full.' In the evening, the family participated in the Torchlight Procession. Whilst Fr Emmanuel was pushing his wheelchair, Gregory said, 'Father, Father, today is the best day of my life.' When his aunt Zosia asked him how his day had been, he repeated it adding, 'If I had just lived for this one day, it would have been worth it.' Fr Emmanuel claims that 'from the room in the hospital to Lourdes', there was a transformation in Gregory: 'There was not one moment of unhappiness.' In Lourdes, Gregory said to Zosia, 'If God wants me in heaven, who am I to argue?'

Gregory came back from Lourdes with gifts for himself and for all his loved ones: peace, understanding and acceptance. Joanna confirms, 'Gregory was very peaceful after Lourdes.' Weronika believes that it was 'almost like he was ready to go, and waited for the right moment.' One of the first things he did when he arrived back was to text all of the people listed in his mobile phone with the message, 'Smile, God loves you. Love Gregory.'

The impact on the pilgrimage was phenomenal. As Zosia states, 'In every single homily, Gregory's name was mentioned. There wasn't a time when people weren't talking about Gregory.' One of the pilgrims tells of his personal encounter with him: 'Whilst I never spoke to Gregory, I did look at him and he looked at me. He had the most piercing blue eyes. It's very difficult to put into words what it was to me. I think it was a look of love. It's that type of look which you would have from Jesus: seeing you as you really are and loving you. It can only have been for a short instant but that was Gregory's gift to me."

Bishop Kieran believes that Gregory 'brought a focus' to the pilgrimage: 'Lourdes can sometimes be a little too busy, too big… the experience in that year focused many of the people there on what Lourdes offers to so many people.'

One pilgrim states, 'I think that Gregory was very close to God. His very presence in Lourdes that year brought a closeness to each other and to God. I have this very strong memory of 2003, of a kind of hush and of an awe that existed that year. We felt very close to God, with him and led by him.' Joanna believes that Gregory touched so many because, 'Everybody knew that he was dying. Death is now so often hidden away. We take the sick to Lourdes but we very rarely speak of the dying. Gregory was simply an example. In a way, he was a bit like Pope John Paul II. He had a very open death to the world. That's why people were so drawn to him and to his death. It's because they were actually seeing him living those last moments. And to have people who can live these moments with dignity is so inspiring for our own death. When I think of Gregory, I think we can all live and die like that.'

In the end, Gregory was the pilgrimage's link to heaven: 'He was going to be knocking on heaven's door any day.'

Mission accomplished

'Gregory's mission was accomplished in Lourdes,' marvels Zosia, 'not in getting his A levels or a degree, not playing in an orchestra. His mission was to touch people's hearts. In some of those people's hearts – that is just a seed that has been sown – it's not germinated yet. See how God has acted in this one person's life and how, when he died, he had fulfilled an amazing mission!'

Sunday, 3rd August, 2003, 2.17am, a suspended moment in time, an unreal moment: Gregory Tobiasiewicz passes away, aged sixteen, surrounded by his mother and father, stewards chosen by God, whose breast he had just returned to.

Just a few minutes earlier, he had asked with the little strength he could muster, 'Dad, I want to sit up.' They were his last words. Bernadette believes, 'It just showed that he never gave up.' Gregory would not die lying down. In his death lay the paradoxes of a young boy going ahead of his parents on the greatest journey of all, an almighty strength born from a crippled body, the 'Keep Smiling' t-shirt, marked by a large 'smiley face', which continued to smile up at his parents after its owner ceased to breathe.

Monday, 28th July, a day after their arrival back from Lourdes, Joanna and Richard sat Gregory down in the garden on a beautiful summer's day and prepared him for the inevitable. His legs were swollen, his need for blood almost insatiable: the hospital had said it was time to stop.

They recall, 'We decided that we'd better make it plain to Gregory that his days were numbered because nobody else had. We told him that the blood transfusions were going to stop. We sat in the garden and we read the passage in the Bible of the raising of Lazarus. We chose it to encourage Gregory, because death isn't the end, because there is something after death, because Jesus cried when his brother, Lazarus died. We told him, "You understand that you are going to die. You're having your last blood transfusion tomorrow." He was not a boy to suffer fools gladly or to keep quiet. We felt that if we chatted to him and he wanted to raise something, he would feel at ease to do so. We said, "Is there anything you would like to do?" He replied, "I've got a few friends coming round. Can I invite a few more?"'

On Tuesday, Gregory was taken to hospital for his last blood transfusion. Jenny was entrusted with all of his medicine and left by his side to enjoy a quiet and privileged moment. 'He was just lying there and he looked very sweet. He was asleep. It was nice to have some time that was just quiet – everything had been so busy – just to sit and think about things.' When Jenny's mother and sister came to pick her up, her sister saw Gregory lying asleep and burst into tears because he looked so ill. It was not only his family being confronted by the fatal illness of a sixteen year old youth: it was all who met him.

Zosia recalls being telephoned by Joanna and told that Gregory was dying. When she arrived, she was asked to lead the prayers. She recollects her last moments with Gregory: 'He was just sitting on the sofa, very, very weak: you could tell he only had hours to live. I thanked him for the privilege of being able to spend so much time with him and told him how much I loved him. "Gregory," I said, "I've got something to ask you. When you meet Jesus and Mary, do you think you could give them a kiss from me?" He just nodded.' She remarks that she could only ask Gregory such a favour because she was sure that her nephew was 'completely at peace with the understanding that he was going to die.'

Bernadette affirms that Gregory's last word to her was 'cool', after she had been talking to him about her guide camp. She states, 'I realised how much energy and effort it must have taken just to say the word "cool". He wasn't eating. He couldn't walk. He didn't even have enough energy to sit himself up. It was like a whisper.'

Maks recalls the strange and comforting feeling of that last night: 'It was as if someone was standing at the doorway but there wasn't.' Gregory's intimate moment of goodbye to Jenny has not faded into the hazy past. It is still real and vibrant: 'The night he died, he woke up and then held his hand out. So I held his hand and he pulled me closer and gave me a hug. I think he was saying goodbye.' By that time, all knew that he was dying. They took it in turns to sit with Gregory. Jenny relates, 'We knew what was happening but we were a bit scared.'

The last time Gregory was sick was at midnight, after which he simply lay peacefully. At 1.30 am, Gregory's godmother and her husband arrived. Gregory was leaning against his mother when he died. The children came down to be by their brother's bedside. His face was lit up by a candle burning nearby and the air was filled with the scent of white lilies. Bernadette says, 'I just sat there.'

His death initially came as a shock. His mother states, 'I expected him to be sick in bed for longer than he was. Nobody had prepared us for what the signs are of a body dying. In fact, a lot of people are sick because the stomach says, "I've had enough."'

'Born on a Sunday, died on a Sunday,' marvels his father. Sarah Clutton recalls that night very well: she had received two red roses from Gregory as a gift of thanks for his short but blessed pilgrimage. When she was called just minutes after Gregory had died, she noticed that one of the roses' heads, both blooming before she went to bed, had drooped.

Last wishes enacted

Before he died, Gregory spoke openly with his sister Weronika about what he wished for his funeral, oblivious that it was to be the hottest day of the year and that four hundred people would be present.

Gregory's spirit entered into the logistics of the funeral. He asked for the colour of his coffin to be pine rose and for the people attending to be dressed in clothes of colour. Rather than a Polish-spoken funeral, he wanted the dominant language to be English, which many more of those present would be able to understand. The hymns he wished for were the ones played at his Confirmation. On a more social level, he asked his sister to keep an eye out for his friends and wanted people to feel comfortable. Finally, he asked that everyone should be handed a sticker with 'Smile, God loves you' written on it. On the coffin was a wreath in the shape of a 'smiley face', chosen by Jenny. The Lourdes choir sang to the memory of Gregory.

A passing felt, reflected upon and lived

Though they differ in their reactions, each person left behind has learnt about life and their faith on a deeper level and has, in one way or another, come out a little wiser.

Weronika's message is 'Just be there. Keep smiling,' adding, 'It's different for everyone." Gregory's parents have learnt: 'Nothing came naturally. You have to make a conscious decision about how you feel and how you are going to feel and then you have to pray and ask for God's grace to help you. People come and say, "How do you do it? I couldn't do it." The reality is that everybody can do it. We could direct our lives much better if we thought about it.' The expression, 'life is what you make it', can be true even in coping with death.

Richard adds, 'Jesus Christ was God's son and God went through the hurt that I went through. Maybe the only way to get to heaven is suffering. It was Abraham's attitude that taught me what should be my attitude. I can say to God, "You took my child away from me", but I've never had an opinion that said that these were my children, a possession of mine. We have always believed that we are the stewards of God's children, of individuals that are free.'

Such a rupture and change sends fragments of differently shaped emotions into all parts and areas of people's lives. 'I've never really understood any of my feelings,' Bernadette says. 'I never thought that he'd die. I think that I never thought he'd be gone. It took me about two and a half, three years to realise it, what had actually happened, and that's when I got more moved by it and felt it more... All the time that it took, it builds up even more.' Bernadette shows how disbelief and shock can prevent someone from fully assimilating the fact of death.

Jenny had to have bereavement counselling: 'I wasn't crying; I wasn't doing much,' she reveals. The counselling and her trip to Lourdes the following year both helped her to experience the emotion of her boyfriend's death. Luke recalls, "It was quite difficult to get over the fact that he had died. It was very up in the air.' Weronika remembers anger invading her thoughts a year afterwards; the first year was 'a blur.'

Anger became one of many uncontrollable emotions. Weronika recalls not being 'the nicest person' after her brother passed away, having felt that they had grown apart during his illness – his life standing still and her life continuing – that she was replaced and not missed. She claims, 'At the time, I would have said it was just anger at other people because of what they were doing, rather than anger at the situation, but then if I look back on it, if I honestly had to say, there must have been something more in there—probably a lot of anger at myself as well.' Bernadette echoes this statement in declaring, 'It's an anger with myself rather than an anger with anyone else.'

Gregory's premature passing, for which there is no easy explanation, has led family members to deep questioning in their faith. Maks finds it hard to face people who suffer and survive: 'It just makes it a lot more difficult: why didn't Greg suffer and survive?' He concludes, 'There are just no answers.' Luke explains that despite being outwardly serene, he asks many questions: 'Why did it happen to him? Why would it be in God's plan for it to happen to him? It was a bit illogical for him to die so young. I've found it difficult since his death to find solace in my faith. It's not answered my questions or calmed my anxieties.' Weronika observes, 'I wasn't mad at Him. I just didn't get the same comfort out of going to church. I didn't feel close to God at all.'

The absence of son or brother is perhaps the most difficult concept to grapple with. Maks comments, 'I feel like there's a part of me missing— not broken. You have a little tear in a piece of paper and you don't really know if it's whole. It's a piece of work and you try to repair it but it's just not easy.' Joanna reveals, 'The difficulty for me has been the hole that is left and finding a way of living with it. It's unfillable.'

Gregory's death has given the family an understanding of suffering and the desire to reach out to those faced with it. Joanna and Richard have since engaged in a lot of charity and voluntary work.

Weronika confesses, 'After Gregory passed away, I went and worked in the home for the destitute and the dying in Calcutta. I saw people dying every day. I don't think that is something I could ever have coped with had Gregory not passed away.' Luke remarks, '… the experience has helped me to empathise more. I think I've gained more of an understanding. I see the opportunity to help people more.'

To aid someone who is grieving for a loved one, Bernadette would say, 'You've just got to see that they're still there. They're still in your hearts and they're still part of you. Even if sometimes you feel as if you want them there, then you take your memories. Don't worry if you feel down. Don't worry if you want to cry. It's natural. If you cry, cry it out and then you can feel better.'

2003 was the year that Fr Ian Byrnes took over as spiritual director of the Arundel and Brighton Lourdes pilgrimage. When he returned to his parish and was asked what it was like to be the spiritual director of the pilgrimage, he answered, 'I have no idea. Gregory was.'

CHAPTER 4

A Hidden Treasure

HOLLY KEEN

Tragedy transforms

'ALL THE TIME WHEN I'M WITH HOLLY, I THINK THERE'S SOMETHING else,' says Chris Xerri. Hazel Plastow feels, 'You know that her smile is from the centre of herself. It's from her heart. There is a real depth to it. That's got to be the God and Jesus within her.' Nick Harvey confesses, 'I don't think of her as being disabled as such: she is just Holly.' Charlotte Burnell adds, 'You will always wonder, 'What is going on in there Holly? What are you thinking about?'

Holly's mother Joy starts by telling us of an apparently ordinary day with her husband, two daughters, Holly and Shannan, and son, Angus, whilst they lived in Australia. 'She was just something very special. She was a very loving little girl, very good. I never had to do more than raise my voice to Holly. On this day, we went swimming in the morning. Holly seemed to be all right. She was tired. She'd had the first four weeks at school and you think, "She's quiet. She's tired because it's a full day." She was just five. We came home and she wouldn't eat her lunch and I put my hand on her and she was very, very hot. So I took her from the table and sat with her and she was getting hotter by the minute. We couldn't afford a phone so I got in the car and drove to the shopping centre and phoned the doctor and he said, "I'll be along in the afternoon." By the time I got back, my husband said, "I think she's unconscious," which she was. I rushed next door. I knew they had a phone but I wouldn't go in for something small. The doctor said, "I'll come straight away and if she starts to fit, do this, do that."

'I came in. She'd just started to fit so I was looking after her. The doctor was there within two minutes. Holly fitted non stop for two and a half hours. That was when her breathing was wrong and oxygen starvation to her brain happened. This was forty-two years ago. Holly is forty-seven now. They didn't have anything like the gadgets to find out what was wrong with people in those days. They said, "It's a virus. We don't know what it is." They didn't know what a virus was really. "She's just been unlucky." That's an understatement. It could have given her a cold or gone to her kidneys and just given her a fever. As a general thing, she got encephalitis but it never got named.

'Holly was in hospital eight weeks, three and a half weeks of which she was unconscious, comatose. The family didn't see her all that time. When they went back to fetch her, she didn't look the same. She'd had a huge operation on her skull to see what the matter was because they didn't have any way of looking in in those days so she was shaven and her head was still swollen. Shannan, who was not yet four, looked at her and said, "That's not my Holly." From the time she was born, Shannan was waiting to follow her sister. She stood when she was seven months and was walking at ten months simply because she needed to catch up with Holly. Suddenly, that was over. She grew up over night: it was absolutely appalling to watch. She was talking about it a while ago, in tears still: "I thought she was a monster." Angus was just coming up to two and clinging to his mother. I hadn't time for that. I had a helpless baby of five unexpectedly. If you're expecting a baby, you're excited and the baby's a pleasure. This was a tragedy.

'She hasn't lived with me since she was seven. She was at home for a couple of years. Forty odd years ago, there were no home care facilities, no special school, no understanding of the needs to keep people at home. I don't know how I kept the house going. She was home 24/7 and I was up with her all night having fits or getting out of bed because I got her walking again. At five years old it's quite easy. You hold the child under the armpits facing the same way and you kick the feet: gradually I got her used to the idea of using her feet. I loaded a doll's pushchair with books and invented the first Zimmer frame! Holly walked around holding onto the Zimmer, or else holding onto the furniture. She lolloped. I don't know what she would have been, but they told me that more than half of her brain was destroyed. It's possible with a child now, with practices, to stimulate and persuade new synapses and new brain paths to develop. In those days, Holly was nursed in a side room so it was quiet: on her back for eight weeks. Whereas now it would be efforts all the time to try and force the brain to start working again.

'Angus doesn't see her. He was four when she went: he never had a relationship with her before the illness because he was less than two years old. Shannan has not got over it. Shannan, now forty-five, is at university doing clinical neuro-psychology to try and learn how to help people who are brain-damaged. She always comes to Holly if there is a crisis. She finds it hard but she comes.'

How did such a trauma impinge on Joy, who was brought up as a Catholic, and how did it affect her faith?

'I didn't think in terms of God. I think I thought in terms of my loss entirely. The realisation took a year because I couldn't get my head around it. I had her and I lost her. I find myself involved in informal bereavement work because people somehow know that there's pain inside me. You seem to carry some sort of scar tissue that you can't see. The change from that bright, sparkling little girl over night: it's just almost too hard to understand at all. I've lost the babies that she would have had, the grand-children. I had a bit of a time with Our Lady but that's nearly over. I don't find it that easy. I put Holly into her arms and she never gave her back.'

Her husband was very affected by the sudden change in his eldest daughter. Joy states, 'Holly went into care in a huge institution in Australia, ninety miles from us. That was the worst thing. I didn't see much of her because we never had any money for train fares. You had to write ahead to say you were coming. You had to report to the gatehouse to say you were there. My marriage broke up in 1972. In 1974, we came back to England, partly because it was uncomfortable living in the same country as him and partly because my parents were separated and both getting old and I was glad to be back in time for my father's death early the next year.'

Before leaving Australia, Joy could not find a place in a home in England for Holly and, when she was there, found herself with no money to go and collect her daughter. Joy recalls: 'I nearly died with the awfulness of having her so far away. It was just a dreadful time. I came over without any money. Within six months I was working in social services. I was a social worker for ten years and then I retired. Having Holly made me want to do it better than the woman who looked after us. I knew I could do it better, and I know I did.'

Rescue mission

Back in England, Joy was dissatisfied.

The break in the connection with her eldest child was too painful: 'I used to write and say, "Please give me news of Holly," because it was pretty desperate being in another country. I didn't get an answer to the letters. This went on in several letters. Eventually, I began to think, "They've written a letter to say Holly had died and I just haven't taken it in, because why aren't they writing?" One term of my second year, I didn't have to go to college at all. I had by then been to Lourdes in 1979, my first year of college, because it's something I had always wanted to do. I went to Lourdes and came back determined to get Holly. I realised, "This is the moment. Go and get her." That's my Lourdes miracle for you.

'At the beginning of the second year, I went to my tutor and I said, "I'd like to have a placement in Sydney for my final placement." He nearly died! He didn't know why I was going. He came back and he said, "I've talked to the examiners. They think it's a marvellous idea and more people should do it."

'I applied for a bed in a big institution in Redhill and got a place guaranteed for her. We left in 1974 and I came for her in 1980: for six years I hadn't seen her, from fourteen to twenty. I missed the teenager. It was November. She was going to be 21 in the December. I got to know Holly again. She knew me! Immediately. The warmth that came to me! She was still there. I went off the plane, met my tutor, had a shower and went straight up to where she was, just north of Newcastle and stayed a weekend, then went up two or three times more in the four months, then flew her back. Another little miracle: we went to the plane and they gave me a seat right at the front with access to first class loo. There were spare seats for Holly to lie down on. I had to give Holly medication every eight hours. She was very easy. She had no trouble settling on the plane, or in the new home."

When they returned and Holly was settled in the home, Joy was spoilt with the time she could spend with her beloved daughter: 'I was working in Caterham. I used to pop in on my way home in the evening and help bath her, or feed her, or just see her.'

The disability

Holly is now with seven other people who have suffered severe brain damage from birth, in one of sixty homes run by the National Health Service. Though Joy describes the home as a 'lovely, homey house,' where

Holly is doing much better than she was in the institution she lived in previously, it can nevertheless be very upsetting for someone who is not used to that type of scene. Joy reveals her internal battle: 'I've struggled with being in that home every year. I have to say that, just occasionally, I'm sitting in there with everybody and I think, "What am I doing here?" Even now I hardly see the other residents: I just have eyes for Holly.'

Despite the trauma of being plunged into an unfamiliar environment through her daughter's disability, Joy does not wallow in self-pity: 'I was asked in Wonersh one year, "Have you ever said, Why should this happen to me?" and I have always answered and still do, 'Why shouldn't it happen to me?' I don't see it as a question. These things come out of the blue. Why shouldn't it be?'

She has always spoken out where necessary: 'I go once a year to Wonersh to talk to the seminarians to tell them what it's like to look after a handicapped child, telling them the good things and the bad things that we have experienced from priests and the Church. Once a very attractive young man lay back in his chair and he said, "Oh! Mentally handicapped: it's not my scene!" And I sat up and I said, "It's not my scene either and I'm stuck with it!" He sat bolt upright for the rest of the afternoon. There are some things that young priests need to know, that it's a not good idea when you're standing by your daughter's bed thinking she's about to die when she's five and he comes in and starts wittering on about the difficulty of getting parking! Little things like that...'

How does Holly communicate? Her mother reveals: 'With her eyes and her face and her pleasure in you. She hasn't got any sign language. She's not clever enough. She has an unassessable IQ. No speech.' Nick Harvey, a helper who has nursed Holly on several occasions, has learnt: 'If she's cross, you know because she screeches. She puts her hand in her mouth and jumps up and down in her chair. And if she gets excited, she screams but it is quite a joyous scream and she has a smile on her face then. As she's got older, she's definitely got more melancholic. She has a lot more of these little ischaemic attacks where she just drifts off and she gets sleepier than she used to. When I first met her, she was a real bundle of energy but then she was in her late twenties. So, as she's got older, she's got a lot quieter.'

Joy talks us through her daughter's disability: 'She's paralysed on one side, she's epileptic, doubly incontinent and wonderful!' This devoted mother adds, 'Sometimes her epilepsy is hanging about in the back and then she gets sulky and bothered, so you never know if you're going to get a happy Holly. She's on a lot of medication. It stops it being worse. They're very small, her fits. She walks like somebody who's had a stroke, she throws her handicapped leg. She puts a lot of things in her mouth because she has only got the one hand. She bites her hand with frustration. You can understand it. She hasn't got the language. She's just completely dependent upon what other people do. Now, they bring something to signify what is going to happen: a plate of food, an incontinence pad and she knows that that's what she's going to do. One of the difficulties with her degree of handicap is for her carers to know when she is in pain, or when she is ill. It must be very frustrating that things are going on inside and not coming out.'

Joy comments on eating, which is one of Holly's favourite activities: 'She hasn't got very good table manners. If she doesn't get food, she will snatch. One carer said, "She is part of the family. She will sit at the table. Holly gets a teaspoon, and everyone else gets a dessert spoon and yet Holly finishes when everyone does!" She has no initiative at all except to pick up a toy, play with it with one hand, feel it. If I finish a book, I go and get another one or go and dig in the garden or get on the phone: all the things she can't do or doesn't even know about.'

Holly stands out within the home. Her mother affirms, 'She's the only one in the house who helps the staff with her own dressing. She can't manage the wobbly arm. She puts her arm through the sleeve. She lifts her legs for the shoes and trousers. The others are just like dolls to dress. They were all born that way, born either integrally that way or at birth, damaged. I don't think there is anybody there who has suffered a later trauma. So the five year old is still there, you see! It's extraordinary. Those five years of ordinary life have made her different.'

Charlotte Burnell, who knows Holly well through caring for her, concludes: 'There is an individual who relies on everything from other human beings and therefore is at the whim of those who would take advantage of her, or belittle her. She is like a baby who is at the mercy of life. Therefore, at the most basic level of humanity, she deserves to be protected and taken care of, kept warm, clothed, fed, made to feel safe, made to feel loved, because she is not able to go and search for any of that herself.'

Joy tells us, 'Even though we don't live together, we are about as tightly knit as a mother with a one year old.' Is such a person as Holly misunderstood by others who do not have the same connection? 'Yes,' confesses her mother. 'It takes people a while to understand. Nobody treats her badly.' Joy concludes, 'There's no change to be expected from Holly.

ot suddenly going to wake up and go and get a degree like her sister. She just trundles on. Life trundles on. I just hope that she lives healthily and dies very suddenly so that she doesn't have long suffering.'

Discovering Lourdes

'After about five years, I was in there one day and the sister said, "Holly's going on holiday," and so I asked, "Where is she going?"

"Oh, she's going to a hotel."

I said, "Is it in the Suffolk place?"

"No, people with money don't have to go there."'

To Joy's surprise, Holly had a hidden Australian pension. The reciprocal arrangement signified that the English government had no access to it. This sum of money had grown over five years and became enough for Holly to be able to finance five people's pilgrimages to Lourdes with Arundel and Brighton. She did this for fifteen years until her Australian pension stopped, when she was able only to finance one person.

Sarah Clutton marvels, 'She paid for over fifty children to go to Lourdes.' Joy finally recalls, 'I thought, if she's paying for all these people, she might as well go herself, and that was the beginning of Holly going to Lourdes.'

'The first year I went with Holly,' begins her mother, 'I was absolutely terrified. I was terrified that she would be healed, because what do you do with somebody of twenty-five who has no social graces, no education? Thank God she wasn't. She doesn't need to be. That's how she is to be.' According to Joy, the first Lourdes 'only broke the ice.' Despite Holly's noisiness and agitation at the time, Joy maintains that the people in the *Accueil* where Holly stayed were 'extraordinary', 'loving of her' and 'so accepting'.

Lourdes soon became the annual routine for Holly. 'I tell her for a while beforehand and we sing a few Lourdes hymns, but she twigs when we're in the coach,' states her mother. Lourdes is where Holly is happiest: 'She's busy all the time. Here, she sleeps a lot of the time. In Lourdes, there's always somebody or something happening or coming and going. She walks with me in Lourdes. She is more interested in life. I think she's more aware, only because there are things to be aware of. So Lourdes is life for her.' Charlotte, who has become close to Holly and Joy over the years, adds, 'I think it's being away in a different environment: there is music and laughter and happiness, colour, people, touch, a real sense of warmth.'

Lourdes is indeed filled with services, events and additions which make it a wholesome, exciting experience. Joy testifies, 'Most of the hymns, she thoroughly enjoys. When she gets really excited, she rocks and the wheelchair sets off. Somebody else hangs onto her things while I hang onto Holly!' She tells us of Holly's experience in the Baths: 'It is a cold shock but she is hardy.'

The Anointing of the Sick is a strange experience for Holly and her mother. 'She doesn't understand that one,' testifies Holly's mother. Do any of us? For Joy, it usually means 'Floods of tears, a great release. It's just us. It's a sort of sacred moment.' She recounts: 'Twice, I've been anointed. There was a very odd one once. We were in the *Accueil*¹ circle and Kieron O'Brien was our priest and he came round and anointed Holly, passed me and did two more and then there was this noise: "Do Joy, do Joy, do Joy." I could hear it coming from all around me. And he came back and anointed me and then he did it the following year… the first one was very moving because I didn't have a card and it wasn't planned or anything. Just amazing. I am always determined not to weep but then suddenly I find that I am. I come out and think, "Did they sing?"' Chris Xerri, a helper, adds, 'You see the love that Joy has for Holly and that Holly has for Joy. It's amazing. She gets so overwhelmed, Joy, but you'll see Holly just reach out and grab her arm. At that point, you can almost sense the affection she has for Joy because she gets very, very calm and it's almost that she's comforting Joy.'

The love that Joy and Holly received was given back generously. Joy's care for others ultimately reflected the dancing surfaces of a deeply rooted love for Holly. Helpers saw the special relationship that both mother and daughter shared. Charlotte says, 'Joy always welcomes every helper with a big smile and she makes it easy for you by bringing you to Holly and telling you about Holly and talking to Holly about you while you are in that environment.' She comments, 'Joy keeps Holly immaculate. Joy dresses her in pretty feminine, summery colours, bright colours, whites, all those lovely colours that any young woman would pick for herself. She treats her like a lady.' Finally, Charlotte recounts, 'When Joy got up to go to Communion, Holly was just sitting there on her own. She knew her mum was coming back and she didn't get agitated. Joy is everything for Holly that is security, warmth, love, care.'

How has Joy lived through Lourdes, a place which awakens buried and quiet suffering? 'Are you reconciled to God?' I asked.

'Yes, I think so.'

'And to yourself?' I added.

'Yes, I think so,' came the reply. 'Coming to Lourdes fills my tanks with courage,' Joy explained. She adds, 'I always find it difficult to settle back because it's so different and you come back to people who are not behaving towards you as others do, with that tight family-like feeling you have in Lourdes. I think that's the most difficult thing: coming back to indifference really.'

Has Lourdes helped to heal the sores of tragedy? 'Yes, certainly. It doesn't last. By the end of the year, I need it all over again. And now it's just a rich aspect of my life: always different, always the same.'

Perhaps the most significant healing is that of her perception of Holly. Joy states: 'I've come out of Lourdes much more positive about her and about what has happened. Her place in the world is so extraordinary. I do love having all that time with Holly. Before, I thought, 'There's nothing there.' Although she was mine and I loved her, nobody else could be bothered with this. I began to see what a treasure she actually is.'

Holly has gained a loving community through Lourdes. She receives at least twenty Christmas cards every year and is invited along with her mother to many social events. One of Holly's dearest friends, Hazel, who knows Holly through the parish but has never seen her in Lourdes, can testify: 'It's what has helped to cement her as part of the community. What the home have said is that, often, if they take her out into Redhill shopping centre during the week, lots of people will come up to her and say, "Hello, Holly," even if she can't even say hello back.'

Joy recalls: 'Once, on the last night in Lourdes, there was a French scout group who got to know the *Accueil* people and offered to come in en-bloc and take over that evening so that the whole of the *Accueil* could go down for the farewell. Holly was put to bed as it was the safest place while these strangers were in and the Chief Scout there came in with an accordion and started playing. In no time at all, bare foot and in her nightie, Holly joined the party!'

A candle in the night

'The more time I spent with her, the more time I wanted to spend with her because she's just such an interesting person,' reveals Catherine Gorman, a Lourdes helper. She remembers, 'On the train on the way home, I was just walking past her bed because I was going to do something else and this hand just reached out and grabbed me: "Hello, Holly! Lovely to see you." If she's in a good mood, her face just lights up. It is humbling. I think Jesus said, "When you look after the least of my brothers, you're doing it to me," and people like Holly are that: if you're helping them, then it's like helping God.'

Joy adds, "She's certainly been a gift to most of the people she knows. There were good moments when I saw the youngsters fighting over looking after Holly. There's so much to get from her, so much of that gentle love, that gentle sweetness: take what you can. You get back more than you give, always.' Her mother declares that the best thing about Holly's illness has been 'seeing the love she generates in Lourdes'. Nick states, 'Holly is just pure joy,' whilst Chris admits, 'I've always maintained that the *Accueil* would not be the same without her. The Pilgrimage would not be the same without her. She is one of those people who has become synonymous with the Pilgrimage. Her enthusiasm, her uniqueness, her love of life: she brings something else, she brings another aspect of life. She brings herself.' Hazel concludes, 'When Holly smiles, you can't help but smile. And I think that's got to be something about spreading happiness in this world.'

What has this burning candle's impact been on those who have been led to her in the night? 'I've grown enormously,' confesses her mother. 'I'm not what I would have been.' Holly has increased her mother's 'understanding of other people's losses,' and opened Joy's eyes to the true gifts that are faith and life. Nick confirms, 'Holly has taught so many people how to be with people with disabilities.'

This is testified by Catherine: 'I think I never thought I would make a connection with her. I judged her horribly when I first met her and thought there's nothing to make a connection with. It's just an horrendous thing to have thought but it's what we all do in everyday life. Having moved beyond that judgement and really got to know her, I feel that it's given me quite a lot of confidence, that I can deal with things that I would never have thought I could deal with. It doesn't matter what your disability or hardships are. You can bring joy to people and you can still give an awful lot to people.'

Catherine also muses, 'You have a different face with whoever you're talking to, but you can't have that with Holly. At the beginning, I found that slightly disconcerting. You feel quite naked because you can't pretend and you have to be brutally honest. She knows what's going on. Once I felt I'd make a connection with her, I thought, "She likes me for exactly who I am."' Chris says, 'She does sense when you are feeling a little bit down because there have been times when I've sat down with her and she's sensed that I'm not the jovial person that's usually looking after her. She'll just grab your hand, grab your arm and that will just lift you a little bit.' Nick believes, 'Holly is a great witness to humanity.'

Sacramental wonder

Through the many sacraments which Holly has been allowed to share in, she has reinforced their mysterious essence, surprising, delighting and enlightening all who bear witness to God's invisible workings.

Catherine recalls an occasion during which she saw Holly transformed: 'Every year we have a Reconciliation service in the *Accueil*. I was with her in 2006 at the Reconciliation, pushing her. I never really thought of it but my leader said, "Are you going to take Holly to Confession? She normally goes", and I said, "Oh, Okay. Yes, fine." I pushed her over to the priest and then retired to a safe distance like you would with anybody else and she just sat there for a couple of minutes and then the priest absolved her. She rocked while she was being absolved but I think that was pleasure. When she came away her face was just all lit up, like a weight had been lifted.'

Holly's total acceptance of the Sacrament of the Eucharist is neither clear nor tangible. It began when she was twenty-six years old.

Joy recounts: 'In those days, people wouldn't even consider people like Holly having Communion. I'd always wondered if she could. Holly went to Mass until she was five, until she was ill, and I used to whisper to her at the elevation, "Jesus is coming now." That was her entire religious education. I said to this nun, "I wonder if she could," and she said, "I'll find out." We had the monthly Mass at the hospital, went up for Holy Communion and one of the catechists said, "Holly will have Holy Communion when it's finished."'

Holly's disposition during Communion has been witnessed by many onlookers. Nick comments, 'Whereas she grabs food from anyone else, as soon as the priest comes up with Communion, she takes it with incredible reverence. It is quite beautiful to watch. She is all quiet and calm.'

Charlotte testifies: 'Holly has this thing where she looks slightly down. She's got her head angled and it's very reverent. She is not confrontational with her eyes. She's not directing her eyes to the priest. It's very accepting.' Catherine adds, 'During the Eucharist, she knows and she goes silent. She waits and she just sits and opens her mouth and lets the priest put the host in.'

Not only does Holly accept the Eucharist but she is fascinated by it. 'Once,' declares Joy, 'I brought her to Mass. She ran to the church at top speed down to the front. When we took her out, the priest said, "I wish everybody ran into Mass!"' Joy adds, 'She just knows the second half of the Mass. She isn't too interested in the first half of the Mass but as soon as it's the consecration, she is unordinarily glued to the altar: very, very strange. People on the other side have commented on it.

Canon Seamus Hester said, 'We love it on the altar: watching Holly at Mass. We talk about it! She has this one word for Communion. When she's about to be given Communion, she says, "Foo", and it's the only word she says and she doesn't use it for real food. She only ever uses it for Communion. She's completely aware all the time of what's going on.'

Jesus led Holly to a lifelong friend. Her name is Hazel Plastow. Hazel and Holly truly met in the Sacrament of the Eucharist and have remained there together, forever at the heart of the mystery of God's love.

This is Hazel's testimony: 'I hadn't actually read the newsletter at the weekend but I was reading it on Monday, and there was an item that said, *Holly needs a friend*. It really felt as if it was God... I don't have children but I'd had a series of miscarriages and Holly was the name of the first baby that I lost and it would have been my Holly's second birthday on that Monday. So when I opened the newsletter and saw that Holly needed a friend, I didn't really have much choice. I left it for about three weeks and then I thought, "Well, I'll just phone up and there'll probably be somebody there now already." I phoned up and nobody else had come forward and they said, "That would be great!" And I thought, "What have I let myself in for?"

'The first few times I took her to Mass, probably about six or seven years ago, I was absolutely exhausted and I came back thinking, "Wow." Holly and I gradually got into the swing of it. From being her escort initially, I feel there is much more of a friendship and there is a real recognition and contact between us. It is very special sharing Mass with her and you do get really good eye contact with her, especially during hymns because she just loves music. She's not so bothered about the words... I just give up on the words and just "la la la" to the hymn and she loves that.

'I think that she takes me as much as I take her. There have been lots of times in the last few years when I've thought, "Going to Mass: a bit of a bind." But because I've made a commitment to Holly, I think, "Oh, well. I have to go because of Holly," and when I've got to church, I think, "Yes, that's why I am here." It is the simplicity of her relationship to the Eucharist that is really inspiring. It's not only inspired me but other people have come up to me and told me that just watching Holly has been a real inspiration to them, so I think that she's touched an awful lot of lives. I think I find that I probably tend to get more out of Mass when I go with Holly than when I go by myself.

'Now we sit right at the front so that Holly can get a good view. She really watches what goes on during the Mass. It is very much that Holly is her own person and I think people around the church accept that. People can see her enthusiasm. Sometimes when you walk into the church in the foyer, it takes a little while to sink in and then she'll start jumping up and down on the spot and start squealing very loudly so everybody knows that she's around. When we go into Mass, so many people will say "Hello" to Holly as they come in and I am more known as "Holly's friend" rather than people knowing me by my name. I had one lovely time when a nine year old came up to her and she asked me what Holly's name was and then she turned to Holly and said, "You sing really beautifully." Maybe it's the honesty of her lived experience. One of the priests said he always knew when his sermon had gone on too long because Holly would let him know!

'I think it gives people an understanding of what it means to have all sectors of the community represented at Mass, that Christ didn't just go for one particular type of person, that, actually, it's for everyone. It helps to give people an understanding and that someone with a disability does interact with the church, is a part of the church and has their own religion that they express in their own way, that is just as important as anybody else's way.

'I think one of the things is that she inspires other people through the directness of her responses. In the *Alleluia*, she will start rocking. I suppose you might tap your foot or something and we learn to be quite restrained, but with Holly, she goes, "Yes! It's an Alleluia! I love an Alleluia!" The bits where she lights up are bits where everybody is joining together, whether that is singing or praying together. It does feel that she comes alive. Often, after Mass, the organist practises and it is hard to get Holly to leave while the organ is playing; I've given up now, so we just sit and listen to the organ.

'She's had three epileptic fits with me in Mass. It's not only her arms but her whole body goes very rigid so she sort of goes into complete spasm. And then she comes out of it. It only lasts a few seconds, but when she comes out of it, it is just, "Wow!" Her face lights up. When it's happened, people don't realise she's having a fit. They've just thought it's Holly having a little moment. But people have commented on how happy she's looked afterwards. Each time, it happened during the *Ave Maria* or the *Hail Mary*: it may well be coincidence but I don't know. When I've worked with other disabled people and whenever they have a fit, afterwards, they are incredibly washed out and tired and it really takes it out of them. But for Holly, you would say that it is some sort of ecstatic experience and she just looks at you and goes, "Wow!"

'Her eyes will watch people receiving Communion: she will watch the Host and watch it going into their hands. That's when I've felt really close to her. Last week, she was very tired. It was Sunday morning and she'd just had a rather large breakfast and she is also on anti-convulsing drugs, so she was a bit tired during the Eucharist. After she had received the Eucharist, she sort of came to and then she looked at me and without me saying anything, she said, "Foo".

'I feel that she is a conduit for Jesus coming into my life and also that I am a conduit for Jesus coming into her life so that, together, we can help to keep Jesus alive for each other.'

The mystery of Holly

Chris recalls, 'I remember one time doing night duty on the ward and I went round and I got told, "With Holly, just poke your head in every couple of hours or so to make sure she's all right." It was two in the morning. I poked my head in and she was sitting up in her bed looking at me. She'd probably been watching the door waiting for someone: looking at me, smiling her head off. I just looked at her and I thought, "Oh God, what have you done?" She had completely messed the bed: myself and one of the nurses had to change her, change the bed, wash her at two in the morning. I thought, "You could have saved it!" She was just grinning away. She completely loved it. She was trying to drink the water out the shower; she was trying to eat the shower head.'

Who is this person who can be so playful yet so serious? Can she speak to us through her limited expression? Can we find meaning in a seemingly tragic transformation which occurred in her fifth year of existence? How could God turn a weakened, severely brain-damaged little girl into his messenger and a guide to the path of heaven?

Behind her mischievous smile is a child-like innocence. Catherine comments, 'There is something about her that makes you want to reach out and protect her because she's so very innocent and very child-like. There's no spite there at all.'

Chris confesses, 'I couldn't believe it when somebody told me, "Oh, do you know that she's actually forty?" "What? She can't be! She looks about late twenties or something!" The spark in Holly is prominent and always present. Charlotte believes that such qualities attract others: 'I think she has an innocence about her that makes people want to spend time with her and sit with her. I think she's one of the Church's special children.'

Non-believer or believer, all can sense the intangible fact that Holly thrives on love. Nick testifies, 'She hooks her arm round your neck and pulls you towards her, so, if you come close to her, if she is in the mood, she will rock towards you. If you give her a kiss, her face lights up.' Catherine adds, 'She is very loving and very easy to love. She absolutely adores being cuddled.'

For her mother, 'Holly is a person of integrity.' Joy explains, 'It's a very funny word to use for her. She just accepts what is going to happen to her. There's no indignity about even changing a pad or any of the personal things that have to be done. I think that's the thing I find an inspiration really. Despite all of that disability and that one-sidedness, there is a woman there. It is hard to explain. She is a true person.'

Holly lives in the present and is not tempted by the illusion of tomorrow, which perhaps may never come. Her mother avers, 'She is not looking forward and not looking back: "This moment, I'm having a great time walking." Holly is living totally in the moment.'

Nick relives the image of Holly bathed in contented silence: 'She is always the first one up in the morning. You go into her room before the end of a night shift at around 6am and Holly will be sitting up in her bed, waiting to get out of bed, quietly looking out the window.' Charlotte adds, 'I just think her humility is quite amazing. She sits there sometimes with everything going on around her: noise, bustle, confusion...There is an incredible patience with Holly.' Charlotte concludes, 'We used to sit below her wheelchair at Mass sometimes, on the floor, and you did feel she was right behind you, but, despite her movement, she is a very gentle lady. I think you feel very close to her like that because it is very peaceful. Sometimes, you catch her and she has her head tilted to the side. She is in a very special place when she is like that. It is very beautiful. My interpretation of that is there is no fear, no agitation: that is her.'

How have others responded to the tragic and the beautiful in Holly's situation? Heaven, which is 'quite tempting sometimes', puts things to right for her mother: 'I'm looking forward to having chats with her and seeing what she thought and getting to know the thinking person.' Chris finds a larger meaning in Holly's situation: 'You could say Holly symbolises Lourdes because she's full of emotion, she's full of enthusiasm, full of these conflicts of emotion that everyone gets in Lourdes and she just shows it more than other people do, more vocally.'

Hazel admits, 'I think, initially, I used to pray for a miracle for her. Perhaps my learning through that has actually been: what am I praying for, for her? Praying for her to be like me? Is that the best thing in the world? That would make her into the same as the rest of us, who are sitting there whilst Holly is watching the Eucharist, thinking, "Oh, I must remember to buy this or remember this for work." Actually, it feels like she has a very special relationship with God.'

Nick adds, 'Holly, undoubtedly, is very special in the eyes of the Lord because Holly has been put in the unique position, through her own misfortune, as are all people that are suffering, to teach others.'

Through Holly's example, the community has perceived clear messages which can speak to many. Hazel believes that Holly teaches us: 'You can have quality of life no matter what the disability is.' She feels that believers can learn: 'Prayer and relationship with God isn't complex, or it doesn't have to be complex. I am sure the depth of Holly's relationship with God is as deep as any Jesuit. You can study and understand all the different types of depth of experience but Holly has her own depth. Everybody's relationship with God is different but everyone is just as valid as each other and there isn't anything that stops us having that ability to have that sort of relationship.' For non-believers, she suggests, 'I think there is a message about the value of individual life. I would like to think that, in the community, when other people around Redhill who aren't religious see people going up and saying, "Hello Holly, how lovely to see you," they see that what's brought those people together is Lourdes and the Church, that there is a common bond because of the shared faith.'

Others have searched deep down for the invisible truths woven into Holly's existence. Catherine believes, 'If there is a message, it's that no matter how little physical ability you have, it doesn't mean you can't achieve great things and that you can't be a valuable member of society and you can't be loved or you can't love because she does all of those things.'

Chris feels that Holly continues to tell us: 'If I can get through my life, then you can get through yours. If you just trust in people, trust in God, life will be all right.' Her mother testifies, 'In bringing up the rest of the family, I just can't be bothered with the little ills that don't kill us. I think that comes out of Holly. There is no side, no show. Maybe that's the message. She's saying, "I can live without any sham and showing off and posh clothes and fast cars and all these things."' Joy believes that we can all be inspired by Holly's 'acceptance' and 'patience'.

In Holly's face is sketched a hidden world. Her eyes compel and intrigue those who can bear to look straight into their depths and, in doing so, be faced with their deepest selves.

Joy reveals: 'The eyes are still full of expression... beautiful blue eyes. There's so much person in the eyes. She's not blank in the eyes. They just stare at you and you think she can see right inside you. I think she probably can.' As well as judging Holly as 'very expressive,' Chris echoes Joy in stating, 'She's got really piercing eyes. They're probably the first thing you notice about her when you look at her.' Hazel adds, 'She is just so intense. I would say that, when I look into her eyes, there is a depth of relationship that isn't based on any formal communication, but it is there. There has to be that depth that the eyes are a window to the soul.' Nick testifies, 'Sometimes, and it's happened probably only ten times since I've known her, she will just stop and stare at you and it's really quite unnerving because she'll look straight into you.' Charlotte concludes, 'I think it's haunting in the beautiful sense.'

The last word belongs to Holly's source, eternal friend and mother: 'Something comes out which is attractive and I don't know what. It is extraordinary. There's another dimension. Who knows what is going on inside her? Her knowledge is better than mine. Her spirit is certainly very strong and knows more than we do about it. Oh, she knows it all! Because she's living with the angels, isn't she? If she's got any life at all, it's with the angels.'

CHAPTER 5

Amazing Grace

HARRY HUGHES

A young man lost

H ARRY WAS TWENTY-TWO WHEN HE ATTEMPTED TO TAKE HIS OWN LIFE. One dark night, swamped with feelings of uselessness and despair, lost in the current of life and the vulnerability of his age, Harry jumped out of the window of his large, Victorian family home in Hampshire. His mother, Peta, was alone in the house. His father, Bobby, and two elder sisters, Veronica and Tessa, were away in France collecting Tessa after a car accident. His youngest sister, Julia, a student teacher aged nineteen, was playing the board game *Twister*, at a friend's house in Roehampton. She suddenly felt very ill at 10pm, having to retreat from the game and lean against a radiator. She wondered whether she was developing flu. This was the time that Harry jumped. A friend's mother decided to drive her back to college as she felt too weak to walk. There, a message of horror was awaiting her. 'I grew up over night,' she recalls.

Harry Hughes was not destined to die that night. He was destined to a life in a wheelchair, brain damaged and tetraplegic (paralysed in three limbs, all but his left hand). When he jumped, he fell on the grass, just missing the rockery. His survival was incredible.

Harry was born on 20th March 1946 into a Catholic, British family. His father was a career naval officer in the Second World War, which left him a prematurely retired man due to his war wounds. He died in 1971, three years after his only son's tragic fall. Veronica would die young of heart failure years later.

Harry's mother, Peta, describes Harry as 'a generous, cheerful personality, a very good communicator, sporting, a leader, not very serious minded, a good wit and a jolly friend.' He was named 'Hearty Harry' at his school, Downside.

After studying at McGill University in Canada, Harry was unsure of his path. Soon he found a religious cult-like movement which aimed at converting people. His mother explains, 'He did that for a year and when he came back home, his health had gone down very much. We were very, very anxious. All this preyed on his mind. All the time he was involved, I was writing to him, keeping up the links with the family. I could see that this was not the right course for Harry but he was completely convinced that this was his way. That led to his mental breakdown. Harry thought he could change the world. He had seen it at the wrong time when he was very impressionable and naïve.'

Tessa adds, 'When your heart opens to that magnitude, you want everyone else to find that same wonderful gift of joy and he came home full of enthusiasm and vigour to convert my parents, but my parents didn't want to be converted.'

During that time, relations became very strained with the family, particularly his father, who became exasperated with Harry's unwillingness to settle down. His mother continues, 'Finally, I began to get replies that he was beginning to understand what was going on, and realised that he had been very foolish, and that it was not what he expected. By the time he got back, he had missed out on a lot of things. He was in a very low state of mind. He had lost faith in himself. He had been brought low by this movement and was completely disillusioned. He thought he had let the family down. Everything was wrong. He had lost his friends. He had lost everything.'

'How does an atom bomb affect a family? It blew us all into smithereens,' says Tessa, talking of the aftermath of that fateful night. She recalls, 'It was just the biggest tragedy for a beautiful young man to be struck down in the prime of his peak condition...' Julia has thanked her friends for keeping her level at such a strenuous time: 'Over the years, I've become more and more aware that the support my friends gave me was crucial. My family were in a mess. I really would have been unable to cope if they hadn't all been there for me.'

'Where there is life there is hope'

After the fall, Harry was in a coma for several weeks and was eventually sent to a rehabilitation centre for brain damaged patients in Wimbledon. The consultant did not show faith in any possible recovery and shared this belief with Harry's parents. Harry's father let this reality sink in very quickly, whereas his mother was determined that her son was going to recover. She employed a speech therapist to come and sit by Harry's bed and simply speak, in the hope that it would reawaken Harry's abilities to communicate.

His mother describes her son's experience in this centre as 'an absolute disaster.' The matron was convinced that his case was 'hopeless', according to Peta. When she decided to apply for Harry's first trip to Lourdes with the Raphael Pilgrimage, the matron sniffed, 'Oh, I don't see that this is going to help him very much.'

In the summer after Harry's fall, Julia had planned a holiday. Although Julia felt that she should be by Harry's bedside, her parents advised her to go. Peta had to experience the same torment and guilt: 'I said to the priest, "Maybe I should not play golf." I felt I was deserting him, and he said, "You must play two or three times a week. You must. You have to think of your life as well."'

Julia vividly recalls that strenuous period: 'I used to go to Mass every single day when Harry was ill. I hung onto my faith like a lifebelt.' Receiving the Eucharist gave her 'the strength to live.' She says, 'My prayer was that he would live: he did live.' Julia was 'deep down thrilled that he was alive.' She explains, 'He became the most important thing in my life, not obsessively, but it was there in my heart.'

Her mother's attitude of 'where there is life, there is hope' kept her going during that time. Indeed Peta tells us that as a result of the near-fatal disability, her relationship with her son 'became more intense, more loving'. She reveals, 'I got very close to him. His whole face would light up. I would talk all the time. I believed in carrying on. Even when he was very ill, I always believed that he understood. I was grateful that he was alive.' Where there was life, there was hope.

Rebirth at Holy Cross Hospital

After his pilgrimage to Lourdes, Harry was transferred to Holy Cross Hospital in Haslemere.

His mother admits, 'It was agony for me. I was trying to bring his mind back to normal. He was incontinent. He was under a lot of medication.

You would go for a visit, and you would not be sure whether he would be awake or not. At the beginning, they did not know if he would live or not.' She confesses, 'I could not have gone through the things I did if I had given way to emotion every time. The only time I gave way to emotion was with Sister Rose Mary. She sympathised with me one day. I was feeling rather low and I burst into tears. I could not have visited Harry if I had been in tears all the time.'

Sister Rose Mary became one of the nuns who nursed Harry at Holy Cross Hospital. She recalls, 'He was bedridden. We couldn't get him in a chair. His legs were all contracted, touching his bottom almost.' Harry loved this special nun who comments: 'As a matron, I was like a mother with children.'

Sister Mary Agnes, a nurse in the operating theatre, recounts her experience of Harry, which occurred when his tendons had to be cut to straighten his limbs.

At that time Harry had not yet spoken since his accident: 'For people who stammer, one of the ways to get over it is to sing. For something to say in the anaesthetic room – *The Sound of Music* had just come out – I began to sing "Doe a Deer". Harry drifted off to sleep. He went back to the ward. Some time later, I was called back to the ward in a great commotion and Harry was singing "Doe a Deer"! After that he began to speak.' Sister Rose Mary remembers such a turning point in Harry's illness with joy: 'As soon as he came round from the anaesthetic, he started singing out loud *The Sound of Music* songs! I sent a message to the theatre nurse and I rang his mother. It was immediate. He started to talk. It was a breakthrough for the family.'

Sister Mary Agnes recalls the next time that she saw Harry, years after he had recovered his speech: 'I went off to another job and didn't see Harry for fifteen years until Peta brought him to Midnight Mass. After Mass, I said to him, 'Harry, you won't remember me.' He began to sing at the top of his voice in the middle of the church "Doe a Deer"!'

Although the recovery was difficult and took seven years, Harry's ability to speak broke the unconscious silence he had been immersed in. Sister Rose Mary states, 'You couldn't hold a full conversation. He could be very clever. His speech was hesitant but always very funny.' Tessa adds, 'It was very difficult to understand what he was saying sometimes because he couldn't co-ordinate breathing and speaking.' Julia explains, 'There were different stages of speech. Giving him a drink of water would help.'

Despite being able to talk, Harry had no memory of what caused his disability. To the family's delight, however, he could remember his childhood and, according to Julia, was 'always good with connections between people.' Being the youngest child, Julia had been nicknamed "Squirt" by Harry in their youth. She was now able to playfully joke with Harry, 'Don't you dare call me Squirt now! You need me!'

Sister Rose Mary reveals that Harry was 'a big, happy person', adding, 'He was mostly very cheerful. He was a deep thinking man. There were never any depressive actions. He never looked morose or sad.' Tessa tells us of the change in Harry: 'The man who grew out of the unconsciousness was a very different being to the child I had known as a teenager or a young man. There was a combination of idiocy and total seriousness. There was nothing much in between.'

Julia claims, 'He was happier. He reached out to the God of his understanding. When he was in hospital, he used to absolutely insist on making the sign of the cross, saying a little grace before a meal. That wasn't like him beforehand. He had a lot of reverence.' Sister Rose Mary reveals, 'He had a strong faith. He would follow the Mass very reverently.' 'He was able to take the message of Christianity and to hold it,' adds Tessa.

Harry's mother concludes of Harry's years in Holy Cross Hospital: 'They were very wonderful there. By the end of the time, he had made great progress. One Midnight Mass, Sister Rose Mary was a Eucharistic minister. I pushed Harry up to Communion and he looked at her and started laughing and said, "Are you here?" "Hi, Harry!" she said. She laughed and was pleased that he was happy.' Julia simply states, 'Sister Mary Agnes and Sister Rose Mary brought him back to life.'

'I want to go to Lourdes'

Lourdes soon became a runway where Harry could spread his broken wings and be freed from the chains of physical disability. In this place, he was as whole as he could be. On one occasion in Lourdes with the Knights of Malta Pilgrimage, a monk from Downside congratulated Harry on how he interacted with his helpers and on how hard he worked during the week in Lourdes. This monk offered Harry the job of being a 'professional pilgrim'. He told Harry that he would like to pay for him to come on pilgrimage to Lourdes every year. Having suffered greatly from the fact that he had never had a job, Harry was thrilled beyond words. In Lourdes, he was acknowledged.

Fr Stephen Ortiger, who knew Harry through Easters at Worth Abbey and then through Lourdes, declares, 'I never had any doubt that he was totally present. It was hugely important, a highpoint of his year. He was looking at Lourdes for a strengthening of his spirit on his particular journey,' and this, according to Fr Stephen, was always done with 'a twinkle in the eye.'

Thus from 1978 to 1993, Harry travelled to Lourdes on pilgrimage every year. His mother confirms, 'He always insisted on going to Lourdes. "Harry, we could go to Spain." "No, I want to go to Lourdes."' She maintains, 'He lived for the moment to go there. For three to four weeks he was on a high when he got back.'

Sister Rose Mary, who regularly travelled to the little Pyrenean town, observes, 'He felt so much at home in Lourdes.' Julia recalls thinking after Harry had returned from his first trip, 'Oh my God, he has found somewhere he wants to go!' To hear Harry's laughter again was similar to hearing that of an infant. Both are music to the ear. Tessa believes, 'I think it meant a lot to him because he was loved, he was fussed over, and it was probably the highpoint of his existence.' She adds, 'It allowed him to heal emotionally and spiritually.'

It was first and foremost a place where Harry could feel part of a wider community and experience a sense of togetherness. He delighted in teasing the female helpers, or 'handmaids', as they were called then. Fr Stephen confirms, 'A handmaid would appear and he would light up like Blackpool Tower!' Charlotte Burnell, who came to know him in 1986 when she was a leader in the hospital, states, 'He liked going for a beer with everybody else. He was amongst friends. He was in a place where he was special.' Mike Carver, a pilgrim who became very fond of Harry, gives his opinion on why Lourdes was special to him: 'It was full of love for him. People loved him unconditionally in Lourdes. I think and hope that he knew he would never be alone or unloved...'

In this heavenly place, Harry's sense of humour and wit were at their best. His mother recalls one amusing incident, 'At the Torchlight Procession, Harry was in the fourth row and started waving his candle, using it like a baton, singing away and conducting! The candle broke: was it going to set fire to someone else?' Julia will never forget a moment on the train on the return journey. 'In those days, we had these terrible mistrals – hot winds – going home. Jane, one of the other pilgrims, had been sick. It was a complete projectile! She was on a bunk bed and Harry was nearby. It was stinking hot weather. There was this huge smell. Iona Kelly, a nurse, came along with the rubber gloves and rolled up her sleeves and got down to clear it all up. And a voice just surfaced: "And I hereby declare that you shall from now on be called, St Iona!" It was Harry!'

Occasionally in Lourdes, Harry would say sentences such as, 'I really love God.' This phrase was a sign of the spiritual workings within Harry during the week in Lourdes. This physically burdened man was 'spiritually refreshed,' as Charlotte suggests. He loved the singing, which took his spirit, amongst the many hundreds, to another level, and he always had his rosary beads. Charlotte recalls, 'He was quite humbled at the Anointing of the Sick: he'd always have his head down. It was a significant part of being there and being blessed.'

Mike Carver recalls, 'I was privileged enough to be with Harry in his last year in Lourdes at his anointing and it was a peaceful, very moving time for all of us... I am sure in my heart that he knew and was comforted by it. Certainly, he would roar out in the quiet moments but then be still and, as I say, "know".'

The Grotto and the Baths were two places where he could find sanctuary. Charlotte simply recalls, 'When we had Mass at the Grotto, I often remember him really looking up at the Grotto.' Mike echoes this with his belief that Harry came to be very close to Our Lady and Bernadette: 'When we were at the Grotto or the Baths or any of the places associated closely with St Bernadette and the Blessed Virgin Mother, he was always greatly affected and I took his tears as "proof" of affection rather than the opposite. He was capable of being very calm at these times.' Mike heard faith's drum pounding in 'our prayers together and his visits to the Grotto when one could see a well-defined "light" within him.'

One touched, others fed

The family were able to find Lourdes through Harry. The first time that Harry's mother went to Lourdes was with Harry on a Raphael Pilgrimage: 'I found it too painful. I cried all the time. I couldn't bear it. I went to the meetings in our group and everybody would say what they wanted to say and, some time in the afternoon, I couldn't stop crying. I felt dreadful. I couldn't take it at all. But since then, I've been back. Now, it's quite different. Julia and I went down quite late one night to the Grotto and we got caught by the Torchlight Procession and we stayed and watched and I found that terribly moving. There were so many international people. It was simply wonderful. Some people were very elderly. Also, in the Baths, where you have to wait for ages and ages, it's very calming. If you have anxieties, you feel peaceful afterwards.' Harry's mother's admits that her relationship with Our Lady was strengthened by Lourdes.

Julia was brought to the essence of Lourdes through Harry, and to the heart of her brother through Lourdes. Although she had been once before and found herself being quite cynical about the experience, it was with Harry that she began to appreciate the hidden beauty of Lourdes, so much so that she avows, 'I do look upon Lourdes as the oxygen for my life.' She explains, 'I think Lourdes was the key. Lourdes gave me the spiritual energy to continue.'

Reflecting, Julia adds, 'It's strange. I've been given lots of challenges and then the challenges seem to become something wonderful and I don't quite understand it.' She recounts one example of such a transformation: 'I was anointed by mistake when leading some pilgrims up to the Anointing. The next thing I knew our chaplain was opening my hands and anointing me. I was trying to say I was not sick but I just ended up accepting it. It had the most incredible effect on me. I felt as though I had a bucket of water chucked over me. I remember I looked over at Harry and he had just been anointed too. It was a bit like a spaghetti junction with all the hands on him all over the place... and that is my memory of Harry, that he had this wonderful effect that people wanted to put their hands on him to help with his healing. I remember just bursting into floods of tears and tried to find a bench in the Underground Basilica to calm down and the next thing I knew was that my friend Luan de Burgh and his father, Michael, my godfather, put their arms around me.'

Discovering Harry

Through Lourdes, many pilgrims received the gift of Harry's presence. Fr Stephen testifies: 'He was easy to communicate with.'

Charlotte adds, 'He allowed you to get to know him. He was a very warm person. He knew everybody's name. He always held your hand in a Mass if you were standing next to him. He told me he loved me. He was quite loud and he had a big hearty laugh, a very big heart. Because he gave back, we just got the opportunity to get so much more from him. I think everybody was always happy to have Harry in their team because he was never difficult, he loved taking part. He was part of our Lourdes: one of the characters who made the time for us special.'

Mike in turn suggests that he was so attractive 'because he was a great and kind man and great and kind men's souls have a way of never going away, even in the worst ravages of earthly existence. You could feel the goodness of the man and sense the kindness and mischievousness that was there still, despite all. That laugh! The incipient naughtiness that refused to be driven out! His face when he slept and the care slipped away...'

Harry was always poignant and generous with his contributions in discussions. Charlotte states, 'He was inspirational although he couldn't get up and shout out his story.' Julia reveals, 'He would make some remark and we'd sit up and listen.' An example of his profound thoughts is his phrase, 'God is the eternal Now,' one appropriate for almost all religious traditions and full of divine wonder and magnitude.

Those who were assigned to care for Harry playfully enjoyed his clumsiness. Charlotte recalls, 'Harry had a particular way of holding things because his disability meant that he could only use his left hand, so we used to laugh and help him with hot drinks because he'd be throwing loads all over the place.' She adds, 'He was a big man. He needed lots of help. He must have weighed about eighteen stone at one time.' She concludes that Harry 'made you very aware of the frailties of human life.'

Harry's joy in the face of the circumstances and constraints of his disability touched many. One man told Harry's mother how Harry would be 'lustily' singing all the songs as he pushed Harry in his wheelchair to Mass which was a two mile walk away. This man also told his mother how much of a gentleman Harry was. From his mother's point of view, 'That put it in a nutshell. He would not have anybody badly treated.' She claims that 'faces light up when you talk about him.' Julia states, 'When he had the spiritual strength and when he built this rapport with people, he had huge charisma.'

Indeed Mike testifies: 'Harry was a wonderful man who had a profound effect on me and on most of those who met him. After all he had suffered, he could still be human and affectionate in his own way. Harry, despite the tortured life he had had after his university days and the trauma of his fall, still retained a sense of what I will call "soul." It was an indefinable quality that he kept: big-heartedness and a laugh that made us realise that there was still joy there within this big, lovely man. He would roar and set us all going!'

Many people have been personally affected by Harry but here is Mike's testimony: 'When I went first to Lourdes and met Harry, I had had a very bad crisis of faith. My partner, my mother, two of my relatives and a great friend had all died within six months of each other and I was traumatised, if the truth be told. I had decided that God really wasn't worth bothering about any more and I had really given up going to church and so on. Harry was certainly part of setting me back on the path. He made me take a good look at my life. He brought me into contact with situations and people I would never have known and which have stayed with me all these years.' Mike's life became forever bound to Lourdes because of Harry: 'I wanted to remember him there in my prayer life and I wanted others to remember him, too. He was proof that a pilgrimage is about being together and sharing.'

St Giles

After five years in Holy Cross hospital, Harry was moved to St Giles, the West Sussex County Home for the Disabled. It was a small home, with only thirty residents.

Harry's mother, who found the idea of such distance between her and her son very difficult, had to be advised that she was not expected to visit him every day and that she would have to accept the most painful maternal challenge of taking a step back.

Nevertheless, she remembers that 'Harry developed tremendously.' She clarifies: 'There were a lot of activities in the home. They had boys from Lancing College who would visit and sing carols. They had an occupational therapy department.' Sister Rose Mary visited Harry a couple of times and confirmed that 'he was very happy' with his new found mobility and freedom. His mother concludes, 'It was at St Giles that he learnt to be happy.'

'In the home, he had a wonderful influence on people,' Peta reveals. 'He had a code of behaviour that was honest and upright. If anybody at table cursed the helpers, he would get very angry, so he was respected by the rest of them. I found it very painful to think that he was with a group of people who were not educated. That should have had a bad effect on him, but it didn't. On the contrary, he raised the level with humour. If you think he had to spend the rest of his life with people using four letter words, it could have had a bad effect on him.' The times that Mike saw Harry were ones which left a deep impression on him: 'I was totally bowled over at the way he was treated: almost as if he commanded great respect from all who came into contact with him.'

When Harry moved to St Giles, he would be picked up most weekends by his mother and spend them at home with his family. Although, as his sister Tessa, suggests, it may have been painful to 'come back to witness what you've lost,' Harry was still able to laugh in the face of adversity and enjoy special moments with his family. His mother recounts one particular occasion: 'Whenever anything happened, he would laugh about it. I had a Saab, and a hoist fixed on the roof to lift Harry in and out of the car. It was electric, on a system like air-sea rescue. I pressed a button and this wire came down with a hook, and I would hook it onto his jacket. On one occasion, he got back to St Giles at the end of the visit and I got him on the hoist and suddenly the thing stopped. He was hanging there. Harry roared with laughter! I was appalled. I rushed into the home and asked for help, and someone said, "We are not allowed to lift."

I said, "But the hoist is broken: you can't leave someone hanging there!"'

His time at St Giles was a period during which the seeds of his faith were watered and blossomed. Julia recalls that the home was linked to a proactive St Vincent de Paul society, a group of benevolent people who would regularly accompany Harry to Mass on Sundays. His spiritual life was not starved by negligence or indifference. One 'angel' in his life was a woman called Pat Smith, who paid regular visits to Harry at St Giles. Together, they would pray and discuss the meaning of life. As well as this, Pat organised a Mass in the home every two or three weeks. According to Harry's mother, Pat 'was a very good soul.' Julia adds, 'Spiritually, they seemed to have quite a rapport.'

Pat informed Julia of Harry's great reverence for the *Nunc Dimittis*, the words of Simeon when Jesus was presented in the Temple, which they often said together. Julia claims, 'I think he used to open up to her and talk to her. He was very profound in his own way. He had time to reflect.' Away from the transitory things of our world, Harry could enter a deeper and clearer world enlightened by God's presence.

The lasting consequences of one desperate act

In the aftermath of the fall, Harry was faced with regular physical suffering.

At St Giles, one of his kidneys died. This left his body full of poisonous toxins yet all failed to notice: 'We were becoming quite concerned at that time,' recalls Julia, 'because he was always leaning to one side in his chair. He never seemed to look comfortable. My mother was concerned. He had check ups and he had x-rays. He was always sighing deeply. He hated his catheter. They hadn't catheterised him in hospital. Once that happens, you do feel a bit dehumanised.'

A friend of the family ended up examining Harry. After leaving the consultant to talk to Harry, Julia returned, only to find that, instead of discussing Harry's catheter, they were in deep conversation about the Holy Spirit! In the process of the operation that followed, Harry suffered a stroke. Julia comments, 'We noticed that one of the eyelids was drooping. The stroke had affected his throat. He couldn't swallow. He couldn't write. He very soon became dehydrated." Despite the trauma, Julia felt the Holy Spirit guiding them.

Harry did not help his health by smoking heavily. 'He would smoke in a disgusting way right to the very end,' observes his mother. 'He was always setting fire to his shirts and scorching himself. In the end we had to say that the cigarettes were kept in the office and handed out when he wanted one. It was one of his only joys.'

The light and darkness of realisation

One of the most trying times in Harry's life was when a part of his memory came back.

Julia recounts, 'Fr Dominic Gaisford from Worth Abbey used to get gangs of brancardiers to come and take Harry to the Baths every day—unheard of! I used to think, What is this thing with the Baths? Why are they taking him again and again and again? One day, somebody said to me, "What's the matter with Harry? He's in a terribly dark mood. He looks very depressed. He's not responding."

'I said, "I'll go and see him at lunchtime." I was helping him with his lunch and he kept saying, "I've been such a fool, I've been such a fool." I thought, Oh my God! Your memory is coming back! I felt that in some way he couldn't really progress significantly until he had looked into the abyss. One night, I had a long chat with Dr Kevin Kelly, (then the Pilgrimage Chief Doctor). I remember saying, "Kevin, do you think it is possible for your memory to recover after you've had such severe brain damage?"

'He just said, "Julia, I've seen some pretty strange things happen here, but I think that's a healing." I agreed. None of us ever thought that he would get this far. When we came back to Newhaven, my mother was meeting us there, and she could see he was in a very dark place. She turned to me and she said, "What have you done to him?" I remember saying, "Mum, I think he has to go through this."'

The light of realisation, which Julia describes as 'shattering', led to an internal war in Harry. Anger at himself led to anger at his Creator. Reconciliation with himself could only be achieved once all calm was restored with God. God had watched Harry sink to the pits of despair, rise from the near dead and live in his state of paralysis. In his anger, Harry could not see the shreds of goodness already formed in the depths of his survival. Harry's mother recalls one of her first experiences of Harry's anger which was to be one of many: 'Veronica and I took him to church at Lancing one Good Friday. Harry started roaring out terrible things during the Veneration of the Cross. He had to express his emotions. He could not control them.'

Tessa states, 'He went through an agony. I've only heard that cry of agony one other time but he howled. He was sitting in his wheelchair in my mother's house and he was looking up at the sun and he was talking to God – it looked as if he was having a conversation – and he howled. He made an absolutely blood-curdling noise. It was just the agony of knowing what he'd done to himself.'

Julia remembers, 'Once, we were at the Grotto and Harry started shouting. I fled. I couldn't cope with it. I was running off and I was crying...' She confesses, 'I remember thinking, "I must do something. I feel so powerless just watching him in this state." So, when I was around Harry, I just used to rub some aromatherapy oils into his hands and arms. I would ask him, "Do you mind if I just rub your arm?" and he allowed me to do it. It gave me a sense of purpose too. I think he felt comforted as well.'

Despite the pain of Harry's anger, many received it in a positive or understanding light. Mike says, 'I think it must have been appalling for him: such a strong, big and handsome man to be suddenly a "survivor" in a world that had become complex and awful for him. I called it his "roar" and I loved it. I felt it was not always negative but full of desire. So many complicated things had happened to him, so many things that were frightening, bewildering and frustrating for him, many of them connected to faith and religious practice. Who knows if sometimes the Mass did not bring to recall in him some aspects that were still terrifying or upsetting?'

Charlotte assures us, 'He wasn't a disrespectful man. He felt comfortable enough to do it. It makes me smile really because we all used to laugh. I remember praying at the time, "Just give him stillness and calm."' Julia, in turn, explains, 'I remember being drawn to a prayer group at that time, and I remember realising very strongly one night, I must go to St Giles. I remember going down there that night and a woman said he had been howling at the moon. It was very dark.'

How do Harry's loved ones explain his attitude? Julia calls to mind a scene from *The Archers*, broadcast on Radio 4 a few years ago: 'The Vicar's wife was killed in a car accident. In the church, he was having a rage against

God. One of the characters, an older woman, went into church and heard him and listened from the sacristy. He cried out. She waited. When he saw her, he was overcome with embarrassment and shame.

She just said, "Is God your Father?"

He said, "Yes."

She said, "Don't you think He has got broad enough shoulders for your anger?"'

Julia comments, 'It's what you do when you have a trusting relationship with your father. His degree of trust in God had got to a point where he was raging. He had been patient enough. Maybe he just couldn't be patient anymore.' Tessa adds, 'I think that that was the dirt that had to come out before the acceptance could level... maybe healing is enabling those dark and dirty emotions to surface so that they're purified.'

Harry eventually managed to unglue himself from the dirty and sticky waters of isolation. One of the carers at St Giles told Julia, 'There's something different. It's like he's painfully living in the present.'

Julia adds, 'We were able to enter into life more.' She recalls one of the first breakthroughs in Harry's anger: 'After Harry had been in the Baths and he was so low, we went to the Prairie. I intended to say something so resonant to him that it would shock him out of it. I said, "Harry, if Pa could see you now, I think he'd be very proud of you." He looked at me as if I'd stuck a pin in him, like, "What are you saying? Don't be silly." He used to feel ashamed. I said, "Pa had great respect for courage."'

'We must do our best then accept and rest in God'

'Once he had worked through that,' declares Tessa, 'I think there came the acceptance, and with the acceptance the peace, and the ability to be happy.'

His mother reveals, 'He accepted his life as it was. He accepted his situation. For the last five or six years, he never asked again about his future. He had answered all the questions himself. That was Lourdes. He only remembered the happy things. He remembered his friends and family. He lived in the present. That's why he was happy.'

'He felt loved when he was in Lourdes and I suppose he felt healed from his awful experience of shame,' adds Julia. 'If we do have God's help, it is like an extra duvet to wrap around ourselves or fall down on when we are exhausted.'

'We must do our best then accept, and rest in God.' Is the man who uttered these words the same man who was aggressively shouting at God, oblivious of all around? Harry, who had known anger, resentment, guilt and self-hatred, could truly appreciate the comfort of God's bosom, the saving light of peace and the notes of tranquillity whispered by God to calm an agitated soul. This inspired phrase was heard by many. Julia recalls Harry's claim that his acceptance of his situation manifested itself most clearly through his claim that he was happier in a wheelchair than he had been as an able young man. This was perhaps the greatest sign that Harry had found peace in his situation.

Complaint was not an attitude Harry was familiar with. Charlotte confirms, 'I never heard him say, "Oh, I should never have been like this."' On the contrary, Charlotte recalls that he often said afterwards how happy he was that Jesus and Mary had found him, that he was so lucky that he had been saved. Sister Rose Mary echoes Charlotte in declaring, 'He was a joy to look after because he was always grateful and happy. For someone so young, healthy, intelligent, highly educated to be left in such a condition: that took some acceptance and humility.'

Harry's happy resignation shone a light through him. 'He was a very humorous man,' asserts Charlotte. 'To find humour means you must be at peace, so he probably did have very big inner strength.'

Tessa concludes, 'Siblings aren't always easily inspired by their siblings, but you couldn't not be inspired by Harry because he had that incredible quality of spiritual radiance about him. Harry was an athlete. He was a sportsman. He was in all the school teams. It grieved him deeply to realise that that ability had gone but he could sublimate that and transform it into an inner strength that gave him the ability to bear with fortitude what he went through.'

Permission to go

The beginning of the end is recounted by Tessa: 'I was putting him to bed one Christmas. I said, "If you want to complete your journey to go to God, don't feel that you have to stay in your physical body any longer than you have to, out of fear of causing more pain in the family. Cancel that fear. We will grieve for you. We will miss you. We will be sad that you have gone, but you and I know that you will be around and that love continues to reach you through the airwaves. We'll always love you. We'll always pray to you. We'll always talk to you. I will certainly continue to love you after you've moved on, and you have permission to go."'

'Thank you, Tessy,' he said. 'Do you mind if I call you Tessy?'

I said, 'No, that's fine.' After I said it, I didn't know how deeply he had taken in what I had said. The following February, Ash Wednesday, he started shouting in the middle of lunch and they pushed his wheelchair out to the coffee space. Suddenly his head fell forward and he had gone.'

On 16th February 1994, Harry Hughes passed away, aged forty-seven. His family members have several interpretations as to why Harry slipped away on Ash Wednesday, the beginning of forty days of penance and longing before Easter.

Tessa admits, 'I like to think he was told it was Lent, it was forty days, and he said, "I've done twenty-five years of Lent! I'm off!"' Julia, however, believes that, 'He died on Ash Wednesday just to remind us, "Don't forget your penance!"' Like a child unwrapping a Christmas present before Christmas Day, he received the reality of the resurrection forty days before its celebration.

His mother reveals, 'It all happened so suddenly. We think that he had probably been suffering all day and nobody knew. I felt relief for him. Of course I felt unutterably sad because, in spite of his disability, he was a lovely person to be with. He was my son. You can't take that away.'

Charlotte believes, 'For Harry, it was peace. I was glad that God took him having given him quite a few years to find a different path of life.' Tessa voices, 'I was very shocked when he did pass away. There were a lot of trapped feelings that had never been allowed to be expressed. When Harry came out of the coma, I related to the new being but the old one had never been grieved because there was this new physical presence. When he died, I was deeply relieved—a completion.'

'I knew he had gone to where no-one could harm him,' concludes Mike, 'where he was to be healed forever and where his laughter would please God and the angels forever and ever. He was with Our Lady in peace and love and walked with Christ as he had done all the days of his life.'

At the funeral on 24th February in Worthing, Fr. Edmund Arbuthnott, a family member who often brought Harry Holy Communion, preached the sermon. Julia, who always prayed for Harry's continual recovery, recalls with laughter Edmund's words: 'He said, "Harry reminded me of my first car. It was tied together with string. I used to pray so hard that we would get to my destination because I never knew if we would get there. Harry went through phases of ill health. Twenty-five years is a long time! There would be a crisis and what would we do? We'd all be praying!"'

Fr Stephen made a special blessing over Harry's grave. Much of the food ordered for the reception was left over. Julia recalls how a woman took a box for the homeless centre in Brighton, someone else took a box for the homeless centre in Guildford, her own family took some. She claims, 'Harry would love it that the bread was being shared.'

Harry's siblings were left with sums of money in his will. Julia used hers to buy a big car through which she was able to help out many people. Tessa could do her qualifications thanks to her brother's gift. She states, 'Every time I go to get money in the wall, I say, "Thank you, Harry."'

Many of Harry's loved ones maintain their precious link with Harry through prayer. Until her recent death, Pat, who suffered from severe arthritis of the spine, would pray to Harry every day and claimed that he was a saint. She kept his saying on acceptance on the mantelpiece and looked at it every day as it had been distributed to everyone on funeral cards. Finally, his mother asserts, 'I pray to him rather than for him. I think he has much more to give us.'

A life redirected

> Amazing Grace! How sweet the sound
> That saved a wretch like me!
> I once was lost but now I'm found.
> Was blind but now I see!

In the end, Harry was grateful to be alive. He realised, after once trying to end his life, that death's finalities and beginnings did not belong to him. They belonged to God. He would not be remembered for a gesture of despair. He would be remembered for his charisma, for his fight to the end and for his love.

If money, mobility, and work were what kept man happy, Harry, who lacked in all of these, would have been an extremely miserable man. Amidst his paralysis and total dependency on others, Harry proved that happiness is found through God and love alone. All else dissatisfies. 'Faith is a gift and I think that Harry, who had once been diverted from the path of his birth-faith, had come to terms with his belief being gifted back to him in some way,' reflects Mike.

Charlotte comments on Harry's faith and his return 'home': 'He'd wandered away from it for a while but had come back. I think he was quite a blessed man.'

Fr Stephen examines the paradox of Harry's attempt to take his life: 'The fact that he was driven to such an extreme is a cautionary tale: how could that happen? The way that he rose from the almost dead is inspirational. One is a horror story, and one is inspirational. Within the inspirational there is acceptance, the lack of self-pity, the honesty, maintaining the *joie de vivre*.'

Charlotte adds, 'I would say that the irony of his life is that in trying to end his life, he truly started a very different type of life. There was a man looking for a way out. He was just shown a different way that he wasn't expecting, by living and by embracing the church again. He found a reward that was very different. The message there for me is that if you are on a path and you think there's no other way, there is always another way and there was another way for him. It brought him a lot of joy. It brought him friends. It brought the ability for his family to have more time with him and, for him, I would have said it gave him humility that none of us will know. He was one for whom there was comfort, there was light.'

Tessa comments on the change his fall induced on him: 'He had found his true self. He had connected with his soul. He wasn't living in his "image of "— "This is the person I think I should be. This is the person people want me to be. This is the person I think is acceptable to other people in order to be loved"— he got to the point where he had nothing to lose.' Harry's life was a life redirected along the path of truth.

Such tragedy required adjustment from many surrounding Harry. Multiple lives were changed by the incident. 'As his younger sister,' says Julia, 'I could feel keenly on his behalf because I knew what was going on. It changed my life hugely. I'm sure that a lot of that pain has given me understanding as well. It's given me the broader picture. We've had a difficult journey but I was alongside him. It was a tremendous apprenticeship. It made me. If I hadn't had those years of walking alongside Harry, I don't know if I could have got through my difficult years later.' She recalls an unforgettable moment with her brother on the way back from Lourdes: 'A year before he died, I was sitting on his bed and we were going back in the ambulance car and I said, "I think it's about time I thanked you." He looked absolutely shocked: "What are you thanking me for?" "If you and I hadn't had a care for each other and a love for each other, I wouldn't have wanted to help you to get well and we wouldn't have had the Lourdes experience."'

Peta learnt a lot from her son. 'Now I am a good age, ninety-three, and people say, "How marvellous!" and I say that all that time with Harry has strengthened me. I am being blessed to enjoy my life, which I do. I attribute that to the time that I spent with Harry.'

When asked what she learnt from Harry, she replies, 'Patience, I suppose. To put up with things. Endurance. Compassion. I had to learn a whole new way to treat people. I had no idea of how to treat people. I had to learn that you touched them, held their hands, hugged them. You may think that doesn't sound much, but it didn't come naturally to me because, in my time, we did not show our feelings. I was brought up with a stiff upper lip. I did learn about how you can communicate with people, people that I didn't feel particularly warm to at all. I learnt from other people how wonderful they were.'

Tessa believes that a very precious message springs from Harry's life: 'Just keep doing the work and moving towards love: that's all you can do.' Her attitude and perspectives were changed in the process: 'I learnt to look at other people's journeys with a less judgemental air. I learnt that you can be very spiritual while you're brain-damaged. Don't keep your suffering to yourself. Tell your truth quickly to someone who is safe. There are two ways of dealing with your feelings: you can bury them alive or you can bury them dead. If you bury them alive, they'll come back. I think it's important to externalise your suffering so that you can free it and let it go.'

The messages in Harry's life continue to speak to pilgrims as well as family members. Mike has learnt: 'Be patient; allow yourself to be helped: both horribly difficult for me personally. See prayer in all things and see joy in terrible sorrows.' He concludes: 'It was what he taught us about patience and perseverance that will stay with me. I think what his later life taught us is that there is nothing in despair worth having. Hope is all we have and we must cling to it with every prayer and the very fibre of our being. Here is Christ the human being who "went about amongst us" and who knew Harry thousands of years ago. In people like Harry, we see clearly the humanity of Christ.'

Approximately one year after Harry died, Tessa visited Harry one night in her sleep: 'In the dream there were flowers and music and colour and beautiful people and food: whatever you want paradise to be. It was just wonderful and Harry was standing with his arm around two pretty girls. Harry had no further use for a wheelchair. He was standing up. He was looking brilliant. He said, "Don't worry about me, Tessy. Look! I'm fine." So I said, "Great! I can't stay here yet. Where are my keys? I've given my keys to someone. I've made my mistakes and I've got to go back down." I woke up in my bed and the feeling was like being wrapped in silk velvet, being completely safe, being completely loved, being completely joyful. It was that incredible moment that fleetingly we get a little taster of every now and again. I can still tune into it. If anyone is frightened of death, it is heavenly!"

CHAPTER 6

The Passion

ANN COLLARD

I am about to leave, my last breath does not say
'goodbye', for my love for you is truly timeless.
I leave myself not to the undertaker and the grave, but
to your memory with love. I leave my thoughts,
my laughter, my dreams to you whom I have treasured,
I give you what no thief can steal, the memories of our
time together and the road we have walked side by side.
I also leave you a solemn promise that after I am home
In the bosom of God, I will be present in the communion
Of saints, wherever and whenever you are in need,
Call me: I will come to you with my arms full of wisdom and light
To open up your blocked paths, to untangle your knots
And be your avenue to God.
All I take with me as I leave is your love and the
memories of all that we have shared. So fear not, nor
grieve at my departure, you whom I have loved so
much... for my roots and yours are forever intertwined.
(*by Edward Hayes, a piece loved by Ann Collard and used in her funeral service*)

ANYONE WISHING TO FLEE SUFFERING OR DEATH WOULD CERTAINLY not embrace Ann's story; one of violence, separation, disability and loss. Her encounter with suffering and evil stirs an instinctive sense of unfairness. To the question, 'Do you ever wonder why me?' she offered the answer, 'Why not me?'

A soldier does not survive a battle without ammunition in his rifle. Ann was a fighter. She knew that if she was to win the combat life had challenged her to, she needed resources. She drank deeply from the cup of faith, squeezing every drop out of it. She inhaled every breath of friendship. Her heart beat with the hearts of her sons. A seed of goodness amidst a quilt of darkness will shine stronger than a blast of summer sunlight. Though the loving and joyful person of Ann and the life given to her seem to belong to two opposing battlegrounds, together they show the fierce power of love, the shattering force of God.

The event: Ann Collard's funeral. The day: Thursday, 10th August 2006. The place: St Joseph's Catholic Church, Brighton. Hundreds of people, at the heart of the beating pulse of love within the church; or outside, desperate to be part of this solemn beat, all wearing a red item, in honour of her favourite colour, the symbol of passion. The Bishop of Arundel and Brighton and twenty other priests find reason to attend, bound by their love or admiration for this woman. The Lourdes Choir sing, representing a place which transformed and shaped her life, and a people, numerous in the pews. The impressive Lourdes diocesan candle, lit in Lourdes and brought back in honour of the event, shines as persistently in the church as the light of Lourdes did in her life. As with any funeral, faces are tinged with apprehension and sadness but many more shine with happy memories, uplifted by the event. If a funeral is a testimony to a person's pilgrimage on earth and Ann's epitomised suffering, then why is there such joy of reunion, such excitement of commemoration?

One friend said, 'She would have been really proud... We didn't cry. We were all there together.' Pain and despair did not have the final word. Goodness did. This was Ann Collard's victory.

Ann Parker was born on 16th July 1953 to an Irish mother and English father: an only child. Ann married Nigel Collard in 1979, with whom she had two sons, Daniel Alexander, born 10th August 1981, and Joseph Liam, born 4th September 1985. One night, after her youngest son had his MMR (Measles, Mumps and Rubella) vaccination, Ann suffered a night of screaming with Joe, who was just starting to say 'Mum'. Tests and investigations followed. Joe was diagnosed with severe autism. He developed epilepsy later on in life. He was left with no speech, limited understanding, few social graces and no fear of danger.

In 1991, Ann travelled to Lourdes for the first time with her son Joe, on the Arundel and Brighton Pilgrimage, the first of fifteen visits for Ann. Ann and Nigel separated soon after. By this time, Ann was living with her Irish mother, her father having passed away from a heart attack aged 54. Late evening, Friday 22nd March 2002, a week before Good Friday, Ann's elder son Danny was murdered in an unprovoked attack, aged twenty, in a street in central Brighton by an illegal immigrant and drug dealer. Danny died from a single stab wound to the heart. Ten days later, Easter Monday 1st April, Ann's mother Sarah, devoted to her eldest grandson, died of heart failure, or 'a broken heart', as Ann later testified to Meridian Television. On Wednesday 26th July 2006, one day before the Arundel and Brighton Pilgrimage set off for Lourdes, Ann, aged 53, was found at the top of the stairs of her house, dead from a heart attack.

Who was Ann Collard?

'Ann's story gives me a huge amount of hope,' says Fr Dominic O'Hara, an old friend who was ordained a year after Ann died.

'I really cherish the fact that I've known Ann, and spent so much time with her because she's brought a lot of laughter and happiness to my life', declares Edward Constable, a member of the Arundel and Brighton Hospitalité.[1] Her oldest friend from primary school, Sandra Williams, tells us, 'What Ann had was inborn'. What exactly was special about Ann was almost beyond her grasp: 'There was something about Ann', she sighs.

Her next door neighbour of twenty years, Elaine Soudain, says that about six months after Ann's death, she realised that she hadn't really laughed since: 'She touched so many people with her sense of humour. That was what shone. She could light up a room with her personality.'

'How can humanity be so extraordinary?' wonders Maggie Wright, mother to Danny's friend, Tom. She marvels, 'She was in the depths of despair and yet she came out immaculately dressed, immaculately made up and she'd have everyone rolling around laughing in five minutes.' When asked by Fr Dominic Rolls, a friend of many years, on the day after Danny's death, how she was going to manage financially, Ann's off the cuff reply was, 'I'll just have to go on the game!' At his startled reaction, she laughed, 'Who would want me, Father?'

Ann's girlish giggles were full of honesty and transparency. Edward Constable, a Lourdes helper who helped to look after Ann's son, Joe, claims, 'You knew where you were with Ann, always.'

'There was nothing false about her,' confirms Kath Parsons, a very good friend who came to stay with Ann for ten weeks after Danny died. Unlike so many of us, Ann did not feel a mask shadow her face, or robes of white clothe a churning body of emotion. She embraced her stings and aches and allowed them to be a part of her friendships, offering them up for cleansing.

The key to Ann's survival was her inner strength: 'Somehow she still seemed to be so strong. She's one of the strongest people I've ever, ever met.' Edward's confession is one of many.

Maureen declares, 'I couldn't say that nothing ever got her down because I know it did. But she would pick herself up and dust herself down and get on with it. She fought right from the beginning for Joe. Parents with children with learning disabilities have to fight for their children and she was a real fighter.'

Ann was committed to having her voice heard when she believed there was a need for it. Not long before she died, she was interviewed by ITN on television, following the state's decision to unquestioningly accept all surrendered knives. Courage, a quality admired and worshipped in countless civilisations over the eras, found its place in Ann. Cardinal Cormac Murphy O'Connor, who knew Ann when he led the Arundel and Brighton Pilgrimage to Lourdes as Bishop, describes her as 'somebody who accepted her lot, which was a very difficult one, with faith, with courage—great, great courage.'

Perhaps there was something more substantial which kept Ann's friends glued to her till she drew her very last breath and which made her a part of their past, present and future. According to another priest very dear to Ann, Canon Seamus Hester, 'The real Ann was the one that was out to carry on and keep people together, continually lifting them up and giving them courage and strength to persevere.'

This was not just someone with a sense of humour. Fr Dominic Rolls reveals, 'I've experienced a deep level of love. In the sense that she loved me, she also loved my priesthood as well and would therefore affirm me in that, and we all need that as priests. She prised me open which is quite a difficult thing to do.'

Fr Chris Spain, who accompanied Ann through many of the difficult episodes of her life, adds, 'There was something very special that would rub off...' He talks of Ann's support in his early years of being a priest: '...your first four years as a priest, you've got a lot of questions and anxieties about what you do. She had a great gift of affirmation. Even if you felt you hadn't done very well, she picked out the positive of what had happened. I hope that's something I've learnt from her because I think I've found that affirming other people in as many ways as you can is very important.'

Ann's was a love story, beginning with her parents, then growing with her children and blossoming with friends and strangers alike. Elaine recalls, 'When she walked into a room, she'd be the first person to speak to people,' adding that Ann was almost 'childlike in her innocence' by thinking that 'everyone was the same.' Perhaps there is more wisdom in Ann's 'childishness' than in another's cynicism. The glint in her eye could only betray a deep belief that everyone can respond to the love of God which all are entitled to. Vicky Cumming-Bart, a friend from the later years, asserts, 'She hated it when people were horrible to each other. She would be compelled to write to people who have had these bad experiences. Ann only had to meet you once to be able to care about you.' This was true and manifested itself most acutely when the builders assigned to Ann's house felt compelled to buy her a present, after being perpetually mothered. By regularly buying *The Big Issue* despite her constant financial problems, it was as if Ann was saying to the seller of a magazine stained with poverty and desperation, 'Whoever you are, whatever you have done, you are loved.'

One of Ann's most famous traits was her generosity, through which Fr Con Foley, another priest who knew her well, saw Christ in Ann: 'If you did something for Ann she would repay you ninety times over. Anything you do for God, God multiplies. Anything we get, we won't have deserved.'

Such generosity shone through her ability to welcome: 'Even after Danny died, there was still so much warmth in the house. It was a very warm place to be,' says Elaine. No birthday or anniversary was ever forgotten. Another friend remembers receiving a Mass card from Ann every year on the anniversary of her child's death: 'You get so many at the beginning and so many the next year and in the end, it was just Ann's.' Indeed her sensitivity was one of the aspects of her character which compelled those around her. 'She had such an insight into people,' says Vicky, who often benefited from Ann's words of caution or advice on people.

Having been her parish priest at St Joseph's Catholic Church in Brighton for several years, Canon Seamus was often stirred by her compassion for people: 'She talked and spoke to the heart of many mothers, who were going through very, very difficult times with children or young teenagers who had learning difficulties.' Above and beyond her efforts to share her story with others, Ann was always a keen listener: 'You seemed to be the only person that mattered when she was talking to you,' the priest adds. Ann slipped into the shoes of a 'spiritual mother', as expressed by Fr

Dominic O'Hara. Indeed, we are told by Canon Seamus that on the Rite of Christian Initiation of Adults (RCIA) programme which Ann sponsored, she would engage with the aspiring converts 'as if she had been a convert herself.'

'Love thy neighbour as thyself' became alive in Ann. Fr Chris tells us, 'Ann really saw life as a gift and I think that she valued that gift very greatly.' She always wore 'sunshine colours' remembers Charlotte Burnell, one of Ann's many Lourdes friends. Canon Seamus adds, 'She always presented herself well-dressed, well-prepared to go out to meet the public. She didn't do it for show but she realised that it was important to present oneself well, whether she was just going round to the corner shop or she was coming up to church on Sunday. She was a dignified person who knew she was God's creation.'

The elixir of life

Ann once wrote,

> I know for sure I am very loved. Thank God for that! Thank You God for the people who have stayed with me—they have been my lifeline. Friends are such a comfort. Instead of blaming You, thank You for giving me these 'guardian angels'.

Ann's soul was like a candle at the centre of her life: people gravitated towards her, despite having to journey to and through those mysterious and lonely depths. The policewoman assigned to Ann and the remaining family when Danny died said that she had never known anybody with so many friends. They became one of the sparks which kept her faith alight. Ann herself wrote, 'All those people were showing me the love of God and, as the words in the poem *Footprints* say, He was carrying me!' Fran Backhouse, a lady who knew Ann since Danny's first day at school in 1985, soon became her companion in Lourdes, sharing a hotel room with her and Joe.

For Ann's 53rd birthday, which was a week before she died, she went out with some friends. One of Joe's carers had recovered from a stabbing, and Ann was very supportive to him, though she could have been bitter at his lucky survival. That night, he performed a song which he had composed for her. Vicky remembers, 'Watching her, seeing her, it was one of those beautiful moments. I felt that even though Ann's open wound would never heal, I did see a change in her. She really didn't want to go home and I really didn't want to leave her. That was the last time I saw her.'

Perhaps the ultimate proof of friendship is people's love for Joe. Ann's friends have taken up her purpose, her devotion and her unconditional love. Sandra, Joe's legal guardian, declares, 'He's our purpose in life now,' as does Fran Backhouse, the lady who shared a room with Ann and Joe in Lourdes: 'The most important thing that Ann left us is Joe. We were friends before but we're all closer now because Joe is at the heart of our friendship.'

Ann left no-one lonely. Perhaps it is because she understood the value of friendship. At her funeral, one of Ann's friends read out some scripture about the gift of friendship, requested by Ann in her funeral wishes. The following is extracted from it:

> A faithful friend is a sure shelter. Whoever finds one has found a rare treasure. A faithful friend is something beyond price. There is no measuring his worth. A faithful friend is the elixir of life and those who fear the Lord will find one. Whoever fears the Lord makes true friends, for as a man is, so is his friend.

> (Ecclesiasticus, 6:14)

'The very centre of her reason for living'

'If Joe had died, she couldn't have lived', affirms Maureen. 'With all the friends and all the love, Joe was at the very centre of her reason for living.' Maureen comments, 'She loved Joe with a love that only a child like Joe can bring out. It just comes right up from the guts.' Although Joe caused her worry, 'She was so beautiful with him,' smiles Vicky. "The song she used to sing to him was *You are my Sunshine*. She used to get up at five o'clock in the morning so that she could bath him, wash him, shave him.' One of the last text messages Ann sent to Vicky epitomises her devotion for Joe:

> Just on my knees clearing up sick and poo...a mother's love!

Ann always had to fight for Joe, to the extent that, on one occasion, she found herself in the High Court over the possible closing down of the children's home in Brighton that Joe belonged to. It was a case between Brighton Council, willing to close the home down, and the home itself, which had the parents' backing.

A group of friends accompanied Ann. Sandra recounts: 'When they were making the ruling, it was all going against the home: Brighton Council was winning. Fr Dominic Rolls was there and he said, "Pray while you're waiting." When it resumed, it all turned around and they won!' Joe was guaranteed a place in a home of the same quality, if not of a superior one, right the way through his adult life. Such an achievement thrilled Ann. Joe's rights had been recognised.

Despite his lack of communication, Joe is capable of much more than people would give him credit for. Fran says that 'When you really need it or least expect it, Joe will give you the biggest hug or the most disarming smile that will melt your heart. He seems to sense when you need that extra bit of love.'

Joe has shown that he is a deeply spiritual individual. Canon Seamus recounts the events leading up to Joe's First Holy Communion at nine or ten years of age, at St Joseph's Parish in Brighton, where, if Joe did make a noise or play up, Canon Seamus would say 'We thank Joe for his prayers' and would include him as part of the congregation: 'We had a Saturday Mass at twelve o' clock every week. A reasonable number of people came to that Mass, maybe twenty or twenty-five. Ann started taking Joe because she found taking him on Sunday was very disruptive and people used to find it unpleasant. So Joe used to come, and we used to call it "Joe's Mass", the Saturday Mass. He began to get to know the little community and they would come and talk to him. Ann had often said to me that it was painful that she saw no future in him receiving Holy Communion. One day, he kept on looking up at me at the readings and the Mass and at some stage the Lord said to me in no spectacular way, "Give Joseph Communion today". After the Lamb of God I sent a server to Ann to say that Joseph was to make his First Communion. Of course, she didn't know what hit her. She came up with Joe as usual. I gave him the host. I think Joe was standing. He took the host so reverently and he immediately broke it in two like Jesus did at the last supper – "He broke the bread, gave it to his disciples" – then he very reverently put both pieces into his mouth. Normally, if you gave something like a biscuit to Joe, he would smell it, and then throw it away if he didn't like it, but he never smelt the Sacred Host. He just put it straight into his mouth and then went back to the seat, and was looking up at me, his two eyes focussed on me. He always had Holy Communion.'

Ann claimed that her main reason for going to Lourdes was her 'very special son Joseph'. According to Sandra, Lourdes was 'the turning point for her with Joe.'

Ann described her very first pilgrimage: 'Our first visit in 1991, when Joe was just four years old, came at a time when I, as a mother of a recently diagnosed autistic child, was at my most vulnerable. However, we were immediately surrounded by a great warmth, friendliness and strong sense of unity which prevailed throughout the entire pilgrimage and continued on our return. My faith in human nature was restored as I realised that Lourdes is a complete acceptance of what you are and not what is considered to be normal and Joe was accepted unconditionally. Joe has always sensed when the Lourdes trip is imminent, searching the photo albums and constantly checking the suitcases.' As far as Ann was concerned and as she stated in her Lourdes appeals, 'This, in itself, is a miracle.'

After losing her son and mother, Joe's Confirmation in Lourdes was the first time that she felt 'a surge of happiness'. Ann declared to the parishioners to whom she addressed her appeal for the Lourdes Sick Fund, 'My heart was lifted and I strongly felt the presence of God that day and was very aware that my darling son and mother were watching in approval from heaven. Where there had been darkness, now there was light; where despondency and depression, now there was hope; where turmoil, now peace.' What Lourdes brought out in Joe was perhaps what gave Ann the most joy and comfort. Lourdes showed Ann and others alike that anyone, including a boy like Joe with very little communication, can be spiritual.

Edward remembers a moment at the Grotto with Ann, Joe and Fran that same year: 'Joe was being really quiet, really still. Ann said, "That's Joe praying too."' Ann's friend Kath recalls: 'I can remember going through the Grotto with Ann and she had Joe with her and when we got to the statue of Our Lady, Joe looked straight up at the statue and she said, "I shall never forget the expression on my Joe's face. I'm sure he saw something that I didn't."'

The year after Ann died, Joe's depths were truly revealed to all in Lourdes. Edward remembers, 'He had really contemplative moments where he just sat quietly and he was the most emotional I've ever seen him. At the Anointing of the Sick, he was reaching out... Tears were just rolling down his face. But it was good. In previous times it would normally come out as anger or frustration. This time, he just knew he could let go.'

As Fr Dominic O'Hara says, 'To be a Christian, you don't have to have three and a half theology degrees. You just need to have a heart.' How has Ann's effort to integrate Joe and "share" him benefited others? Edward would answer, 'It's shaped the rest of my life, knowing about and learning about disabilities. It taught me a lot about not looking at someone and just seeing their outward appearance, but seeing their inward appearance as well.' Edward qualifies it as 'a humbling experience.' Elaine now knows how someone like Joe deserves to be treated. She has decided to go to

Lourdes for the first time in 2008, after years of hearing about it from Ann: 'I want to see Joe treated as he should be treated.'

Although some find it sad that Ann died before she could see some of the fruits of her groundwork with Joe, many others draw comfort from the extraordinary progress that Joe has made in the last year. Indeed, his behaviour in public has improved, he has left his wheelchair and has lost a lot of weight. Fr Dominic Rolls comments, 'Joe has flourished, reached a new level of maturity, his relationships have deepened...' Sandra adds, 'Every day he's doing something better; he's increasing his walking or he's going out in the community.'

Vicky believes, 'Joe is love. We went up to Ann's grave. It was to bless the stone. Joe came up with us. Joe had gone back to the car and I went up to him. I said "Joseph Collard, I love you" and what he did was so amazing because he hit his chest twice... that's almost like "I love you".'

'Aren't we ready for Lourdes?'

Though Ann's friends may differ, all are agreed on one simple fact: Lourdes was Ann's lifeline. Ann said in her appeals: 'My one week a year spent in Lourdes helps me through the other fifty-one and gives me a tremendous spiritual and emotional boost.'

Fr Dominic O'Hara believes that 'Lourdes really fed her, watered her, nourished her. Lourdes probably kept Ann alive. It was like a mother.' Sandra, Ann's oldest friend, confesses, 'I can't express how much Lourdes meant to Ann. It was so important.' A week before Ann died and the Pilgrimage set off to Lourdes, Maureen received a phone call. It was Ann. She was overwhelmed with excitement at the prospect of returning to her "haven", as Canon Seamus once put it. In that phone conversation, one of the last they were to have together, Ann said, 'Aren't we ready for Lourdes?'

The Anointing soon became one of the sacred occasions where Ann could be loved and healed. After Danny and Sarah died, Ann, Joe, and three of Ann's friends, Kath, Sandra and Fran, were all anointed together: 'The Anointing was an unexpectedly healing experience,' recalls Fran. 'We had not anticipated this opportunity but Father Colin's suggestion that we receive this sacrament was, in our eyes, an unforeseen blessing. We all felt so strongly that Danny and Sarah were there with us. It helped tremendously.' Canon Seamus reveals, 'Ann would be in there, at the centre, with a large group around her.' Ann describes one special occasion in her 2006 appeal: 'Stuart, a twenty-one year old with a learning disability, on seeing my distress and tears during Mass, gently touched my shoulder during Communion and pulled the corners of his mouth up into a smile.' He said to Ann later on, 'I just wanted to make you happy.' Ann told her friend Fran that his hand on her shoulder was like the little touch of an angel.

Ann's experiences in Lourdes were so intense partly because she had so much hurt to release. Away from social constraints and people's cold disinterest, 'she could be herself' in Lourdes, according to Chris Evans. Fran adds, 'Lourdes freed Ann. She often felt that she had to control her emotions in public, put on a brave face, especially when people were responding negatively to Joe—that really hurt her. But Lourdes is the place where all emotions can run their true course. You can unburden your heart. No-one asks questions, just sits with you or holds you for a while when you need it.' This letting go of her suffering allowed a place for healing in Ann's life. Ann stated in one of her appeals, 'The mention of Lourdes to the "unconverted" conjures up images of sick and dying people, miraculously cured, but in reality the greatest "healing" I have witnessed is the inner healing of a crushed and bruised spirit.'

Fr Dominic Rolls states, 'Ann proved that it was the quiet miracles that were the profound ones.' In the same way that Gerard Manley Hopkins wrote

Let him easter in us [2]

he concludes, 'In Ann, God eastered in the ordinary and her miracle was the fact that it all went on and lots of people didn't realise, even her close friends, that she was being transformed.'

People formed a key part of the Lourdes experience, both spiritual and human for Ann. When Danny and Sarah died, Ann would spend many evenings and nights alone, despite the constant support from friends. Such loneliness never burdened Ann during the week in Lourdes. Fran soon became her companion in Lourdes, sharing a hotel room with her and Joe: 'The three of us began sharing a room so that Ann would have support with Joe as he was often up and about for many hours during the night. It didn't seem right that Ann was managing on her own as she had had to do that for years. We were good friends anyway and this only helped us to become closer. We were always laughing and singing so that anyone who passed by felt the urge to come in and discover what was going on... that in turn meant that Joe was making new and true friends.' As Fr Dominic Rolls states, 'It was the love of other people: looking after and loving Joe opened her to what Our Lady was doing in Lourdes. It was the love that led her into a deeper faith.'

One of the ways in which Ann and her story were heard was through the appeals she made to raise money for the Lourdes Sick Fund of the Arundel and Brighton diocese, which offers financial support for any sick or disabled people unable to afford the trip. As well as raising large sums of money, Ann touched the hearts of those listening to her, often reducing them to tears. Fran thinks that 'Ann's appeals really opened people's eyes as to what Lourdes is about, why people need to go. It helped people to understand what it's like to have a child like Joe, and raised awareness of how isolated parents and carers can feel.' Ann always ended her appeals by thanking the parishioners 'for allowing me to share my wonderful experiences of Lourdes, the place where ordinary people give God enough room to operate through them.'

A double funeral

'Danny was such a friendly boy, really outgoing and friendly,' affirms Elaine, whose children he would baby-sit. She reveals, 'Ann was really proud of him. He used to stand up for old ladies on the bus. They used to love him.' Maggie, mother to Danny's good friend, Tom, does not differ: 'Danny was the most loving boy. Danny was a very short little boy and he was famous amongst his friends for his extreme courage: he would stand up to anyone. Underneath that, the reason I liked talking about Danny was his absolute affection for his mother and his brother Joe. Come Sunday morning, we'd say, "Oh, he's gone to Mass." He'd run in and sit next to his grandmother and his Mum. I thought, "What a lovely lad, he's out there trying to be the big, hard man and he's racing off to Mass with his Mum on Sunday."'

It seems that Danny inherited his extreme courage and pride in his family from Ann. Canon Seamus recalls, 'Danny became an altar server and struggled through in teenage years and was still altar serving when he died. He served the evening Mass on a Sunday. Many young lads that age wouldn't be serving. I think he was very proud of his mother and of what she was going through. She was respected by so many of his peers.'

Tom's mother Maggie vividly recalls the night of the 22nd March 2002, when Danny was stabbed in company of three friends. The group included her son, Tom, whom the knife was aimed at first: 'The night Danny died, Tom walked in here and his first words were, "This'll kill Sarah."' Little did Tom know how prophetic such words would be. Maggie tells us, 'Sarah worshipped the ground Danny walked on. He was her golden boy. Sarah was the mother in the family. She really looked after Ann and Joe and Danny.' Elaine describes Sarah as 'a tower of strength, typically Irish,' adding, 'She would giggle!' Chris Evans remembers seeing Sarah the day after her beloved grandson was murdered: 'She just looked absolutely broken, like I've never seen anyone.'

The day after Danny's death, 'Ann's house was like Victoria station in the rush-hour', recalls Kath, who spent the best part of the next few days making a stream of cups of tea. Disbelief was the first emotion that hit Ann's friends and family, amongst whom was Maureen: 'To this day, going on that journey, I recall it every time—that lack of belief that this could have happened to her. We just held each other. I hadn't cried like that, not with anybody.' Sandra recalls that 'Danny's close friends came over that day and they came over with a bunch of flowers but they were so upset. So she was comforting them.' Sarah Clutton remembers going to the house on the Saturday afternoon and seeing it 'full of Lourdes people.' This horrendous situation still had some shreds of light in it: 'Though it was the most traumatic day of my life,' says Fr Dominic Rolls, 'it was also one of the most uplifting... because it was like seeing love and compassion in action when you would have thought that it would be a time of despair and despondency.'

Sandra recalls her moments with Ann as she was making the arrangements for the funeral: 'I remember sitting at the dining room table with her and she was streaming, crying. I felt totally helpless, not knowing how she felt. Ann said, "Sandra, if I could explain this to you, it's like somebody has ripped open my chest and torn my heart out."' Ann wrote, 'My light went out that week.'

With incredible, hidden strength, Ann managed to keep giving. Elaine's son Luke idolised Danny. When told about Danny's death at thirteen years of age, he turned around to face the wall in his bedroom and refused to talk about it. On Sunday, he went to Mass with Ann. Elaine spoke briefly about Luke's reaction to Ann. Sunday afternoon, Ann came round, barely two days after Danny died, leaving a house full of people, to talk to Luke. Elaine declares that Ann sat in Luke's bedroom for three quarters of an hour, during which time Ann asked Luke if he would like to help carry Danny's coffin. 'Ann was there for Luke,' Elaine comments. 'She was there for everybody. Everybody was crying and she was comforting them.'

The court case soon arrived and left Ann and Danny's friends and their families feeling devastated. According to Maggie, who describes it as 'another death; the papers sensationalised and lied about the boys and really didn't behave well towards Ann. All of the boys felt incredibly let down by everything, by society, by the law... Ann always felt that was a huge injustice. It just broke her heart. She had no money, she was destitute and nobody cared. Yet the person who killed Danny was in jail. He was having counselling, further education, and was receiving every support with psychiatrists. He was also having a whole support package in jail, which was costing thousands and thousands of pounds, plus an extraordinary court case with a top barrister.'

On Good Friday, 29th March 2002, a hundred people gathered at the spot where Danny had been murdered one week previously, to support Danny's loved ones in a vigil which was organised by St Joseph's Parish. Twenty candles were lit, prayers echoed, hymns lulled. 'It was surreal,' wrote Ann, 'especially because it felt peaceful, especially as the previous Friday there was violence and murder there and a week on there was love and prayers.' At the time, Ann spoke of an 'amazing sense of peace' and said, 'It brought me a great deal of comfort.'

On Easter Monday, 1st April 2002, Ann's mother, who had been admitted to hospital and was suffering organ failure, passed away. At this point, Ann was beside herself. Suffering from violent sickness, she needed people to physically support her as she was no longer capable of doing it herself. This grief-struck woman claimed that her son's murderer had now murdered her mother too. She had lost another lifeline, her precious rock and her sanity.

On 19th April 2002, Ann and Joe attended the double funeral of Danny and Sarah. Elaine comments, 'To see two coffins on that altar that day and how dignified Ann was. She carried that out with great dignity the whole time. Apart from Ann's funeral, I've never seen as many people in St Joseph's. It was packed: there were people inside, there were people outside. You couldn't help but shed tears. She held herself together so well.'

Where did Ann draw such strength and courage from? Elaine remembers Ann's opinion: 'She said it was as if God had lifted her to a different level so she could get through it. He had actually taken her up from where we all were, sobbing wrecks, and she was supporting other people. She did get her strength from God because there's nowhere else she could have got it from. She was the one lifting people, helping people.' Ann said in her 2006 Lourdes appeal, 'The person that entered the church feeling bereft of any family was the same one that left feeling confident that I indeed was blessed with families, my parish family and my ever increasing Lourdes family who were there in force, the Lourdes Choir providing the most beautiful music which touched the hearts of everyone present.' Ann watched the funeral video many times afterwards. Why? 'She was proud,' says Vicky, 'she was proud to think that so many people loved her son, loved her mother, loved her, loved Joe. She was very proud of her mother and her son's achievements. She was a very proud woman.'

Ann wrote about one particular incident which left a deep impression on her, occurring soon after Danny's and Sarah's deaths:

> The day I sat opposite Joe, me on Dan's bed and him on the sofa and saw one tear trickle down his cheek, I knew he knew something had happened. The pain in my heart was probably like the pain Dan felt when the knife went into his heart on 22nd March 2002.

In her Lourdes 2006 appeal, Ann explained,

> Joseph's lack of understanding of death led to weeks and months of him self-harming, biting his arms until they bled, smashing his head on any sharp corners within the house for hours on end, wailing, physical attacks on me and extreme ritualistic behaviour. In his eyes, half of his family had just disappeared, apparently abandoning him...and his endless searching from room to room was heartbreaking to see. He could not be pacified. I vividly recall an evening, after many hours enduring his behaviour, I looked to heaven and verbally begged God to help me.'

Three years after her son's murderer was put into prison, Ann received a letter from him, or 'words of contrition,' as Ann put it. This letter tormented Ann, feeling bitter and angry, but desirous to make the right decision and be true to herself. 'Bitterness wasn't part of Ann,' states Maureen. Having always appreciated the value of friendship, Ann felt compelled to ask for her friends' advice, who provided her with mixed replies. Some advised her to not have anything to do with her son's murderer. Others encouraged her to write the letter and try to forgive him for her sake and for Christ's sake. Elaine believes, 'She did listen to her friends. But ultimately she did what she wanted to do.' Thus Ann decided to write him a letter, dated 18th April 2005, in response to his letter of a month previously, dated 14th March 2005, 'and then in a sense she became Ann again,' highlights Maureen.

The following is an extract from Ann's letter:

> What does a woman say to the man who plunged a knife into her beloved son's heart, then ran away leaving him to bleed at the roadside?! You tell me you pray to God each day for forgiveness. God asks no questions, offers no criticism but will rejoice that you have come back

to His house for forgiveness, assistance and the chance to try again. I want to be able to say I forgive you, but for now, all I can TRULY say is that I am trying to forgive you and that's a good start, I suppose! My bitter heart has softened somewhat since I received your letter and I no longer wish bad things for you. Yesterday I received Our Lord in Holy Communion (I am a Catholic) and before I knew it I had offered it up for you. For the past three years I have never been able to recite the whole of 'The Lord's Prayer'. The words 'And we forgive those who trespass against us', I have chosen not to say—but I will say them now, so I guess I am trying! But I'm not a saint and I do still feel a certain amount of anger towards you. I pray that God will guide you and that he will help me lose my bitterness and remaining pride and resentment.

Finally, she ended her letter by saying,

If there is a hell on earth I know I have been there and I'm sure you are in your own hell! One day maybe we will both find peace for our souls.

One of the sadnesses for someone who has lost a loved one is people's often unconscious distancing after the first few months. So how did Danny and Sarah's deaths affect Ann in the long term? Loneliness was Ann's dreaded demon. Fr Dominic Rolls confirms this: 'Her big struggle was living by herself in that house. She was the sort of person who would cope with grief by surrounding herself with other people, but there always came a time where you had to live with silence in yourself... she didn't thrive on it.' Danny and Sarah's deaths changed the entire dynamics within the household. Maggie explains, 'Ann's relationship with everyone had to change because she'd been the child to her mother, this really loving, protective mother, and Ann suddenly had not only lost her son but she was plunged into the role of being the mother, the chief carer. Now she had lost her main support.'

Some of Ann's friends have gone so far as to claim that Danny and Sarah's deaths did not only cause her deeply rooted pain, but that they contributed to her premature death. Maggie recalls, 'She was destitute for affection. I think the whole pain, constant pain of it, literally wore her out. She always said she'd die at fifty-two.' On her fifty-third birthday, a week after which she died, Ann rang round her friends and joked, 'I've made it.'

Ann's gravestone is now with her mother's and son's at the cemetery in Brighton, overlooking the sea, on a vast grassy area. By the time that she died, Ann had become very familiar with that peaceful haven. Maureen claims, 'She went to that grave so frequently. That gave her consolation. It was always like a garden. If she couldn't get up there, she used to fret.' Fr Dominic Rolls suggests, 'Maybe she was halfway to heaven.'

'...the disciple took her to his own'

Now there stood by the cross of Jesus, his mother and his mother's sister, Mary of Cleophas, and Mary Magdalen. When Jesus therefore had seen his mother and the disciple standing whom he loved, he saith to his mother: Woman, behold thy son. After that, he saith to the disciple: Behold thy mother. And from that hour, the disciple took her to his own. (John 19:27)

After Danny's death, Ann introduced Tom Wright to this powerful passage from the Gospel of St John, which shone a divine light on their relationship, born from pain and loss. Tom testifies, 'Not many people are so lucky as to have two mums but that is truly how I looked upon Ann and how she looked upon me.'

On the night of the 22nd March 2002, Danny's killer attempted to stab Tom before he finally stabbed Danny. Tom spent virtually an hour trying to resuscitate Danny without success.

Sandra remembers how Ann spoke to Tom in his devastation and 'made him feel that it wasn't his fault and that he did everything he could... even though inside she was dying.' Tom's mother, Maggie, observed from a distance how Ann and Tom's relationship evolved, as well as how Danny's death had a profound impact on her son: 'Tom remained absolutely firmly, firmly closest to Ann's affections because he never stopped being in contact with her.'

The Saturday night following Danny's death, after being heavily questioned and having had no sleep since the murder on the Friday evening, Tom told his mother that he had to see Ann. The two of them went together to Ann's house and were plunged immediately into a sea of grief. 'She just put her arms around Tom,' recalls Maggie. 'Some mothers could have been vindictive or aggressive or questioned him but she just literally put her arms around Tom, and the two of them just sobbed and sobbed and sobbed. It was the most shocking and moving sight.'

Tom recalls, 'I started popping round to visit Ann and Joey... and my Mum and Dad became as much a part of her life. She was so infectious as a friend and we considered her part of the Wright family. His mother comments on her family's developing relationship with Ann: 'It was almost like I'd been thrown into this immediately very intimate relationship with someone I hadn't really had any stepping stones of the relationship with. We immediately became supportive to Ann and Tom kind of adopted the role of a surrogate son and was just completely there for her. She and Tom had a unique understanding that I couldn't even share in. Tom had shared intimate last moments with her son. So that put Tom in a very special place with Ann.'

When the Lourdes Pilgrimage approached in the July after Danny had been killed, Tom was asked whether he would like to accompany Ann, Joe, Ann's friends, Fran, Kath and Sandra and Danny's two other friends to Lourdes. The idea was that Tom, like the others, would find healing amidst the devastation. Tom recounts, 'When Ann asked me to think about coming to Lourdes with her the first time in the year of Danny's death, I jumped at the chance because I knew it would be good for me to be there for Ann and Joe but had no real expectation of the place itself.' Maggie recalls her first impressions: 'I thought, "he'll never go." Tom was very disillusioned with anything religious. He was going through all the things that young people go through...'

Despite all assumptions, Tom went off to Lourdes with Ann. He admits, 'I needed to feel I was helping Ann because I needed to take my mind off what had actually happened but she was actually helping me by showing me the strength someone can actually have in a moment of pure hell.'

On his return, his mother, ready for 'a real blast of anti-Catholicism from Tom', had given his sisters strict orders to 'say nothing, just be completely quiet, let him say what he has to say'. Maggie describes her first impressions of Tom: 'He shone. There was a light from him that I had never seen. Life is far more extraordinary than any fiction. Tom was this golden, beautiful child who everyone wanted to have a piece of. It was almost like he had had a charmed childhood. People used to stop often and say, "Oh, isn't he beautiful." And then he grew to be an awkward teenager. He was just this big, long, gangly, spotty teenager—cruel things nature does to boys. When Tom walked in from Lourdes, he was like he was as a child. He had this glowing beauty about him.'

They made two pots of tea as Maggie 'could not stop him talking about this experience of Lourdes.' Tom recounts the experience: 'I came to Lourdes with a feeling of guilt on my own part and confusion as to the incident with Danny, but by being in an environment such as Lourdes, we were all able to release our demons together without fear of embarrassment or awkwardness. I'm lost for words as to tell you how I felt and feel every year... We were mob-handed, to say the least, the first year.' He recalls, 'I think I wasn't the only one during the Anointing that year to have a truly spiritual experience. We were all just recharged that week and it got me through the following year.'

Having never been to Lourdes herself, all Maggie can do is recount what she heard and understood from Tom: 'Basically, what he said at the end of it was, "Oh well, I'll go into Brighton again tonight and it'll be like hell, because I've got to put up my guard."' Tom describes the feeling of arriving back in Brighton as 'walking on a different plane of reality to everybody at home.'

Maggie pursues, 'When they were in Lourdes, all those young men, they let down their guard and they were children of God. They let themselves be seen for how beautiful they really are at heart. But you can't do that in the middle of Brighton on Saturday night. You have to be the tough guy who goes, "Yeah, what if... I'm not afraid of you." But in Lourdes, you could cry, you could have a hug. Everyone was telling their story which put their experience into perspective and everyone's story is the most beautiful gift they can give you.'

One moment recounted by Tom is clear in Maggie's mind: 'Tom had gone down to the Grotto one night. He was ill, probably from exhaustion and everything else. He had really bad flu symptoms. And he said, "All I can tell you Mum is that I was filled with the most amazing heat and warmth and I just sat there for an hour and when I left, I was well."' Tom has returned to Lourdes each year and found the same experience.

Holiness is wholeness

'It was the faith in her that enabled and empowered her to be Christ to other people,' says Canon Seamus. For a talk themed 'Hope in the Eucharist' in Lourdes on the 2005 Pilgrimage, Ann recounted the following story:

> After the terrible events that happened I went along to a bereavement support group. One lady had lost a child ten years previously and she said that she had not smiled since. I asked the person whether she thought that was what her child would have wanted. After being at this meeting, I realised that I did have hope and meaning because I had my faith, my friends, my church and my community.

Only Ann's faith could bring meaning to this terrible ordeal. Indeed, Fr Míceál Beatty remembers Ann as 'clinging very strongly onto her faith.' Ann wrote in a reflection on that strenuous time,

> All I could think of was Jesus' agony in the Garden and I knew this was my own agony in the Garden.

Ann was effectively able to make parallels between her experience and those recorded in the Bible, which she could not have truly understood beforehand. One image that Ann drew consolation from was the *Pietà*, a statue of Mary, the mother, holding her son Jesus' wounded body. The week that Danny died, Ann went to the Chrism Mass at Arundel Cathedral. When her eyes fell on this beautiful and sorrowful statue, she turned to her friend, Jo Harrison, and said, 'That's me.'

In this sense, Fran believes that Danny's death forged in Ann a deeper relationship with Our Lady. 'In the same way that she clung onto her friends, she clung onto Our Lady and St Bernadette. I think they were pretty good friends of hers in the end.' Fr Dominic Rolls is perhaps not wrong. In her humility sometimes lost or forgotten amidst the wonders of the Lourdes experience, Bernadette was 'inspirational for Ann', recalls Fran: 'Bernadette was so brave in what must have been very frightening times. She was an ordinary, humble little girl who stuck to her guns even when figures of authority criticised her and her family.' Like Bernadette, Ann was forced to be a fighter.

One of the opponents she faced was the whirl of negative sentiments and despondency. She wrote:

> I must hang onto the shreds of my faith, keep going through the crucifying experience. God is there. He is with me. I am not alone.

Although Joe was her purpose and kept her going, her faith saved her from desperation and created hope. Ann and Maureen both agreed that they did not know how anybody could survive such a situation without a faith.

In order to understand Ann's faith, perhaps we should understand her mother's. The night that Danny died, one of the people present cried out, 'How can God let this happen?' Though completely shocked by the news, Sarah found the strength in herself to reply to this person and say, 'It's nothing to do with God, God didn't do it, God didn't stab him…' Such an exemplary faith shown amidst indescribable desperation demonstrated that being reconciled to God helps reconciliation with oneself. Although Ann felt tremendous anger towards her son's killer, she did not express anger at God or herself. She would say to her friends, 'I don't blame God.'

Chris Evans believes, 'Faith isn't like a switch.' In Ann's case, her faith was not 'switched off' in one event. It was a solid foundation on which Ann could rely and build. Fr Míceál believes, 'It was tested first of all and latterly strengthened. The lives of the saints teach us that suffering can bring us closer to God.' At the time Ann confirmed this, by stating that her faith had not only been preserved through this shattering experience, but that it had also been strengthened.

One of the ways in which Ann kept it alive was through prayer. When asked what Ann drew comfort from in her low moments, Sandra's immediate answer was 'her missal. She always had those books of different sorts and sayings, and the Bible. She had them by her bed. She valued the Mass enormously, not just because she was a practising Catholic but also because it was very hard for her to get to Mass. The little she had, she valued.'

As a priest Canon Seamus could help Ann through the Mass which was 'her great reservoir of strength, the strength to go on looking after Joe.' Finally, 'Music was one way that helped her pray and prayer gave her strength,' recalls Fr Con. Indeed the music from the Arundel and Brighton Lourdes choir was an essential part of Lourdes for Ann. She would regularly play the 'Lourdes hymns' at home. Even Joe integrated the Lourdes music into his ritualistic behaviour and played the music repeatedly.

'The real thing that comes across with Ann, something that I've heard other people say but I think Ann depicts it, is that holiness is wholeness,' muses Fr Chris Spain. 'With Ann, there was a wholeness. Her spiritual life, her struggles, her sense of humour and love of people and life all became one.' Fr Chris knew that Ann's faith was not shunted into one part of her life. It encompassed everything. She thrived on a faith which was fun as well as reverent.

Simply by living her faith, Ann would inspire and act upon others. Maureen learnt 'the power of prayer' from someone who was 'the living embodiment of faith.' Vicky, a recent convert, remembers what Ann told her once: 'Being a Catholic is not all about going to Mass on Sundays, it's a way of life.'

Not only through her example was Ann's faith a faith in action but also through her quiet invitations to friends to renew their own beliefs. Elaine says, 'It was her fault I became a Catholic. There was something special about Lourdes...' Elaine's daughter suffered severe eczema on her face and body as a three month year old baby, but when Ann's mother, Sarah, gave her Lourdes water and Elaine used it on her scarred baby, the eczema disappeared, never to return again. Elaine soon went to St Joseph's in Brighton, where she met the parish priest, Canon Seamus, and thought, 'This is for me.' She testifies, 'She not only introduced me to the faith but she was there for me all the time. She was my sponsor, she did everything with such a sense of humour.' Ann quietly fed Elaine with signs of support and love: Elaine received her first missal from Ann and always received a gift from Ann's annual trips to Lourdes. This legacy has continued. Elaine's best friend is now following in Elaine's footsteps, having become a Catholic a year ago and is now hoping to come to Lourdes.

Sandra, on the other hand, confesses that she lapsed, though she didn't 'stop believing', but came back when Danny died because she saw all this tragedy and 'saw Ann's faith.' She recalls, 'I was going to mass more, I was having masses said, and I've never, ever had masses said for anyone. I learnt about the Communion of Saints. Ann used to tell me little bits of things. Ann would never preach. When I was little, I remember being forced to go to church but now, I really want to go...' Ann also brought Lourdes into Sandra's life: 'This was only my second time to Lourdes. And now I know I'm going to go every year. Look at what Ann's done! But it's not because I'm doing it for a duty for Joe. It's because I want to.'

'My broken heart'

'We summarise the Passion, whereas Ann's was drawn out.' According to this statement by Fr Con, the degree of Ann's suffering is beyond most people's understanding. Though every year we must live through Jesus' darkest moments on earth, we know that the victory of the resurrection is two days away from our agony.

For Ann, there was no clear exit or light at the end. On one of her notebooks recounting the events of 2002, Ann sellotaped the message:

> My broken heart is in this book. Don't say you understand. Thank God you don't!

Cardinal Cormac states, 'My heart went out to her. She was so faithful in trying to cope with her suffering which was very difficult, very difficult.' Fran claims that you could call Ann saintly because of this 'passion'.

Ann decided, nevertheless, to face up to her suffering, which her son, her faith and her friends were all signalling her to do. For Fr Dominic Rolls Ann coped by surrounding herself with friends: 'She wore her heart on her sleeve.' However, he also notes a paradox in the way that she coped with her suffering: 'On the other hand you could say she didn't deal with it. She internalised it. I'm sure that that's why she died early. She did have a heart condition but she was very tough on herself. She would push herself physically to look after Joe, or Danny, when he was alive.' Fr Chris testifies, 'Those pains, you could see there in the back of her heart, yet she was one very much not to want to draw attention to herself or her needs.' Fr Dominic Rolls concludes, 'She died to the world when Danny and Sarah died.'

'Did suffering bring Ann closer to God?' was the question that many were asked. Fr Con stresses that suffering tends to bestow beautiful humility on its victim: 'The thing that can stop us getting close to God is pride. Humility is something that you learn when you suffer.' Fr Dominic O'Hara explores a paradox deeply rooted in the spirituality of the Christian faith: 'We know for sure that suffering is almost certainly a mark of God's love for us. Look at what He did to His son, or allowed happen to His son. Death and suffering are the single biggest things that we all face and assuming the good Lord doesn't give us paracetamol every day of the week, there has to be some meaning to that. The experience of the saints and the experience of the spiritual life is that suffering borne in a particular manner is not only redemptive for oneself but also can be for other people.'

'Christ himself is the perfect example,' says Canon Seamus. 'Not that we want people, that I, as a human being, as a priest, want my people to suffer, but, inevitably, people do suffer. Crosses come as we journey through life. I think we all have to realise that Christ gives the graces we need. Sometimes we don't believe they're there so we try on our own and don't succeed.'

Even through pain that gnawed away at every limb in her body, Ann was an inspiration. Elaine often uses Ann's story when people are feeling sorry for themselves. Fr Dominic O'Hara remembers the police saying that they had never met a victim family who had been so sympathetic, caring and understanding.

Fr Dominic Rolls comments on Ann's sense of true love, forever at the heart of Jesus' message: 'It's people like Ann who know how to love because they know that it involves an essential self-emptying, and she had everything taken away. She had nothing but she had everything. Ann's Christ-like love involved embracing the cross fully, in a way which was not at all showy. She wouldn't walk down the street with a long face. Her cross was worn internally and in the circumstances of her life.'

Elaine leaves us with these thoughts: 'She'll always inspire me. She always did inspire me and she will continue to inspire me. She's an inspiration not just to Catholics and Christians because her faith was so strong, but to anybody who suffers.'

A mighty legacy

'I think all our lives are richer for having known Ann. It's not just a cliché. We've all learnt something from her. We've all benefited from being close to her,' declares Leslie. Fr Dominic O'Hara simply states, 'I just thank God that I've known Ann Collard.'

'I think Ann has left a legacy to lots of people,' adds Vicky. 'Ann never had wealth, but what she did have, you couldn't buy with money.'

Ann's life raised many questions and gave far fewer answers. Maggie believes, 'She offered us an opportunity to question what's important: material things, human things, pride, hate, forgiveness, love. She just laid it all out there for you. Being a friend of Ann's, you were in the very middle of asking that question: in what way does God have a hand in this? In what way is God to be seen in this? It certainly was a God journey, a God instance.'

Ann's story taught others to review their attitudes towards death. Vicky in particular learnt to 'confront people who were in mourning who really needed that tender hand, that touch, that hug.' She reveals, 'You just have to be there and have that touch. For Vicky, 'Death is no longer a frightening subject. For years it used to frighten me. But I think it gives you acceptance. Life is only a flicker of a candle and it can be blown out just like that.' Despite adversity, Maureen believes that 'with God's help, you can always get through: let go, let God.'

Vicky refers to the letter Ann wrote to her son's murderer: 'It was the fact that she had contact with him and she saw a seed of hope in what he wrote, in his words. In this life, we don't have to rant and rave and we don't have to draw knives on people and we don't have to kill people. We just have to find that seed. Be the bigger person and forgive. It's much better than the person who carries the hatred forever.'

The Church would not progress if it did not learn from its people. 'Ann was someone who was easy to ignore because she was locked up with her autistic son,' says Fr Dominic Rolls. 'I think the Church has a lot to learn on just how to appreciate Ann, appreciate people like that. We can very easily draw our strength from a secular notion of how to live, even within the Church, in terms of pursuing position, power or influence, but that's not how Christ worked at all. When Christ went to the poor and to the sinners, it wasn't in a patronising way because they were poor and because they were sinners, but it was because they were open to him or more likely to be open to him. That's where their power came from and I think it's the same with Ann as well. Don't look for God among the rich and the powerful but look for him among the ordinary people, and there are hidden virtues there.'

Maureen adds, 'I think the Church has to do a great deal more about disability. I think that Lourdes should be re-enacted in each parish. There should be more awareness. Because I'm a midwife, our message is that life is always sacred. Babies in the womb are hugely at risk now. Because we say this, we have to show that we mean it. That means huge support for children that are born with learning disabilities. I think we should be a beacon to the world about this. We can't just say abortion is wrong. We have to value the people that society feels aren't valued enough to be born. We should be valuing them, saying, "You are all so wrong". You see little ones who have Down's Syndrome who are serving at Mass. They're given a place. We can't say to people, "Not under any circumstances" and yet at the same time not be truly valuing people with learning disabilities or physical handicaps.'

Canon Seamus concludes: 'We mustn't give up. We must persevere like she did. Amid the numerous, numerous obstacles and crosses and hardships to bear, she persevered and reaped the crown of reward in the end.'

Ann's final pilgrimage

What did happen in the end? In the months leading up to her death on Wednesday 26th July 2006, Ann became laden with challenges. As well as having to fight with the Brighton Council over Joe's home, she underwent surgery on her knees, which caused her severe pain and would have resulted in her being in a wheelchair in Lourdes. Maggie remembers a moment at Danny and Sarah's graves where Ann's knee wounds opened as she insisted on getting down on her knees to polish the stone. Maggie returned home later that day and said to her husband, 'I know that I sound melodramatic, but I'm convinced Ann will be in that grave this time next year'.

Ann died alone. Though friends had held her and surrounded her during her lifetime, Ann spent her last moments alone. It was a single battle. In the end, it was just Ann and God.

Vicky arrived at Ann's house at six o'clock on the Wednesday afternoon: 'Her house was busy with people. When I got to the top of the stairs, there was this police lady. It was almost like she was keeping watch on her. It was the most horrendous moment but the most beautiful moment as well. I lay down with her, kissed her on the back of the head, and just said goodbye to her.'

When Ann died, her friends and her son's workers were left with the task of telling Joe that his mother had died. Bill, the manager of Joe's home, showed Joe a photo of Ann and signed "finished" so that Joe would clearly understand that his mother had passed away. It was then organised that Elaine would be at Ann's house to meet Joe. Elaine recounts, 'Bill brought him along. Joe went to the fridge, opened it, saw there was nothing, went into the lounge, looked at the TV, went back to the fridge, then went back to sit in the car.'

As Charlotte states, 'There was to be no quintessential happy ending for Ann.' But what meaning could be found in her passing away? Fr Dominic Rolls believes that 'her death was Christ-like.' He states, 'I thought that she was very close to God because she bore the cross right up to her moment of death. Of course I was very shocked and sad but there was a divine justice in it. There was fittingness in her death because she'd done everything for Joe that she could possibly do.'

Fran confesses: 'There were still so many things that she was worried about, her health, finances, growing old alone and not being able to look after Joe. And if Danny and Sarah hadn't died before Ann, then what might have happened? Danny would have had to care for Joe. Sarah wouldn't have been able to manage, which would have left her devastated. In time, everything becomes clear. This was a merciful God, bringing Ann home.'

Maureen adds, 'As Christians, we must never lose sight of the fact that we are pilgrims and we're just on our way back; back to God. It's easy in this day and age to lose sight of that from time to time. The time was right for Ann. It may not have been right for us, but it certainly was right for her.' Finally Vicky's eldest son, Jonathan, aged fourteen, told his mother, upon news of Ann's death, 'Ann was too good for this earth. God took her because she couldn't take any more. I'm not sad because she can't be hurt. If we believe, then this is the way we should be feeling. We shouldn't be sad. We should be happy.'

It is a misconception to believe that a person stops living and having an impact on earth at the moment of death. Edward believes, 'There's still a massive part of Ann that lives on in Joe.' Joe is the greatest source of comfort to Ann's grieving friends. Fr Dominic O'Hara speaks out, 'I carry Ann around with me,' whilst Sandra believes that 'She's still living on,' and has admitted to praying to Ann. 'I believe she's in the Communion of Saints. I pray to her. I pray for her sometimes.' Vicky believes that, 'If you're open enough to your faith, there are certain things that happen for a reason.' She recalls two touching moments since Ann's death: 'We went out on Ann's birthday. A white butterfly was fluttering around our table all during the meal. When we were up at the gravestone, Fr Chris said the most beautiful prayers over Ann, Danny and Sarah's graves. We said the 'Our Father' and three birds flew all in a line over the top of us. I think they're just signs to say, "We're here".'

'The one thing that I didn't want to do was go to Lourdes but everybody said, "Ann doesn't need to go to Lourdes now: she's there, isn't she?" When Ann died, Maureen felt, along with many of Ann's friends that Lourdes would not be the same without Ann. Edward recalls the week in Lourdes as being 'a really tough week'. He admits, 'It wasn't until Lourdes that the emotion started to come out. At the Anointing, as soon as I saw Fran, I lost it, and we were just hugging for a very, very long time. It was the best place to deal with it.' Now he says that, 'You can just feel her around you, especially in Lourdes.' Finally both Canon Seamus, who told one of Ann's friends that Ann had been 'sky-rocketed to heaven', and Fr Dominic Rolls marvel at the proximity between Ann's death and the pilgrimage to Lourdes. Canon Seamus reveals, 'I thought, the suitcase packed and left at the top of the stairs, the day before she was due to go. Somehow, there was a spiritual message in it. She was so close to Lourdes and it meant so much to her and Joe, that, I suppose, it was happy for her that her departure was in some way connected with the proximity of another pilgrimage. She went on the best pilgrimage of all then. She went to her maker. Ann didn't have an exceptionally long life, but she went well-prepared, I think, for that pilgrimage up to heaven.'

'She swapped the image for the reality,' adds Fr Dominic. 'You can receive God in Lourdes but she received the reality in heaven.'

Footnotes

1. Hospitalité is the name for the helpers' organisations in pilgrimages which go to Lourdes, and in Lourdes itself the Hospitalité of Our Lady of Lourdes is made up of volunteers who give up a week's time to welcome visiting pilgrims, often continuing over many years.
2. A quotation from the final stanza of 'The Wreck of the Deutschland' by Gerard Manley Hopkins, published in *Poems* (1918)

CHAPTER 7

Still Fire

STUART MURRELL

'Plenty of hopes'

'CAN LOURDES CHANGE SOMETHING FOR YOU?' I ASKED. 'Yes and no,' came the reply. 'Apparently, it can make me more of a believer but I believe anyway. I believe in God, in Jesus and the Holy Spirit, so what more can it make me believe?'

These were forty-five year old Stuart Murrell's thoughts in July 2007, before his first trip to Lourdes. "Any hopes or fears?", I questioned. 'No fears. Plenty of hopes.' He stated, 'I'd just like to go,' adding, 'In my head, the voice of God told me that it would be a good idea. I thought, "Yes, I want to go." The more it was said in my head, the more I wanted to go to Lourdes.'

Immobile on his bed, unable to help himself, slow at speaking, Stuart voiced, from the bottom of his weakened body, words of fiery desire and inspired longing to go and be a part of Lourdes. After meeting this recent convert, Vicky Cumming-Bart asked him whether he would like to come. His mother and 'chief carer' reveals, 'Going to Lourdes was quite a difficult decision to say yes or no to because one half of you says, "What would you feel if anything happens to him?", and the other half says that you're not really entitled to take away that experience. Nine times out of ten I'm inclined to say "Yes". It's just being alive. That's all it is, isn't it?'

Sister Collette Davison, a Rosminian nun, one of his regular visitors, adds, 'He kept saying when I said he was going to Lourdes, "Where did this come from?" And then I think he was a bit overcome by it all and said to his mother, "Why don't you go instead of me?" and she said to him, "No, this is for you." And he said, "Maybe I'll be healed," and she said to him, "Stuart, the miracle is that you are going." He said to me about being healed and I said to him, "It is very rare and I don't know what the Lord's plan is for you but I think that the very fact that you are going is a gift."'

A born fighter

Born on 4th February 1962, Stuart always was an extraordinarily strong individual, a born fighter. He recounts his battle against various forms of weakness: 'I was put in the lowest set. I taught myself to read. I taught myself to write. I was moved to a higher class. I said, "Yes! Now I'm back!"' He adds, 'When I went to primary school, I was always looking after my brother. My brother was always being picked on. I was always there for my brother and my sister.'

Stuart's mother, Pat, was brought up an Irish Catholic. His father belonged to the Church of England, as did Stuart, though he never practised. 'When I was young,' recounts Stuart, 'my Dad lifted me up and said, "This is my son and I love him." I loved him beyond belief but he started cheating with other women. My mother is brave. She's got a good heart and I love her to pieces! I've never said that! She is a really nice person.'

He recalls the various jobs he exercised in his late teenage years: 'First job I had, I worked with my father in the butcher's. My father said to me, "Go out there and sell it!" I was enjoying it. He said, "Come back here. You're enjoying it too much!" Then I got a job in Fortnum and Mason's and I was working in the receiving department. I got to the top of the receiving department. I left because I got a job on the railway, working on the tracks. You had to be quick to move out of the way. Then I got bored and got put in for a promotion as supervisor, aged eighteen. I passed. I was given two gangs of men. I treated the men with respect and I got it back.'

His mother remembers, 'Stuart had lots of friends and our house was always full of people. He was very strong willed.' Physical strength not only gave him the skills to be a good football player but also led him to be an accomplished rugby player. Providence, however, ruled against these skills.

Two births and a marriage

Stuart was a good-looking young man and very popular with women. Always able to defend himself and attract others, he was the invincible male stereotype. Soon, he met two girls, Jane and Susan. They each gave birth to a child, making Stuart the young father of two. Susan gave birth to Stacy in 1987 and Jane gave birth to a son, Luke, born on 14th January 1988. Stuart exclaims, 'I thought, I'm not going to bed with anyone! I was going back and forth.' On 23rd February 1993, eight years after they met, Jane and Stuart married. He declares, 'I'd broken every rule.'

From strength to dependency

'I was twenty-one. I couldn't feel anything in my hands and I thought, "I can't work... it just must be me." My walking started to go bad. In Southfields there is a big hill down to the station. I couldn't walk down it. It was like I was drunk and I had fallen over. I said to Jane, "We can't stop here. We'll have to go." I kept falling... I could feel my legs go forward and then they'd go and I'd fall over. It was annoying. It was making me angry. I went back home and I said to Jane, "I can hardly do the work anymore." I said, "If I don't get hit by a train, I'll get electrocuted." She said, "Well then, stop." So I stopped. I put in my notice. That made me angry that I had to do that. I said to Jane, "We cannot stay here. We have to go." We moved to Birmingham. I said, "Does that mean I don't see my daughter?" Susan said, "No." I said, "If my daughter wants me, she'll know how to find me." She's twenty-three now.'

At the time, Pat was living in Birmingham. They moved in with her until they found their own flat. The move led to more than a change of house: 'I went into the hospital. I had lumbar punctures and they really hurt. I came out: I was in a wheelchair. The man in charge said, "You've got multiple sclerosis, Stuart." I said, "Lovely, what else can I have?" I didn't understand what MS was at that time. A lady called Judy who had MS came around and saw me and she explained all of this, my legs going and everything. She said, "You'll probably laugh now Stuart but eventually it will happen." And I said, "Not yet." She was brilliant. She had a wig on. She lost all her hair. That's why my hair is so precious!' Despite this, he adds, 'Bad things did happen and I didn't laugh anymore.'

The strong boy in the crowd, the pin-up, the protector of many was now weak and suffering from progressive corporal deterioration and dependency. At first, he says, 'I could walk. I was told I was disabled and I started going to this centre.' He was only fully diagnosed with multiple sclerosis when he was twenty-six, on 16th January 1988, two days after his son's birth. From standing, he descended to a wheelchair. From the wheelchair, he became used to lying on a bed; eventually he was housebound, bedridden and incontinent.

Like father, like son

Luke was the 'happy' jewel in Stuart's life. Like Stuart, he was of no practising faith. Stuart had told his wife to allow Luke the option when he became eighteen.

Love brims in Stuart's eyes as he utters, 'He did everything that I did.' He recalls, 'I said to Luke, "Do you want to see your sister?", and he said, "No."

'I said, "Why?"

"Because she looks like you, Daddy!"

'I said, "You will. When you get older, you'll look like me." Me and his Mum were sitting in our sitting room in London and we heard, "Yes!" I said, "Jane, What's that?" Luke comes out.

'I said, "Was that you who shouted Yes!?"

"Yeah, that was me, Dad."

"Why?"

"Because I look like you."

'I said, "And that makes you happy?"

"Yes."

'I said, "I told you you would!"

'He said, "I play rugby like you did. I look like you. You're going to teach me how to chat women up!" He said, "Mum's told me all about you. Women falling over themselves for you."'

Stuart, who has always been a passionate Chelsea supporter in football, tells us, 'Luke said, "Who can I support?"

I said, "Luke, you can support whoever you want."

He said, "I'm going to be a Chelsea supporter." I taught him all the songs that Chelsea sing. He was Chelsea mad!'

Luke's grandmother, Pat, says of Luke in her modest way, 'He was a nice person. He didn't like to see his Dad get ill progressively.'

All leads to Stuart's conclusion: 'He was everything to me.'

Until we meet in heaven

On his seventeenth birthday, 14th January 2005, Luke died three weeks after being admitted to hospital where he was diagnosed with a tumour behind his liver. Having undergone many tests, he died of an allergy to the fresh frozen plasma he was given in preparation for a bone marrow transplant. He left his mother childless and his father separated from the one light in his life. Shockwaves immersed the family in grief and horror. The terrifying case was in the newspapers. A friend of Luke's created a website in which she wrote how one of the things she most admired about Luke was his relationship with his father.

Stuart reveals, 'When he died, when I was told he died, I cried and I cried and I cried. I felt like I could get hold of anyone and hit them. I really felt angry.'

Despite this grief, Stuart's mother recalls the transformation she saw occur in her son: 'He wept when Luke died and then he stopped and then he said one day, "He's where he should be: in my heart and my thoughts."' Sister Collette, a regular visitor of Stuart, recalls, 'When he went to the funeral, people were saying "God is so cruel. He's taken your son," and he said, "I don't see it like that. It's not God's fault. It was just time for my son to go."'

Now, Stuart states, 'I accept his death and I live with that.' Luke's mother, Jane, tells us, 'Every day is another day, just as hard as the day before, sometimes harder. The more it goes on, the further away he is. I feel his presence a lot. I dream a lot about him. That's when I know that he's close. If I'm worried or upset or thinking about him, I dream about him. I dream of him when he was little.'

Stuart also feels Luke's presence in a different way: 'I believe that my son talks to me all the time. I've been watching the football on telly and then his voice comes into my head and I think, "Not now! Talk to me in an hour", and he says, "But I want to talk to you now, Dad" and I think, "Go on!"'

Having lost his own son, Stuart feels strong compassion for Our Lady who had to suffer the public, excruciating death of her only son. 'I just don't know how they crucified Jesus. For his mother to sit there and watch must have been heartbreaking. I feel for her.'

Though Stuart has accepted his son's passing, his overwhelming fatherly desire to have his son at his side has not disappeared. The anniversary of Luke's death and his birthday are painful reminders for Jane and Stuart of the unnatural separation between themselves and their son. Stuart affirms, 'Jane cries and I cry, and we talk about Luke. I miss him. If I could have one wish, I'd want Luke back here.'

The following words were engraved on Luke's headstone:

> If tears were a ladder and memories a lane, we'd climb up to heaven and bring Luke back again.

Since Luke cannot be brought back, Stuart's hope rests on joining Luke in heaven. Stuart is eager to be in paradise, a place in God's heart, an area void of suffering and loss, a haven filled with love, deep satisfaction and joy. He concludes, 'I want to see Luke and I want to ask Luke if he is all right. I want to be near Luke.'

The care of the many

Until they separated, and divorced in May 2000, Jane was always there with Stuart when he needed help. Now, she is a phone call away.

Pat reveals, 'He still has, some days, quite a busy life. He probably sees more people some days than I do. He has his carers. He has nurses and he has a physio who comes in and he has the most marvellous social worker. Tilly, the hairdresser, comes in once a month and does his hair...' One of his carers has said how he wished that he was more like Stuart, and many are entertained by Stuart's light sense of humour. He achieves the same respect that he did when he was standing.

None, however, has replaced the tender hand of a mother. His sickness is her sickness. His pain is her pain. His delight is her delight. She reveals, 'If there's something wrong, I do interfere an awful lot. I think people sometimes think, "Goodness, here she comes again! She's going to moan, going to complain, she's going to find fault", but that's the only life Stuart has.' She states, 'They asked me to go to Lourdes and I said I wouldn't go because I'm one of those awful people: if someone asks Stuart a question, I'll answer it for him... I felt I would steal Stuart's limelight and he really could do without me.' She argues, 'I suppose it puts you in a different position because being as he is, not married, there's no other person in his life that takes his attention from you. I'm just in the background, there if you're needed to be there as a mother, but I think he reserves most of the other things for the outside world.'

Where does she draw her fierce strength from? 'I think you have to believe very strongly or it doesn't work. I just have to do it from whatever strengths I've got... really and truly you just deal with it.'

One of the values that she lives by is honesty: 'I've never tried to hide anything from him: whatever's going to happen or whatever isn't going to happen. I don't make up different stories. When he says he's worried about anything, I say, "Well, it hasn't happened yet. Wait till it happens and then we'll deal with it at that time because we can't do anything before that time."' His mother concludes, 'I think we get on quite well. I think that's all down to him. I mean, it's more than that really but you don't like to say it.'

Stuart was living in Croydon when he and Jane separated. He could not settle down and enjoy the independence of his age but was tied down to whoever had the charity or kindness to look after him.

Pat says, 'My sister died so the flat on the ground floor became vacant. Before she died she'd said, "Why don't we go and see the landlords and see if Stuart could have the flat? At least he'd have his own flat." So we did that and he moved back here again.' There, his mother believes, he began to get better. Stuart later moved to a bungalow in Battle, fully equipped and not far from his mother.

Stuart's situation has been psychologically trying on Pat. She finds the situation much harder than he does. Her faith has especially been shattered by the burden of illness and the deaths of loved ones.

She reveals, 'I really don't feel I get anything from God and that sounds awful, doesn't it? I've got nothing bad to say, nor anything marvellous to say about it. When I was a little girl, the Catholic faith was quite strict... It was fear more than anything else. If I remember rightly, we went to purgatory or we went to hell and all these things to a little person are absolutely horrific. You can't even in your wildest dreams imagine these places.' She adds, 'You see, that's when I think, he shouldn't be like that. There doesn't seem a reason for it. I mean, if there was a reason for it, then I would just go along with it, but there isn't a real reason. Most people could say, "Well, that's God's will." I'm not able to do that bit.'

Despite this, there is something in Pat which has not died: 'Sometimes I think that there's obviously something somewhere that keeps us all together. It doesn't matter what you say – you don't believe – you always say, "Oh, God, help me." Whatever happens, you seem to revert to asking Him for help.'

She tells us of her daily intimate moments with Stuart: 'We phone each other about three times a day. So it's like a ritual. We talk in the morning. He phones when the girls have gone and I say, "Are you all comfy and dusted?" Then we talk about who came at lunchtime perhaps and then the last phone call could be in the middle of the afternoon or later and – it's the same every day – I'd say, "Is this your last call?" and he'd say, "Yes." (I'd still say "God bless" to everybody... I suppose the Catholic is still in you). I say, "God bless," and he says, "God bless," and I say, "I love you," and he says, "I love you." And then I say, "Now you know where I am if you need me," and he always says, "You know where I am if you need me." Well, he couldn't really do anything, could he?'

'I always say, "Of course I do," and that makes him still feel like a person who's able, not make him feel like he can't do anything. So when we say that, it's always our last bit before we put the phone down. So, I suppose, it's still in you somewhere.'

Conversion

The change of the soul is always a mystery. It bears multiple fruits but hides powerful origins. Few converts can explain how they were pulled from one lifestyle into another, from darkness into light.

'I heard two Catholic ladies talking and they said that when you die, you can go to heaven. I thought, I want some of that.'

One of Stuart's carers, Audrey, was a Catholic and one of the main instruments in helping Stuart find faith. She came to visit him in the mornings or afternoons and taught Stuart how to pray.

His mother affirms, 'One evening, when I went downstairs to Stuart, he said he'd been talking with Audrey and he'd decided he'd like to become a Catholic. It wasn't just over night. They had lots of talks. I don't know what they said all the time. He said he felt it would be for him and that he'd like to do that. So I said, "Well, if that's what you really want, then let's do it."'

Audrey told the parish priest, Fr Chris Spain, and, as a result, Stuart was put on the RCIA (Rite of Christian Initiation for Adults) list, ready to voyage through the unknown world of theology and the Church, and the mystery of love, engraved on every human heart since the beginning of creation. What Stuart did not realise was that only a few months after he was signed up on the RCIA programme, his son would die of cancer. 'After losing his son, he really needed something,' reveals his mother.

From the moment that Stuart announced his desire to convert, members of the Parish in Bexhill came to visit him, talk with him, or instruct him in the Catholic faith. One such person was Sister Collette, whom Pat describes as 'a leading light in his travels through the Catholic faith.'

Sister Collette came to visit Stuart every week whilst he lived in Bexhill: 'Fr Chris asked me to go and see Stuart and I felt a bit weird about going to see this young man in bed. But after the first meeting with him I was fine, and I thought, "Oh, this is going to be great," and it was. It was only two or three months and then he lost his son and the relationship became close."

Sister Collette reveals how Stuart has helped her to settle into her new job: 'I do think that it has affected my work here because, before that, I was a teacher and I'd never worked in a parish and I'd never had to visit people and take Communion. Having done it with Stuart, I feel that it is a privilege. I used to feel more light-hearted going to Stuart. He was someone who almost gave more back because he was so keen and so interested. Stuart just had that, "Wow! Why me? Why has the Lord? How did I come into the Church?" I'd say he is very open to the Lord. He is almost like a child. A lot of our learning is from the scripture, but he knows nothing really. He comes out with these expressions and I sometimes don't know where they've come from. Because not many people talk to him about these things (so he hasn't remembered what someone has said), it just comes from him directly. I'm sure the Holy Spirit just infuses it. You see how the Holy Spirit can work, and it's always in people who are, not ignorant, but, like St Bernadette, haven't got any preconceived notions. They are open, and they just take it, whereas we say, "Is this really what I am supposed to do?" Our own ideas spoil. In that way, it gave me a boost.'

She allows us a glance at her time spent with Stuart: 'He was very greedy to know more. So, every week I went to him, he would ask me a question. He was quite confused at first about what the Catholic faith was all about. His son had just died and he was asking if it was all right if he spoke to his son. He said, "I know he is in heaven and I know that God has taken him to a better place because he was sick and maybe he would have suffered more if he had lived."

'He said to me, "I talk to him a lot," and I said to him, "Stuart, that's fine, but be careful about it because he's gone to heaven and although he's close to you in some ways, don't hold onto that too much because you have to strengthen your relationship with the Lord." He always wanted to know more, so I was always prepared to spend a little time with him. He manages to get through the Our Father and Hail Mary. I explained about the Last Supper; but he's not very well versed in scripture. I gave him a tape to listen to but he can't turn it on and turn it off, and his concentration span is quite limited. It's ever so difficult. He's very appreciative but religion wasn't here in his life, so it was quite a turnaround for him. I said to him,

"You don't need to say prayers. Just talk to Him. He is your Father in heaven. He loves you."' She concludes: "'It was giving him great strength and inner peace.'"

Once Stuart was ready, he was formally received into the Church. His mother recalls, 'The priest came and Sister Collette, some ladies from the church and some of Stuart's friends were here. They made it possible by coming to the house and making it all so lovely.' Whilst the multiple sclerosis was degenerating, Stuart had lived through one of the most significant transformations of his life.

In becoming a Catholic, Stuart's thirst for community and meaning has been quenched. He comments, 'No-one came and saw me. I felt yuck. Now I feel like a human being.'

His mother confirms, 'Being part of the Church seems to have changed his life by giving him a community. It's brought so many things into his life he didn't have before. I honestly and truly do think that he does take it very seriously and very deeply. Maybe, in a funny way, since losing Luke, that's given him a greater need and now there's somebody there, isn't there? The church: it's there for him.'

Many of Stuart's visitors are from the Parish, in particular two gentlemen. Pat comments, 'He makes me laugh because he says one is open to suggestion, and the other gentleman is very set in his beliefs. Well, I'd never have thought the day would come when Stuart would say something like that, or take it on board that people in that faith could be different as well! It pleases me to know that he does talk about it.'

Indeed, he draws comfort from Jesus' story, an example given to us by God of how to deal with our suffering. Sister Collette testifies, 'When I told him about the Passion, he said, "Oh, wasn't Jesus brave with all that he suffered?"'

Stuart indeed struggles with such a tale of violence and rejection, just as he struggles with his own 'story': 'I don't like the way he suffered. I feel he didn't need to suffer. He definitely didn't need to be crucified. The question I've got is: the men who banged in the nails, do they go to heaven?'

'I say my prayers every night,' testifies Stuart. 'I don't just say them for me and for my family. I say them for everybody. I love the Catholic people. They're brilliant. I say prayers for them.'

Being a Catholic now, Stuart is regularly brought Holy Communion. This has a powerful effect on him: 'I feel stronger. I feel like sometimes I'm gonna get up and I'm gonna have a walk. I think, "No, use your head.

You'll fall and who will get you up then?"' Sister Collette adds, 'It is very beautiful. He is very aware that this is special. He really is very devout. Whenever he receives Communion and whenever I pray with him, he says, 'I get a warm, warm feeling inside me.' He always says, "I get this great warmth all the time," and I think that's the Lord.'

Vicky, also a convert, recalls the first experience of meeting Stuart: 'Sister Collette knew that I was having a really hard time. I used to live in Mass because that's the only place where I got peace, the only place where I could be myself. I said to Sister Collette one day, "Where are you going?" She said, "I'm going to visit Stuart."

'I said, "Who's Stuart?"

'She said, "Stuart's a convert that I take Communion to. He's only a young man and he's got MS." She said, "He's so beautiful. He is just so hungry to learn his faith."

'I said, "That's how I feel. I feel hungry to learn. Next time you go, why don't you ask him if I can come along? Tell him that I'm a convert and that I'd like to meet him." We were going after a Tuesday Mass. I walked in and he radiated because he smiled. I sat by him. I said to him, "It's nice to meet you." I held his hand and he was so cold. I said, "You're cold! I'm going to hold your hand and warm your hand up." So I sat there rubbing his hand. He didn't feel intimidated. He felt very comfortable.'

One moment sticks out in Vicky's mind: 'When I witnessed Stuart receiving Communion, it was one of the most beautiful things I've ever seen. To this day, it shocked me to the core because Sister Collette was saying prayers and she's got this lovely way about her. He was saying after her, "Holy Mary, etc…" Every time she said something, he then repeated it. Then afterwards, if you saw him receive Communion! I said to him, "That was the most amazing thing."

'He said, "What?"

'I said, "It was almost like seeing the face of Jesus. It was so beautiful." I said this and Sister Collette was quite taken aback.

'She said, "Vicky, that's amazing because in lots of the Gospels they say that we should see the face of Jesus in each one of us."

'When I heard that, I thought wow! I'd never heard that before. I really did mean it. It was like you would imagine Jesus' face to be: so beautiful. That is actually what you're receiving, the Body of Christ.'

Stuart's faith is far from passive as he determinedly engages in a ministry to others. In turn, he has become a messenger. Sister Collette observes,

'When he's been in hospital and he's seen other people sick and ill, he's more or less tried to cheer them up and said, "It's only the Lord that can help you. You need to turn to the Lord." He is showing love and, in spite of his suffering, he is still giving out, giving of himself. He is not just receiving—*I am sick and people have to look after me!* He is giving, giving. Because he is totally open to the Holy Spirit, the Holy Spirit can use him and work in him and touch other lives.'

'There's a woman who's a carer,' Stuart tells us. 'She said, "My Mum was not ready for death." For someone who doesn't believe in God or Jesus or the Holy Spirit, she wants me to take her to heaven to see her mother! I said, "You can." She said, "What happens if my mother doesn't want me?" I said, "Well, I'm not going to leave you by yourself am I? You come with me."'

My heart

'My heart is where I get the strength from. Lots of the women that come here think that I'm a hero and I'm not a hero. I just get on with it. I look in the bathroom mirror every day. I blow a kiss! I just stay as I am. I just stay as Stuart. I'm still the same person with the same sense of humour and I just get on with it. I don't think I am special. Of course I don't hide anything. I tell the truth. I don't lie to God or myself.'

When asked if he has blamed God, Stuart answers, 'No, not once. I'm thanking Him. I've asked why. The answer has always been: "Because you can take it."'

Perhaps such an attitude partly prevails from his mother. She recalls, 'I remember him saying when he was quite young one day, "Why me?" It's a difficult question to answer really but the real answer to all of it is: there's nothing you can change.'

'I don't want to be lying in this bed', Stuart tell us. 'That's why I look forward to Tuesdays. That's when I go out. Yes, I have pain and I suffer but that's my pain. I just get on with it. When the pain happens, I think, "It's all you can do! You're supposed to give me pain. You're not giving me anything!"

'A man came up to me and he said, "My wife's got MS." He said, "'How do you cope, Stuart?"

'I said, "I laugh at it. I think it's funny. I don't think MS is threatening. I've got MS and I have to make the best of it. My life still goes on. I've learnt to accept things." There was a time when I didn't accept it. When I wasn't well two weeks ago, when I went into hospital, I thought it was funny. My opinion is the MS turned around and said "Oi! I'm still here. I'm in charge!"

'I turned around and said, "No. You're here but I'm in charge." I won't let the MS say it's in charge because it's not. I am. I'm a human being with a good intelligence. I'm not stupid. I just feel I've got a lot of things I want to say.'

Faced with Stuart

Stuart's attitude has created admiration and amazement amongst his loved ones and those who have met him. Stuart reveals, 'I do exercise! Lisa does it every night. She says to me, "Are we doing it or aren't we?" And I say to her, "I'm really tired."

"Oh, have a go! You're strong!"

"Too strong for you!"

'I have one Catholic man who comes on a Friday. Twice now, he said, "I want to be like you Stuart." The first time he said it, I said, "Get to the hospital. Have plastic surgery but you won't be like me!"'

Stuart's mother is proud of him: 'He's still there. He's come through lots of life, lots of fun, lots of downs, lots of good things, lots of bad things. He's just gone all the way. Even when he went into hospital, a couple of weeks back and when he was in the emergency room, they said to him, "Does that hurt?"

"No."

"Does that hurt?"

"No!"

"Is that painful?"

"No." Slowly now, I think, nothing can change what's happened but he has come through a long way. He hasn't changed a great deal. But then I suppose you can't change who and what you are. Your body might be affected but, at the end of the day, that's who you are, isn't it?"'

Sister Collette remains profoundly touched by the man she prised open to God: 'There is no bitterness about him. He never speaks about his illness, and he never feels self-pity. He is a beautiful soul. I think people who have illnesses are Christ's. He definitely impressed the people in the *Accueil*.[1] They all said that he is so special.

Sister Collette believes that he is an inspiration 'not only verbally but by the way he faces life.' She concludes, 'I think his very life is a message.'

Truths born from suffering

From example to message, Stuart tells us what he has learnt from his experiences of suffering: 'Just get on with life. Don't feel bad. Feel good! There's nothing bad about life. People who have MS: don't feel life is finished, because it isn't. It's just started. It's a new life. People come to see me and they say, "I have a friend who has MS and she's really down." But I don't understand that: why? You should feel life has just started. I don't feel down. I feel loved.' However, he refrains from any message for non-believers, whom he can relate to: 'It's not up to me to judge people. I'm not God. You've got to have it in yourself to ask the question and if you haven't got it, you're not going to ask it.'

Given the chance to deliver a message to the Church, he states, 'I shouldn't give advice to the Church. Understand people. I don't care who it is. I will talk to them.'

How does he feel about death, a reality for him more than for most? 'Death doesn't scare me. I think part of that is working on the railway. I've seen people jumping in front of the trains. When you've done that, your life must be totally boring. There's always a way,' he proclaims. He has lost all feeling in his bones but he has not lost the feeling in his heart, the hope that keeps him alight.

'Do you feel ready for death?' I asked.

'Yes, I am. I don't want it now but if it happened, then I'm ready.'

The awaited pilgrimage

The challenges of the boat and train journey to Lourdes did not prevent Stuart from shining like a newborn star: 'I got on with everybody,' he comments, 'Didn't matter to me if you were disabled, if you were whatever. I thought people didn't think I would listen and I sat there and I listened to what they were saying. To me, you learn a lot by listening. I remember the second night of being there, the girls were singing and there was this girl. She was disabled in her speech and I just said to everyone there, "I want to listen." The place went silent and they all shut up. I thought, "Blimey! What have I done now?" She was really good and when I got off the coach, her Mum came up to me and said, "Thank you, Stuart, for letting my daughter sing." I said, "Don't thank me. I didn't do it." She said, "You did."'

'I didn't feel I was disabled,' Stuart reveals. 'People in the street can talk about me and they'll say, "What's wrong with him?" Nothing in Lourdes is wrong. After a while, I felt like a superstar! I don't know why but this one girl came up to me and said, "I think you're gorgeous!'"

How did Stuart experience his quiet moments at the Grotto? 'It felt weird. It felt strange. I went in and I touched the top bit with my hand, not for any reason. I just wanted to and just felt comfortable, at peace. The whole week's holiday put me at peace.' He reflects back upon the river which faithfully flows through the little town of Lourdes, forever producing the same stirring noise: 'I went down there every morning when it was Mass. That water. Hearing the water was brilliant. I think simple things like that are brilliant.'

He recalls a few memorable events: 'The man in charge said to me, "I think you need Confession," and I said, "Good idea! I'll go now. Where is the priest?"

"Here he is, Stuart."

He sat down and said, "What's the problem, Stuart?"

I said, "Have I done anything wrong?"

And he said, "You've done nothing wrong at all."

I said, "You're sure?"

He said, "I'm positive."

I said, "Thank you," and we went outside.'

The experience was cleansing because it was an affirmation of who Stuart was. The service of the Anointing rang deeply in Stuart's soul and he approved the experience with child-like appreciation and wonder: 'It was strange but I accepted it. Just strange because I've never done those things. Helpers get more worked up: disabled people don't really get worked up for any reason. They accept it.' Lourdes gave Stuart his first ever experience of the Mass since becoming a Catholic: 'I was going to Mass in the morning! I was praying that I wouldn't do anything wrong but apparently I didn't.'

Amongst the people who grabbed Stuart's attention was a twelve year old boy. This is his story:

"I first thought that you needed to put your ear close to Stuart because you couldn't really hear him. I don't know why, I just found he was very serene in his wheelchair, like he had no wheelchair, because he was so active and he wanted to live, to be part of all the fun. I just thought from inside there was this fire burning for more to happen, even though he's a middle-aged man with MS. It was very daunting being next to him because he has MS and he's paralysed and you don't know what you can do which would be proper.

You have to say the right thing because sometimes people who are ill can take it badly, but Stuart is completely different. If you want to say a joke, he'll see the funny side to it.

'When I was in Lourdes, I asked him, for the journey back, "What would you like the most?" and he said, "I would like some cold cranberry juice." So I got him some cold cranberry juice which we iced and he was just sucking it and he really had a glint in his eye and sort of swayed his head a bit as if he was like a child, as if he'd stayed that age even before the MS. It's as if he hadn't grown up and he'd just forgotten about it which makes him a unique person, very unique.

'He's a man with a mission to tell the world to get strength from your heart, which he says a lot and which he does. He's always found that whatever he does, whatever he wants to do, he's led by his heart. It's like his heart is out of his body and it's like the light leading him, casting the shadow of MS behind him. There's a shadow and he's just walking towards his heart and he just believes in what he says. It's the interior where the real power comes from and that's what he wanted to say.

'I told him that I sang in a choir...You could always have a conversation with Stuart and he would always understand you. If you had something on your conscience, he would listen to you and if it was something bad, he would think, "That's in the past now. We're in the present." He wouldn't judge you at all because he can see you as you are which was very nice for me. Even though it was three times that we spoke I felt as if it was like three years I'd known him because we'd gone into chats where we just talked about our lives, about what I did and then I managed to sing two songs for the people in that ward who were having their tea and they were just so happy. Stuart was so happy and said: "I wish I could sing like you!"

'I don't think he was happy or sad. He was just very serene. He was just very graceful in the way he was lying there trying to explain his mission. That's why he was just wanting to tell everyone. He helped me to understand that I'm lucky. For somebody not to have an illness is like a gift because there are so many people who are ill in the world. I just feel I've been given a gift to be healthy and staying alive in a painless way.

'He really inspired me. I think humans, most of the time, think from their brains but he encouraged me to think from my heart which is a completely different thing. It seems hard but if you just concentrate, it just comes naturally and then you can just think of the right decision. He just encouraged me internally to actually think from the heart which really has made me a bit more mature. I've thought, "Is that kind for the person? Will

CHAPTER 8

A Spring of Youth

JOSHUA MILNE

Redshirts creation

THOUGH YOUNG PEOPLE OFTEN WANDER DOWN DARK OR UNCERTAIN paths, sitting at the core of this maze of treachery and dead ends is a fervent source of spirituality, desperate to burst forth and escape its confined surroundings: a meagre stream longing to be a mighty sea.

In the last few years, the Redshirts have become the semi-autonomous youth group adjoined to the Arundel and Brighton Lourdes Pilgrimage. In a time when young people struggle as never before with broken homes, contradictory messages between society and the Church, and increasing academic pressure, God designed one of His many counter forces: an enactment of the Gospel, 'a flower blooming very quickly', as their founder, Diocesan Youth Officer Ray Mooney observes, and an assembly of visionaries, and servants of God.

Since 2004, the Redshirts have travelled to Lourdes separately from the main Pilgrimage, staying in their own hotel and journeying through a week of prayer, self-discovery and service to the Arundel and Brighton pilgrims. The title for the group arose from the characteristic uniform, once worn by just over thirty youngsters, but now proudly borne by fifty-four (though the demand is significantly higher). Helping Ray lead the group of Redshirts in Lourdes are a number of leaders, paired up to manage small groups for more intimate, personal contact. One of the leaders, Sophie Wellbelove, who was there from the beginning, states, 'We're just instruments of God's greater plan. It all works so well. No human could ever do that.' Ray tells us of the place of the Redshirts in his life: 'On a personal level, over the last twenty years, the Redshirts are the best thing that has ever happened. Their witness has really strengthened my faith and given me encouragement to be more open about my faith and to be even more passionate about young people.' Stuart Prior, who joined the Redshirts as a leader in 2006 and abruptly changed his vocation in order to dedicate his life to young people, reveals: 'The transformation between how I was before I went with the Redshirts and how I was when I came back is incredible... I found God on a new level. I had been at the Grotto with my Mum. We'd been praying for guidance for me, for a bit of my life's path to be revealed, because she never thought I should be a pilot, which is what I was training to be. Our prayers were answered. On a small scale that is a bit of a miracle for me.'

Linked arms

A key aspect of such an experience is its community spirit, which allows young people's desire to belong to be satisfied. One Redshirt confirms, 'We are one group. Everyone in Lourdes is all as one.' Fr Rob Esdaile, who has been the group's chaplain since 2005, affirms, 'There is something about group identity that is important to youngsters, especially in their teen years.' Stuart, in turn, adds: 'It is a difficult time after Confirmation because it is *my* choice now. When they see that there are so many people their age who have got a faith and do go to Church, it shows them that they are not on their own.' He recalls the very moving experience of the Anointing of the Sick, a perfect example of togetherness: 'The last few years we have put arms around each other in a big circle. Everyone is there for everyone else and although there are only a few being anointed, I think everyone is with them.' He describes it as a 'liberating' experience.

Ray recalls one Redshirt's words of thanks to another Redshirt who lost her brother to cancer: 'There's one sixteen year old putting another sixteen year old's life into perspective... that sort of peer ministry that goes on amongst young people is immensely more powerful than anything I can give them. Ultimately, the God given strength of the Redshirts is the Redshirts themselves.' One Redshirt concludes, 'It's a family who accept and trust each other, and then it's like, "Bring it on" to the surrounding world!'

Ray recalls a special moment during a prayer time when a Redshirt leading a reflection said, 'Hold hands with your friend.' Expecting people to fumble amongst those present for their friends, Ray was overwhelmed when each person automatically held hands with the person next to them, loving their neighbour as themselves.

A ministry of welcome

What use is the word 'welcome' anymore? How beneficial is a wave or smile? Do we really need angels calling us to God? Is the banquet not sufficient? Two parallel red lines emerge from the distance. As I approach closer, I feel waves of warmth tease tantalisingly at my skin, more and more penetrating, increasingly powerful. Suddenly, I arrive at the foot of this aisle of love. A church looms victoriously at the end of it. The waves and laughs are leading me to an even greater love, to the source of all things. Faces glowing, words brimming with goodness, smiles to drown my feelings of slight bewilderment or uncertainty, cheers echoing love's 'victory'. A ministry of welcome as only God could provide.

'If you go to a party,' muses Ray, 'and you stand there ringing the doorbell and nobody comes, how do you feel? Or if you do come, somebody just slings the door open and walks away, how would you feel? That moment of welcome at the railway station – in the distance you can see this line of red shirts – is saying, "Come here. This is the way."' Sophie adds, 'It is such a vital part of life that's just so shunned by society now. It just makes you feel so special when someone can care enough to welcome you.'

Fr Rob was sceptical when he first heard about this supposed 'job' of welcoming assigned to the Redshirts. Despite such initial thoughts, all reservations left him when he saw the idea in action: 'I think it was quite inspired because it gave them a role, an identity and it turned out they were very good at it. It helps to create a sense of community for everyone else. It has a warming effect on the rest of the group.' How would such a joyous entry into Mass affect our daily or weekly masses, bearers of God's greatest gift to mankind? 'It sets the tone for the Mass,' suggests Stuart. Indeed, all hearts can be lifted, cleansed and filled in preparation for Jesus.

Bishop Kieran, one of many beneficiaries of such welcome, comments on the symbolic presence of the young people and their role as welcomers: 'I think that's a very important image, that the young people are often welcoming us, showing us the way.' Pilgrims are guided by fresh, open hearts into the very heart of Jesus. He adds, 'I was particularly touched this year when we got to Calais and the big Pilgrimage arrived at Calais before the Redshirts. As the Redshirts arrived, the other pilgrims formed instinctively two lines to welcome them. The other pilgrims had learned from the Redshirts how to present service and welcome. The Redshirts themselves were very touched by that. That was a marvellous image of a lesson learned in Lourdes.'

Such love can never reach its limit. Once, Ray recalls, 'an elderly person turned round to her helper and said, "They think I'm the Queen!"'

Somewhere that I never knew existed

'The Redshirts helped me most of all in my faith,' testifies a Redshirt. 'They kind of touched somewhere that I never knew existed and the youth and the people my age filled me with this fire and this desire to serve and worship. As a teenager, the Redshirts are perfect. They are funny but also help you learn that you mustn't judge people by the outside, something I try to do a lot less. In the Redshirts, the shyest of people who you probably wouldn't talk to at school turn out to be the most inspirational! The Redshirts helped me also in my confidence just before entering year 11 because, after leaving them, I knew the kind of person I wanted to be and I kept sight of myself at school, whereas most people changed personality completely.'

Fr Rob views young people as 'naturally spiritual people,' adding, 'It's spiritual questions that teenagers ask: "What is my identity? What do I want to become?"'

Bishop Kieran states, 'The Redshirts find a safe place to be to reflect on their lives, examine their lives, share their lives. They make great personal progress in those few days.' Sophie tells us, 'They can actually have that opportunity to share their faith and to see that there is a God that does care, there is a God that does love them and that there are other young people that believe the same thing. God is at the centre of the Redshirts. We put a lot of time and emphasis on prayer. God will grant anything for you if you pray about it.'

Changed

Though none could be called a miracle, many cases of healing, deep change and signs of God's grace have occurred through the Redshirts; mighty, little or as yet unnoticed. Stuart confirms, 'I think being in the Redshirts helps them to discover their gifts.'

Ray pursues, 'Parents have said, "I don't know what you've done with my son or daughter but they're not the son or daughter I gave you ten days ago." God opens the doors, opens our eyes really to what's possible.' He recounts one particular case of healing: 'A first-time Redshirt this year, a non-Catholic, was at the service of Anointing: she was profoundly moved. She was a girl who, four or five days before, was saying, "What are we doing just moving boxes?"' Ray talks of this young girl 'going up to the priest for the rest of the week to receive blessings at Communion and being able to write about the experience and share it with parishioners in her own parish later on.'

One non-Catholic girl came up to Ray at the end of the trip and said that after going to Lourdes, she wished to become a member of the Church. Above and beyond religion, she had found her heart's calling, a direction amidst loss and a path which seemed right for her.

Fr Rob concentrates on the healing of people's bruised spirits, of faltering self-belief: '...they are given a very strong message: "I'm loved because I am me. I am needed. I am wanted." It's what we all yearn for, to know that we are taken seriously.' Everybody is given a fresh start, a second chance: 'They have been themselves, not judged on what they did last week as there wasn't a last week.' He testifies, 'I've seen people's attitudes change during the week quite remarkably.'

'If a miracle is God changing something,' states Sophie, 'like Jesus changed the water into wine, then I think every young person who's come through the Redshirts has been a bit of a miracle and then part of a bigger miracle, in that God is using them to speak to others.'

Youth ministry

The Redshirts have gradually raised awareness and questions about the ministry of youth in the diocese, and beyond. Ray takes pride, 'I am so glad that the Redshirts have given a new face to the youth ministry in the diocese, a new sense of young people and their presence and their importance.' His message is: 'Invite people. That invitation doesn't just extend to opening the doors. It extends to what goes on once their doors are open.'

He has learnt or been reminded about several aspects of youth in the process: 'Music is a massive ministry. The number of Redshirts who have said my music identifies who I am, it is one of their identity criteria. Youth ministry is a whole community ministry. It's not just two or three people giving up a day a week. They've got special gifts and responsibilities but it must be a whole parish community to take it on board.' Fr Rob underlines one of today's challenges: 'It's very hard for young people, and young

Christians to know that it is okay to be a believer partly because very often there is nothing in the parish that is geared to them... they don't fit in with the groups that seem to be dominant in the parish. It's very unusual for fifteen or sixteen year olds to be in a place where older people are looking up to them and saying "You're great!"'

Impact on Arundel and Brighton

What lasting effects has such an unlikely group of people had on the Arundel and Brighton pilgrimage?

'If I was to take one thing,' states Ray, 'I'd say it has put the spiritual, prayerful aspect of the Pilgrimage at the top of the agenda.' Bishop Kieran adds, 'What we see is that the Pilgrimage is a busy time. You do need space, personal space, to be alone by yourself if you can be by yourself.' Fr Rob confides, 'Lots of people have said that it's changed the main Pilgrimage. It gives people access to the young, observing them doing good, which they wouldn't otherwise have. Our culture can be very negative about young people – they are a problem – whereas actually what you hear in Lourdes is that they are amazing. There is a trust in the young people.' Bishop Kieran confirms this, 'They give people great courage and optimism that there is a younger Church and they're growing. Here are genuinely spiritually grounded young people with profound faith which is developing.'

A Redshirt's story

Joshua Milne, born in 1989 to a Catholic mother and Anglican father, joined the Redshirts in 2005, returned with them the following year and was integrated into the Hospitalité team as a young helper in 2007. This young man embodies the deepest characteristics of the Redshirts: openness, vulnerability, solidarity and love are but a few. Sometimes, the most dazzling gifts hide in silence from the exterior world. When discovered, feelings of shame stir within the souls of those who listened to the treacherous voice of prejudice. It is not the first time that God has played with assumptions. The same God who placed the Redeemer of the world in a stable breathed in to a boy 'conditioned' by Aspergers, bullied and broken by family separation, a fountain of truth and love.

Diagnosis

'When I was three years old, I was diagnosed with Aspergers. Basically, I have that and I've always known I had something. I couldn't particularly pinpoint what it was. I knew I had something because I was always going to see specialist doctors in London and the school nurse used to give me hearing tests but I didn't know what it was. I felt that I wasn't exactly the same as other children but I only found out the name of what I had when I was thirteen years old when I was in hospital.

The only reason I found out was through the nurses in the hospital. While they were trying to explain to me about my hearing test at the time, they mentioned to me that I had Aspergers and I asked them to explain it to me. It was from asking them that I was able to realise more about myself. I felt I had done something horribly wrong when, actually, that wasn't the case. For a while I just didn't feel like an equal. I felt I couldn't relax. I felt I wasn't like anyone else and they put prejudices on me. They thought I was weird. I'm not seriously affected by the condition. Currently, I am at the lighter end of it. Many people have it and no-one is perfect. Some people are in wheelchairs. Okay, everyone is different but everyone should be treated equally.'

Family

'I've always got on better with my Mum,' Josh recounts. 'When I was little, my Dad would go off to work and usually my Mum would pick me up from school. My Mum would take me to the shops. I spent time with my Mum during the day. I didn't have a proper relationship with my Dad until later on.'

In 2003, pain swept over all the family members as Joshua's parents felt compelled to separate. Soon after, his mother moved out, which left his father, his older brother, Sam, aged fifteen, himself, aged thirteen, and his younger sister, Isabella, aged eight, in the house together: 'I was devastated. It was one of those things that you never really think would happen to you. You're not prepared for what will happen. Often I was trying to protect my sister as she was upset and sad to see our parents crying.'

As very often in a separation, the children became swept into the parents' feud. At the time, Joshua was only seeing his mother every few months, though he wanted to see her much more. His relationship became more tested with his father. Neither was finding peace. A mixture of lack of understanding and anger led to a life-changing decision one day in April 2005. Aged fourteen, left an unhappy scene: 'One day, I just walked out of the house. I didn't have any socks on and I was not in a good state of mind and I couldn't think.

'Thankfully, a youngish couple saw me and asked me, "Are you okay?" They were saying, "Let's take you to the police station." They were saying, "Don't worry. You haven't done anything wrong." I was at the police station a few hours while they were trying to find me a foster place. Even then, I asked my Mum to live with her. I kept telling the situation to her but I don't think she fully knew what was happening or quite believed me...'

Years later, in 2006, Josh's mother gave birth to a baby boy, Caspian, of whom Josh states: 'I love to see my baby brother. I think of him as my own brother. The half bit doesn't matter.' Time has helped to heal some of Josh's sores: 'For a time in my life things have gradually fitted into place. I am getting along with my Dad a lot more than I was, which I am really pleased to say.'

His father calls the moments Josh spends at home 'quality time.' Josh comments, 'The thing in Lourdes this year was about reconciliation and about forgiveness and it made me think about my own situation with my family. I felt to myself, 'Okay, I can get angry with my Dad about what has gone on in the past. Honestly, there is not that much to get worked up about. We are getting along quite well at the moment. I felt rather than just dwelling and keeping a grudge, it is much better to take each day as it comes. My Dad loves me and I still love my Dad, even though so much has come between us in the past few years or so. My family, nonetheless, is important to me. They are the ones to see me through university, having a shoulder to lean on in times of upset and generally help you to make the right decisions and care for you.'

Away from home

'The first time I went to Lourdes, I was feeling quite down with myself. I went into foster care. I really wanted to be back with my biological parents. Unfortunately, that couldn't happen. A few months after, I was living with my foster family in a place called Hailsham, quite near Eastbourne. I still wanted to get things sorted out with my Dad. . . It just really upset me. I wanted things to be normal. I wanted to be with my own family and not in a foster family. I got along okay with the foster family but I missed being with my own family. When I was in care they were moving me about because that is what happens in care.' Josh lived with ten foster families in total.

After his first experience in Lourdes in 2005 as a Redshirt, Josh moved to a children's home in Hailsham and lived with approximately eight other children. This marked the beginning of severe bullying for Joshua, who was tried and shattered in many ways. 'When I was living in Hailsham, whenever I went about the house I was being picked on and being called names. I couldn't even sit on the settee without one of the others throwing an apple at me, or one time they even put the bin over my head. They just kept being nasty to me trying to irritate and annoy me all the time. They would often mock me because they didn't understand. A lot of the kids made fun of the fact that I was going to Lourdes because they didn't understand what it was all about. One of them said a really horrible thing, "Shall we all go and push all the spastic people off a cliff in wheelchairs?" and that just really hurt me because they were making a judgement.'

In July 2006, Joshua journeyed as a Redshirt to the place where he felt happiest. Upon his return from Lourdes, he found that his experience of Lourdes had made his life at the home, if possible, even harder to deal with: 'It made me think I was a caring person and I didn't have to put up with the rubbish the other kids gave me.'

Only a few weeks after his return from Lourdes, Josh found that the home was being closed down. As no foster placements were open, he was forced to go to another children's home in Hastings. He recalls, 'When I found out I was going to Hastings, they said in this children's home, "You're going to be beaten up and nasty things are going to happen to you," not trying to advise me but bullying. It made me feel uneasy. I didn't want things to turn out bad as I had hope from going to Lourdes.'

In August 2006, Josh moved to the children's home in Hastings. 'It started off okay... I didn't really have much contact.' He recalls, however, the slow and strong return of the ghosts that had haunted him in Hailsham: 'I would feel really uncomfortable about going home because if I tried to enter the children's home someone would come up to me and start hitting me or throw cigarettes at me. They did say sorry but they didn't mean it. They did the same things time and again.' Josh's studies suffered considerably as a result of such harassment: 'For a while, I couldn't sleep I was so worried and stressed out about preparing for my exams. My concentration levels started to drop and I started to have panic attacks often.' One day, Josh was driven to speak to the doctor about such difficult circumstances: 'The doctor referred me to a counselling service. No-one particularly told me I was depressed but for a while I was feeling so low and depressed. I felt that it almost wasn't worth living.' What did he draw comfort from during these unbearable trials? 'The only way I was happy was going to school and being in my lessons with my friends.'

A wind of change blew into Joshua's life when he was informed by his social worker that he would be moved into supported lodging, designed to help him to become independent and prepare him for university. He reveals, 'I was excited about being with a family because I hadn't experienced it for about a year. I was due to move there a month or two later. During that time the kids at the home were making my life hell...'
He moved in with his new family on 10th May 2007 and greeted this fresh beginning with joy: 'During the weekend, when I was trying to revise, I used to think, 'This is brilliant. I am able to revise. I'm not being pestered. Okay, they would come and say, "Joshua, could you do this?" That is normal family life and I do it.'

Now that he has left behind the misery of bullying which had consumed him, Joshua is able to view that painful time in a different light: 'I've moved on now. I don't see myself as Joshua Milne coming from a children's home. I see myself coming from a family. I see being in a children's home as being one of those really hard obstacles throughout life and you have to learn how to get through it. We all find times in our lives that are difficult. I could say to myself, "Oh, no: all these terrible things have happened to me," and think I'm worthless and terrible but it is a waste of my time. Instead I could be thinking about how I could help people or about getting my essay done.'
Having had all the essentials in life threatened or taken away – his family, his education, his dignity, even his faith – Joshua now realises just what is worth fighting for.

'Knowing that God is with me'

Joshua's faith is not wrapped up in a cardboard box and hidden away in a cupboard, ready to be taken out and have its dust brushed off every Sunday for Mass. It is drawn on and lived. He states, 'It makes me feel happier with myself knowing that God is with me. Sometimes, if I can't talk to my friends on the phone, I do feel quite lonely and it's quite reassuring when someone is there for you. I believe that if you do put your faith in God, God will produce marvellous plans with you. He wants you, us human beings, to be his followers, his disciples, and he wants us to carry on the jobs he did in the Gospel. I'm not saying everyone should produce miracles. Sometimes we should be there to help others when they need it.'
In the same way that Lourdes kept him alive, so did his regular attendance at Mass: 'I go to church pretty much every week. If for example I'm not feeling very happy when walking down to Mass, people going into Mass say "hello" and they are smiling and they make me feel better in myself.

Back in my own parish in Uckfield where I grew up, I talked to other families afterwards about what I was doing during the day—normal stuff. I felt so much brighter and energised, feeling like the Holy Spirit was in me. I just can't bear the hostility that there is... I don't see the need for all these wars. It just seems like something should be sorted out so that everyone should get along in harmony.' The latter is exactly what he experiences in receiving the Eucharist: 'When I went up to Communion at my local church it made me feel as if something special was going on inside me to give me the energy to carry out my day to day living. I feel like there is something special inside me, waiting to become released.'

Prayer has become one of Josh's few peaceful, comforting dialogues in life: 'I pray as much as I can. If there is something I am really uncomfortable with, I ask for God's help. If there is something I am really stuck on, I ask for His help. Things usually get sorted out okay.' When asked if he struggles with anything in his faith, he replies, 'No, not really.' He recalls one occasion when he prayed fervently, 'I did pray to God and after praying I felt God was with me and I felt secure going to sleep.'

Josh's faith is one which skips all theological complications or distractions. It helps to illuminate the Catholic faith: 'I see Mary as the mother of Jesus. She gave birth to an extremely special person who was to be our Saviour. People should have a lot of respect for her because she was the great Mother of the great Son.' He describes the story of Lourdes and the person of Bernadette, whom he understands perhaps better than most: 'Bernadette, because she was uneducated, didn't know about Mary and the Immaculate Conception and so people found it hard to believe her. Mary could have gone to anybody but she decided to go to a poor girl, in the South of France, just like the Angel Gabriel in the Bible saying God chose Mary, a young girl, to be the mother of Jesus. Without Bernadette and the apparitions there wouldn't really be such a thing as the holy place or the Domain of Lourdes. There would just be Lourdes, it wouldn't really be of holy or religious significance. I think it is good that there are a lot of churches dedicated to Bernadette.'

'A calling from God'

If Joshua was so close to having all desire to live sucked out of him, only something great and powerful could have nurtured his broken soul back into health. Did God know that Josh would need Lourdes like a parched man in search of water? Though nothing was stable in his life, Lourdes arrived each July, the first when he had just been placed in foster care, the second when he was living through his first experience of a children's home, and the third only months after he had finally been placed into a family again. He believes, 'God specifically chooses people to go on pilgrimage to live His word.'

'After my Confirmation at Worth Abbey over two years ago, there was a leaflet that mentioned the Lourdes Pilgrimage. I already knew a bit about Lourdes from my RE lessons but it just felt almost like I was called to go on the Pilgrimage. A few days later, I spoke to my Mum about it. A place was available. I was staying at my Mum's house in Haywards Heath and I remember saying to myself, "Hang on, something quite exciting is going to happen to me! This isn't some ordinary trip. This is something significant!" I remember, when I was going, my grandparents and my Mum were taking me to Crawley to get the coach to Lourdes. People were going for different reasons or to find something out to help them with their life. We all had an intention. We were all searching and that is what a vocation is all about. It's a calling from God."

'Going to Lourdes was completely different from what I expected it to be,' Joshua confesses. The Redshirts allowed him to share in a community: 'When I was in the Redshirts, just simply wearing a red top made you feel part of a group as much as when you go to school wearing a uniform. But a lot of the time when you are at school, you don't feel a part of the group. You try to stand your ground but, in Lourdes, everyone is there to listen to your feelings.' Josh tells us of the affirmation he received: 'Lourdes has touched me because it made me feel special in my own unique way. I didn't feel judged by anyone. I didn't feel incompetent in anything. I certainly didn't feel anyone was against me. I was able to get along with everyone. In Lourdes, I felt at home and respected for who I am. Sometimes, we try to be something we're not. It made me feel happier because I was able to go with other people. I remember that weekend, two years ago, when we met up for the reunion and people were rushing up to me saying, "Josh! Josh!" You don't get that every day! I felt like a celebrity!'

The Redshirts also helped him on his path of spiritual development: 'I got a lot of spiritual guidance from being with the Redshirts. Just talking with people about what they wanted to do made me think about my own life and what I could do to make things better for myself and ultimately for other people.' He suggests, 'Although I wasn't old enough to be a helper, I still felt that I was helping, just saying hello to them or meeting and greeting people. It was such a pleasurable experience for all of us. I got back from it and the first thing I told my Mum and foster parents was I just wanted to go back."

Eyes and ears

Josh impacted on the Redshirts in a profound way. Fr Rob states, 'He had gentleness about him. People found that in him and it affected a lot of the young people around him. A kindness too. He touched everyone he met. I think one of the wonderful things was how well he fitted in as part of the group.' Ray adds, 'I think on every single occasion that I have met him, he always comes up to me and in that very quiet way, has that gentle smile and says, 'Hello Ray. Thank you very much for today.' That almost formal thank you, you can see that it really comes from down here.' Stuart admires Josh because 'He's not a judgmental person. I've never seen him look down on someone for anything. He is a humble person.'

A Redshirt recalls, 'Jack Gad was in my little group and we were together on the banister at the hotel looking down on Josh doing aerobics. Jack was next to me and said, "I'm going down." He just went down and joined Josh. When Jack got back, he told me the story of how he met Josh. It was at the gathering in Weybridge and Jack was all moody and sitting alone and everyone was trying to be sociable and ignoring him, but Josh came up to him and just started chatting. Josh brought the best out of everyone. He unarmed us from all the social barriers we had put up, and brought it down to this raw acceptance of a human being.'

In his quiet gestures and disposition, Josh promoted the value of love and acceptance. Ray believes, 'Josh just cemented this whole idea of love in action: that we are all here together and it's not about fifty squeaky clean, goody twoshoes, perfect, one dimensional, boring people. If we are true to the Gospel, true to love, people like Josh who might bring with them certain challenges bring a whole lot more. He was making people laugh, making people cry. The girls loved him! They all loved him. And from my slightly 'round the edge' look, I could see the gifts he was bringing to the group by his mere presence." On a personal level, Josh has helped Ray 'work through that vision, definition and process of the Redshirts.' Ray concludes, 'He is a mirror of love. I think he emphasises what Lourdes is about.'

Fr Rob believes that his companions learnt from Josh 'acceptance of who you are, and awareness that we are all very different from each other and we don't need to point score on who got the best GCSE results.'

He concludes, 'Perhaps the lesson to be learnt is that we are only ever called to be ourselves, not somebody else. Live that the best way you can and I think Josh does that.' One Redshirt relates, 'I really felt that when Josh was there, it was like he had someone with him because he was just filled with grace and acceptance. When he arrived in a room, the atmosphere almost shifted and people would stop their conversations and go and speak to Josh.' Sophie recalls the acceptance and utter contentment in Josh's expression: 'This year in Lourdes I saw him and I thought, "Oh, there might be something wrong. He's sitting on his own at the back of Mass." So I went over and sat with him and instead he was just inside his own head and being still with God. He looked so content.' In Lourdes, Josh lived the knowledge that he is a child of God.

In his honesty, Josh exposed the pains of living a lie and the release of inhabiting a world of truth. Fr Rob calls Josh 'a very disarming chap,' particularly in his 'directness which many people would lack.' Stuart classifies his honesty as 'childlike innocence,' claiming, 'He doesn't mind making himself look vulnerable.' Sophie reflects, 'If you say things as they are, you could get hurt, but he didn't have that barrier, that social confinement... for the Redshirts to see that, it was just quite humbling. They thought, "Why do I ever have to cover up how I feel, what the truth is to me? If this is truth then I should be able to share it." In that sense, he brought a lot of joy and he taught a lot of people by being himself.' She concludes, 'In a way, Josh gets back to basics. He just gets to the core of what it's about. If you want to be a disciple of God, you've got to live a Christ-like life. That's his message to other people, I think. I think Josh just brings home that truth of letting God be the one in charge.'

Stuart reveals Josh's 'mirror' effect: 'Because he is so open, people open themselves to talk to him and get things out: it's probably a good way of releasing things. He talks from the heart.'

Occasions for Josh's qualities to shine forth were both Redshirt talks of 2005 and 2006, respectively centred around *Love and the Eucharist* and *Confirmation*. In both, Josh gave a testimony on how the theme of the talk reflected in his life. Sophie remembers the preparation of talk on *Love and the Eucharist*, which caused many tears and absolute silence from the eighty people who had come to listen: 'He had a look in his eye that said, "I know what I'm going to say. God knows what I'm going to say. It doesn't really matter if you know what I'm going to say or not." He just had such a calm.' One Redshirt who was also giving a talk reveals, 'I was nervous but Josh just had this total freedom and poise. I asked him if he was nervous and he just said, "No, because I've told the truth about how I feel." He had written it all down in felt tip on two sides of paper and hadn't made any edits.'

During his talk, Sophie recalls: 'He spoke with no script at all. It was short and sweet but so to the point and it challenged you so much that you wanted to run away...' She recalls highly memorable parts of Josh's first talk: "Jesus is the Eucharist and if we're taking that on board we need to live it. You can go to church on Sunday, take part in the Eucharist and then go outside the church walls and do something so un-Christlike that no-one would ever believe you'd just been part of the Eucharist. You have to live like Christ if you are going to be part of it. You can't do it half-heartedly. You have to do it with your whole heart." She recalls, 'He was fifteen years old and it didn't faze him at all that he was just about to speak to people that he'd never really met before.' She adds, 'That's what he wanted to do. He wanted to share. He wanted to say, "Look, this is who God is to me and I want you to know that." Josh expresses himself better than thirty of the other Redshirts. He's so deep. There's so much to him and there's so much faith.'

Josh also talked courageously about how the Lourdes experience had left an indelible imprint on his soul and life, what it meant to him to have received such love and acceptance in this place of peace.

Josh tells us of his second talk: 'I genuinely wanted people to have the knowledge, the understanding of how great the Holy Spirit can work with people if you let it. I wanted to help other people have the same experiences as I had.

'For example, I wanted to explain to them the importance of going to Mass, how it helped me spiritually and also the effects of what happened at my Confirmation. I remember saying: I come out of church feeling so much better like something has come out of the blue and shook me and said, "Wake up, Joshua! This is real life! You've got so much to give the world."'

Stuart recalls, 'The way he can just talk from the heart in front of so many people without looking worried, without stressing out about it... he is just willing to share his experience, to share who he is with so many people in such a loving way.'

Fr Rob says of both testimonies: 'They were very carefully thought out and very much from the heart. You could have heard a pin drop. He touched something very deep in everyone who was listening. He inspired a great deal of love and respect.'

Through suffering and trials Josh himself is able to advise: 'My message to others is: although life might seem complicated, there is always a way out. The message may not come straight away. You might have to seek different ways of finding the message, speaking to other people or praying but generally God wants good things to happen to people... God loves us all. Otherwise he wouldn't have put us all on the earth. The sanctity of life... life is holy and sacred. We must take into consideration other people, especially the sick.'

Unravelling the mystery

How does Josh perceive the mysterious, timeless place of Lourdes, which escapes our understanding and runs through our hands like water?

'One of the strongest aspects of Lourdes that did touch me was seeing the amount of sick people and people in wheelchairs. You feel concern. You want to help these people. Here you are going about with two legs, you're relatively healthy, no major health concerns.' He confesses, 'The first time I was there, I was quite upset, seeing people in wheelchairs, but then I thought to myself, "Instead of thinking about what might happen, think: how can we help these people to improve their quality of life?' I feel that everyone should be treated equally, whether they have a blue tongue, whether they have one eye! We should love other people regardless. They are special in God's eye. God makes people how they are for a reason, to help carry out His role.'

The visible presence of suffering has inspired Josh in his personal journey: 'I learnt that in spite of how you might see people, the sick and disabled people, or even elderly people, have a wealth of experience that they can give to us.'

Lourdes allowed Josh to experience compassion without condition or preference: 'A lot of the time we only think of our own desires, which can make us quite selfish... what I feel is quite mesmerising is the amount of help people put on loading the train and offloading the train. Everyone is going and saying, "What can I do? Can I carry this?" It makes me feel happier and confident that I am able to help people. If everyone was the same on the outside, on the inside people wouldn't feel the need to care about other people. But because everyone is different, people want to look out for people and help them on their spiritual journey.'

He calls some highlights to mind: 'When you go into the Underground Basilica, when you are surrounded by the posters of all the saints, you feel at home with the saints. You feel like the saints are watching you, and you can relax and everything is one. The service of the Anointing, which occurs in this Basilica, is, according to Josh, 'a fantastic way of coming together and showing your love.' He also speaks of the famous procession of lights amidst enveloping darkness: 'I felt it was very touching and moving. You were able to reflect on your own thoughts. When you are in a very busy and chaotic environment, you don't very often have the opportunity to think for yourself as you are so consumed by the business of your life.'

Walking through the Domain to the Grotto allows feelings of awe and reverence to seep through his mind: 'I feel as if I had some moral authority over me, as if I am going into somewhere where I have literally been called to be.' The Grotto itself left a deep impression on him: 'I felt that I could be at peace with myself. I knew God, Mary and Jesus were with me. I was able to think and reflect by myself with the candles, especially at night time. Even just walking about the Grotto, placing my hand on the rock or thinking silently to myself really did make me appreciate what a great experience I was able to have. Not everyone has that great experience.'

Finally, he recalls the powerful experience of entering the Lourdes Baths: 'Although the Baths are quite cold to be in, I knew that the presence of God was with me and He would keep me safe and no danger would happen. I felt a sense of trust in God that He wouldn't let anything bad happen to me as far as when I got out of the bath, I noticed the water was suddenly dried off. I knew God was here for me and that He does produce good things if you ask Him for help.'

Joshua has learnt through the mocking of others how very difficult it is to convey the experience of Lourdes to those who have not travelled there: 'I feel that unless you go to Lourdes yourself and experience Lourdes, you never particularly know the true meaning of why people go to Lourdes.' This made the return from this 'other world' more trying and painful: 'In Lourdes, I was able to redirect my thoughts but when I got back to England, that's when a lot of problems in my life started to unfold again. It made me angry that I had lost the security of being in Lourdes, back in Hastings or in my own home. Everything seemed wonderful in Lourdes. It is full of love, but then you get back home and you realise you have changed but the world hasn't and there are still problems in your life.'

Each person's experience of Lourdes is unique: 'I do think people are happy in Lourdes. However, I also believe it works differently for different people. Some, when they go there, don't see anything holy about the place. They just see it as the same as other places but with churches and the Grotto.

They don't really see the symbolic relevance. Others say Lourdes has changed their lives forever.' Could Josh possibly be in the second category?

Indestructible armour

'When I was in Lourdes I felt, 'Hang on a minute. I do have a lot of things going well. I am a nice person. I am caring. Generally, for me, it made me appreciate that there is so much in life that you can offer. I felt happier and more content with my situation. I realised, 'Okay, I have got Aspergers, but it's not life-threatening. Okay, I know it is something to do with lack of communication, but I'm fairly okay with communication! I've got loads of friends. Okay, people have made fun of me in the past but I don't take it to heart. I just try to get on with it.'

Being anointed has left a lasting impact: 'I've been anointed for the past three years. It made me think about my life and it also gave me encouragement. I am a good human being. There is a lot I can offer the world. I was able to feel more at peace with myself. In Lourdes they were saying, "How can you expect to love other people and be reconciled to other people if you are not reconciled to yourself?" The Anointing of the Sick made me feel I can trust God to a further extent than I ever have had in my life. I often feel that because there's so much uncertainty in my life, I don't really see how I can help other people. But sometimes, it can be a gift. If you are more willing to take heed of what other people are saying to you and go along with different experiences, then you are more likely to become a better, more developed person.'

Lourdes has injected him with the hope he once lacked. Even the foster home noticed and told Sarah Clutton how important Lourdes is to Josh. He is now aiming towards the caring profession of homeopathy, though it could change: "I am more hopeful. I've got motivation. I know more or less what I want to do and in which direction I want to go and from that I hope to help other people to find that motivation. I remember coming back having so many great plans which I wanted to achieve. Some, I have achieved, like what direction and subjects I want to study at university and what subjects to study this year. There are still aspects I could make better in my life, such as the people I live with, who I'm friends with. Relationships could get better.

'I feel like Lourdes has helped me in three different ways,' he states. 'Each year I have matured a bit.' After speaking to various people in his first year in Lourdes about his situation, he claims, 'I did feel guilty about talking about my problems with other people in case I was wasting their time and that my thoughts and feelings aren't significant, because people have drummed it into me that I am not important. But they said, 'You're not useless and you have a lot going for you.'

I thought there was a bad stigma against me because I was living in a children's home. In Year 11, my RE teacher encouraged me to speak to the year below me about my pilgrimage to Lourdes to try to help them with their exams. I thought, "Yeah, it will help them."' Moreover, Josh had to write an essay about Lourdes as part of the theme of pilgrimage they were studying in RE. He was awarded an A for his work. Being a helper, Josh states, 'I wasn't really too sure about going but I am pleased I went because I feel as I've fulfilled a duty that God has required me to do.'

Josh sheds tears when he remembers some of the hymns which have comforted him in his times of distress: 'Some of the hymns really did speak volumes to me. I heard one of the hymns we sung in Lourdes when I was back home from my holidays working at a Christian coffee shop in Hailsham and listening to it brought back so many memories: "Jesus, be my centre, be my source, be my light, Jesus." And another one: "There must be more than this".

'That song! Going to Lourdes made me think about the time in the children's home and it made me feel that there must be more to life than a children's home. I can have a better life than this and it is within my distance. It made me feel that I didn't deserve all of the torture that was happening to me and I was a strong person who could persevere with difficulties. I think that if I hadn't gone to Lourdes then I probably wouldn't even be here. I would have given up long ago.'

CHAPTER 9

In the Communion of Saints

JANE BOWYER

'This girl is special'

SISTER ROSE MARY CUSH, A DAUGHTER OF THE CROSS, recounts with simplicity how Jane Bowyer, aged twelve, ended up on Holy Cross Hospital's doorstep in Haslemere, with nowhere else to go: Jane was born in London on the 30th March 1928. She suffered from cerebral palsy from birth and she was blind. 'At the onset of war her parents had to evacuate their children, Jane, and her younger sisters Brigid and Carol. The problem was that they could not find a children's home for Jane, not even a nursing home, as Jane was very disabled. In desperation they came to the Holy Cross Sanatorium run by the Daughters of the Cross. Sister Francis Clare was the superior at that time. She gave the parents a list of homes to try, but she did say, "Come back to me if you can't get Jane placed." Sister then had a dream in which Our Lady asked her to take Jane who was a special child and needed a lot of care.'

Something that the other girls had

Jane became a Holy Cross patient and was given a single room so that she would not contract tuberculosis from the other patients. Sister Rose Mary recalls how this change of location led to a deep-seated change of heart: 'Sometime after admission Jane realised that she was missing out on something that the other girls had. She heard them talk about going to Mass, about Holy Communion and about Confession. She heard them talk about Our Lady and the Rosary. Jane, although blind, had acute hearing. She asked to be received into the Catholic faith and having got permission from her parents was received and made her First Holy Communion. Jane looked forward each morning to receiving Holy Communion. She loved the Rosary and had a tremendous love for our Blessed Lady.

Jane's thirst for God was quenched by one man in particular. 'There was a Colonel Ritchie who came to see if he could visit some patients in the hospital and asked if he could see Jane. Every Tuesday he stayed with her her for about three-quarters of an hour in the evening and read the Bible and the Gospels to her. Instead of having a conversation with her he would read to her slowly and she understood everything. And then some Sundays in the summer time he brought a small mini car. He'd put the seats back so that they could put Jane's stretcher in and take her out to his garden for tea. She loved that. He loved her. He spoke to her about Our Lady. He loved Our Lady of Lourdes too. He could talk to Jane about it and they had something in common, until he died after a couple of years.'

Jane was filled with joy, a convert newly in love with her faith. Sister Rose Mary tells us: 'She loved coming to Mass, particularly Midnight Mass: something out of the ordinary. It took about three people to lift her off her trolley and bring her over to Mass. She loved the very fact of being able to get off her trolley. That was a joy to her. She might start snoring in the middle of it, she was so relaxed in the presence of the Lord.'

Physical bearer of the cross

Jane led her life through suffering. Sister explains, 'She couldn't move. She couldn't get out of bed. You couldn't sit her up, for instance. If you tried to sit her up, her back would arch back again so we had a special trolley for her so she could fit into that and be wheeled about. She couldn't do anything. She couldn't see. She couldn't use her hands. Jane used to get moments of unconsciousness. She was not with you for a few minutes. Her breathing would change. Nurse Peggy Smith reveals: 'Jane was the first person that I had met who was severely disabled. Jane needed feeding and all nursing care.'

Despite multiple disabilities, according to Sister Rose Mary, Jane was very healthy, with a good appetite and physically fit. She had a big bonny pink face. She always had a smile on her face. She chuckled away.' Also this extraordinary girl's sense of people was acute. Sister Rose Mary recounts, 'For instance, Fr Michael Bourne, from this diocese, came to the convent and asked the Sister if he could see Jane and she said, "Yes, Father, I'll bring you over." So he went over to Jane's room and as he opened the door and he said, "Hello Jane!" She caught his hand and said, "My Michael, my Michael."'

How did Jane bear her burden of pain? Karin Harvey, who met Jane in Lourdes as a young helper, confesses: 'I could not tell if Jane suffered. If she did, I never visibly saw it.' Jane's pains were quiet and always laid aside, hidden by her humour and happiness. Sister Rose Mary testifies, 'I've never prayed for a miracle for Jane because it wouldn't be Jane if she was walking around. There was no bitterness. She never spoke about her suffering. She never even said, "I wish I could," but she loved the prayer in Lourdes, "Lord, that I may see. Lord, that I may walk." I said, "Jane, you'll be walking in heaven."'

The joys of nursing

'It was a joy to nurse and to care for her,' reveals Sister Rose Mary, who arrived at Holy Cross Hospital in 1960, over twenty years after Jane did, and became the Ward Sister. She states, 'I felt that Jane needed more than just nursing. She needed companionship as well. I made sure she had everything that she would need: I'd do her shopping for her, made sure she had a nice clean nightie on and I organised her diet for her.'

Jane stood out from the other patients. One Lourdes pilgrim remembers, 'Sister Rose Mary told us that at Holy Cross Hospital in Haslemere, Jane was like the pivot of the whole of the community. She was the heart of the community. Everybody did everything by reference to Jane. She had this very special place: like a beating heart.'

Sister Rose Mary learnt during the time that she nursed Jane: 'She loved her music, she loved her radio on, particularly good music. She wouldn't listen to rubbish! She'd say, "I don't like that. I don't like that," if it was something she didn't want. She wasn't unintelligent. She could mention places in the world and say, "My father was there." By listening, she had a terrific sense of hearing. We know that she understood everything but she could only respond in a kind of pidgin language, a few words. You couldn't hold a long conversation with her but she'd love you to talk to her. She loved company. We got to know the things she liked. She loved tomato and cheese: it was wonderful! Every mouthful you gave, she'd say, "Lovely, lovely." Because she was always very grateful, she was never any problem. She had to be turned over to be washed and dressed and all the personal things done for her. There was never a grumble, she always said, "Thank you" and always said "Please". She was very special.' Nurse Peggy echoes this: 'During the time that I knew Jane she was always the same, a lovely smile she had for everyone and always so grateful for the care that she received.'

Out of all of the nurses who cared for Jane, Sister Rose Mary was the never-fading pearl who shone in Jane's life. Sarah Clutton claims, 'She just loved Jane and Jane relied on her.'

Another pilgrim recalls, 'Sister absolutely adored Jane and you could see that in her, in the care and the love and the respect that she showed for Jane. For anyone who was interested in Jane like I was, she was so happy to tell you all about her and her background and who she was.'

Julia, another pilgrim, marvels, 'I was flabbergasted at her devotion to Jane.' Sister Rose Mary herself was deeply moved by 'her joy, her innocence, her spontaneity, her gratitude.' She testifies, 'The other nurses looked after her too but she always said, "There she is! There she is!" when she could hear my footsteps coming down the corridor. The other staff changed every couple of months but because I was always there, I think that was why. She knew I was very fond of her. She knew she could trust me with everything. She looked on me as a kind of mother figure. She was happy in my presence. I felt happy in her presence too. Though she was always happy, you would feel afterwards, "I wish I could have done more for her."'

Lovely, lovely Lourdes

'Jane went on pilgrimage to Lourdes every year from the mid-Sixties to the very last year of her life,' reveals Sister Rose Mary. 'She went on the National Pilgrimage until the Arundel and Brighton Pilgrimage started.'

A journey from England to the South of France was extremely long for someone who was dependent on others to see, react, and care for her. This did not faze Jane. Sister Rose Mary affirms, 'Jane loved the journey whether it was by air, jumbulance or train and boat. The rougher the journey, the better. When everybody else was sick on the boat and it was rough, because of her blindness she was still smiling away.' She recalls an occasion in the jumbulance which transports the sick and disabled on bunk beds: 'A patient was on top, miserable and grumbling, and Jane was chuckling, "Oh, this does me good!"'

The people brought the experience alive for Jane, as they do for so many others. Sister tells us, 'She loved to be with crowds. She loved to be with a group of people. She loved Bishop Cormac and Cormac loved her.

He used to watch out for her, particularly at the Blessing of the Sick. I think too it was the very fact that there were so many young people around her and they would be making a fuss of her. She loved the excitement and the care that she got from everyone. She was noticed by so many people.'

During the week's pilgrimage, Jane lived through many intense experiences. Sister Rose Mary says that Jane 'loved the Blessing of the Sick,' a peaceful time where all gather around the core of the Lourdes experience, the sick and disabled, tended and comforted by all who are present. One pilgrim recalls, 'We used to take her out. The helpers were there to put her from her bed onto the stretcher, so she always went everywhere on a stretcher. It was no mean feat to move her out of the bed onto a stretcher! We didn't have a hoist.' This pilgrim recalls one unforgettable experience: 'In those days, we did amazing things we wouldn't dream of doing now in Lourdes. We took Jane on the High Stations of the Cross on a stretcher. Underfoot, it's very dodgy! We had to lift the stretcher and carry it all the way round with her.' Sister once again adds, 'The rougher it was, the better for Jane!'

Another unforgettable event was the Baths, which, according to Sister Rose Mary, she 'loved going into' and would respond to with her characteristic "Lovely, lovely." A male helper recalls, 'She went more than once in the week because she loved it so much. She came out glowing.'

All Jane's attention was focussed on Mary. Her devotion to the Virgin was almost tangible. 'Jane always had a small statue of Our Lady in each hand,' recounts Nurse Peggy. Sister Rose Mary recalls, 'When she was bathed and washed, she had little tiny statues in each hand and you had to open her hand, take the statue out to wash her hands but she always wanted them back again.' This sight of Jane with the statues has remained imprinted on the minds of many a pilgrim. Karin Harvey reveals, 'The first thing that struck me when I first met Jane was that she had a statue of Our Lady in her hand. I can remember thinking that this person must love Mary very much. I was very moved by this act of faith.'

Jane's close relationship with Mary found expression in her love of the Grotto. 'Her joy was to be down by the Grotto,' declares Sister Rose Mary. She adds, 'She'd go over as near to Our Lady as possible. She was full of Our Lady and she just didn't have much time for anybody else, or the other saints for that matter. She loved her rosary and we used to touch the statues around the Grotto with Jane's rosary. Jane was always in prayer with Our Lady. She had these two statues and the *Ave* was her prayer. She was in constant prayer. Nothing would please her more than to put on the tape of *Ave Maria*. She just loved to sing and she could sing *Ave Maria* to her heart's content, but she wouldn't remember the words. Jane couldn't remember long prayers, big prayers. She couldn't remember the Creed but the *Ave* and the "Hail Mary full of grace": those were just so easy and so simple and she just responded to those.' Sister recalls that Jane loved her family dearly and would offer them up to Mary: 'She used to pray for them. She used to pray, "Please Our Lady, please Our Lady, give them what they want." For instance, if people would say to Jane, "Say a prayer for her," then you'd hear her saying, "Please Our Lady, please Our Lady, give her what she wants."' Sister Rose Mary muses, 'Whether she actually saw Our Lady, I don't know. Maybe.'

What place did this special town have in Jane's life? Nurse Peggy, who once accompanied Jane to Lourdes, says, 'Jane just loved going to Lourdes and had such a deep affection for Sister Rose Mary because she was able to take her. It was going to Lourdes every year that gave Jane the strength to bear all her suffering and the indignities of nursing care for all her needs.' Sister Rose Mary testifies, 'She lived for it. When she came back, it was, "When am I going again?" As soon as she was on the way back, she was planning when she was going next year. Her whole life centred on Lourdes.' She cannot stress its importance enough: 'This was her holiday. This was everything for Jane.' Cardinal Cormac concludes, 'Being at Lourdes was the highlight of her year. She didn't come for a cure. She came just because Lourdes said something to her, the great message of Christianity somehow is manifested in a particular way and she recognised that.' Sister concludes, 'When she was happy, that's when she was in heaven. Lourdes was heaven to her.'

Touched souls

'I came into contact with Jane on my very first pilgrimage as a handmaid back in the 1970s,' recalls Karin Harvey, now one of the Pilgrimage organisers. She testifies, 'I learned that happiness and love can be found in all situations. Jane was the first sick pilgrim I ever helped feed. I was nervous, but Jane smiled and often said "lovely" throughout the meal. Jane showed me that I could help someone and it felt good. I am always thankful to Jane for her patience with a novice handmaid! From my memory, Jane greatly touched many people.'

Jane left a legacy of 'touched souls' on earth when she departed it. Many felt called by Jane. Sister Rose Mary recounts, 'One year I couldn't find anyone to look after her. I asked one of the ladies who was Secretary to the League of Friends, and wasn't a Catholic, if she would go with Jane. She said, 'I'd love to,' and she came back and she was telling everybody about Lourdes. It was better than sending out a Catholic in a way because she came back with such joy. Sometimes I'd send a nurse from the ward and they loved Lourdes too.'

Nurse Peggy Smith was one such person who was guided by Jane to a great fountain of happiness. She recounts, 'I had the privilege of taking Jane to Lourdes one year. It was a wonderful experience. So many people knew Jane and she was just full of smiles for everyone and a great inspiration to everyone who met her. It was my first experience of Lourdes and I was working in the hospital. It was truly inspirational to be there.' Sister Rose Mary still marvels at Jane's 'inspiration to all the young helpers in Lourdes, by her cheerfulness and patience and happy acceptance of a life of suffering,' adding, 'It is no wonder everybody loved her. We now know why our Blessed Lady said, *Jane was special*. When I'd go in the morning, people were saying, "Oh, Jane was so wonderful...Jane made such an impression on me."'

Sister Rose Mary believes that Jane's life is an inspiration to many, notably to the Church: 'The fact of her disabilities, her inability to move, her inability to see, her inability to walk: Jane didn't look at it as the Crucifixion but in fact it was. She didn't even query anything like that. She didn't query the Lord's suffering, crucifixion. She just accepted that that's the way it was.' Another pilgrim adds, 'I think someone like Jane is constantly reminding the Church that it is in weakness and vulnerability and powerlessnesss that Christ operates and it's the way that he operated. He was not a king in an earthly way. People like Jane are a constant reminder of the fundamental values of Jesus.'

On a personal note, Jane spoke to Sister Rose Mary's soul: 'Her great devotion to Our Lady increased mine. You know you couldn't be with Jane without loving her dearly and without praying to Our Lady, without saying the Rosary: it was part of Jane's life and became part of my life too. Our Lady must have loved Jane, therefore Our Lady must have loved me because I loved Jane—like a triangle.'

One particular pilgrim, a recent convert at the time, recounts his first meeting with Jane, his first year in Lourdes and her last year in Lourdes and on this earth: 'I went to Lourdes for the first time in 1982. I was a little bit curious about her, and couldn't quite work out who this person was lying in the bed. I felt drawn towards her. On one of the first duties that I spent time with her, I found her a fascinating and beautiful person. You'd get close to

Jane. You'd whisper in her ear. You'd talk to her. I think she knew what was going on around her. The thing I remember most was, "Can I have a coffee please?" – she got fed in a child's beaker – and "lovely, lovely!"

'You'd suddenly discover amazing things about her...about her coming every year to Lourdes for twenty years, each year asking if she could walk, and each year getting the same answer, "No, Jane your place is in bed for me." When I heard that story, she was an example to me of hope and of faith. I used to imagine about what it would be like if Jane walked. Her total acceptance of God's will was to understand that that wasn't to be the case.

'One of the helpers, Celia Robinson, bought me a statue of Our Lady like Jane's, so sometimes I would hold it in my hand when I got back from Lourdes, thinking of Jane and this amazing faith and love of Our Lady that she had. She was very, very close to Our Lady. As the week went on, I realised more and more what a special person I was looking after.

'I went through a radical transformation that first year I went to Lourdes. My faith changed. I'm convinced that my time spent with Jane was the catalyst and the reason behind that. What I learnt from Jane is I came with a faith that was more of an intellectual-based faith. Jane taught me to use my heart. That first year, I spent a lot of time praying at the Grotto and I had a lot of amazing moments praying there. I remember being very, intimately drawn in prayer.

'The defining moment which I will never forget was the last night in the hospital. Jane loved hymns to Our Lady and her particular favourite was *As I kneel before you*. Quite often, two or three times in the week, a music group would visit the wards, take a guitar and would sing hymns. They went round the ward and came up to Jane's bed. There was a guitar and violin. Because it was Jane, we asked them, "Can you play, *As I kneel before you*?" They played it. I wasn't right up close to the bed. I was in the second row in the crowds behind. There were a lot of people round her bed because it was the last night. It was a special moment. They started playing *As I kneel before you*, and her face was transfigured into pure joy, pure delight; something I'd never ever seen before. I'd never seen anything as beautiful as her face that night. It was the last moment of her last night on her last pilgrimage to Lourdes. I stood next to a girl who was a helper and I looked at her and I said to her, "Josie, are you seeing what I am seeing?" She said to me, "It is amazing. I've never seen anything like it in my life."'

A visit from the Pope

Sister Rose Mary recounts one of the most intense and special moments in Jane's life at the time of the late Pope John Paul II's visit to England in June 1982: 'Sarah Clutton rang me and said that they had to limit the number of sick people going to the Southwark Cathedral, where the Holy Father was to anoint the sick, and one person from each diocese could go. Jane, from this diocese, was chosen to go. I thought, "That's absolutely wonderful! I'll go as well."

'The whole cathedral was packed with people. He blessed each one as they came up. So it was very special that Jane got that special blessing as well. I was full of joy. It was lovely to be there. She couldn't see the Holy Father. She could sense the atmosphere.'

During that memorable Mass of 28th May, the Pope addressed an 'urgent plea to this nation'. The following is an extract, and illuminates the value of Jane's life:

> Do not neglect your sick and elderly. Do not turn away from the handicapped and the dying. Do not push them to the margins of society. For if you do, you will fail to understand that they represent an important truth. The sick, the elderly, the handicapped and the dying teach us that weakness is a creative part of human living, and that suffering can be embraced with no loss of dignity. Without the presence of these people in your midst you might be tempted to think of health, strength and power as the only important values to be pursued in life. But the wisdom of Christ and the power of Christ are to be seen in the weakness of those who share his sufferings.

> Let us keep the sick and the handicapped at the centre of our lives. Let us treasure them and recognise with gratitude the debt we owe them. We begin by imagining that we are giving to them; we end by realising that they have enriched us.

A pilgrim concludes by saying, 'We've got politicians who are there running the country. We've got bureaucrats and administrators, business people and doctors and nurses who keep us healthy, but we need a heart.'

Unrecognised sainthood

'I was immediately struck by her,' reveals Cardinal Cormac, who speaks of 'a kind of mystic life' that he found in Jane: 'She had a most beautiful smile. I can still picture her. Somehow her life had real significance.' One pilgrim marvels, 'How could a woman with no speech or independence inspire so many people? I don't know. I think it is the mystery of Lourdes.' For Sarah, 'Jane was on everybody's mind. She was special. I don't know why.'

Karin Harvey echoes this: 'She had something about her. Jane was, from what I can remember, always happy. I felt and believed that Jane was very close to God.'

Sister Rose Mary adds, 'Her smile, her gratitude, her simplicity, her nearness to God: these were the special things. She was most unworldly.'

Through her acceptance of who she was and of her life and through her love of Our Lady and her love of Jesus, God was able to shine through her, through her weakness, through her humanity. Someone who's blind often gets a greater sense of hearing, a pilgrim reflects. Maybe for someone who is just deprived of almost all their senses but who is so totally loving of God, their heart just develops into something very special.

On 15th September, on the Feast of Our Lady of Sorrows, Jane died very peacefully in Holy Cross Hospital. Sister Rose Mary tells us: 'She got suddenly very poorly. I think the last few months of her life she'd get a bit chesty and physically she wasn't as well, so in the end she died of pneumonia and heart failure. I wasn't here when she died but it wasn't a sudden death. They rang me and I came back and she had died. I was here for the funeral. We had the Mass in the Chapel. She was buried down in the local cemetery. It was just wonderful that she did die so beautifully and peacefully, in her own bed.'

Sister Rose Mary reveals, 'Her sister Brigid gave me Jane's rosary beads which I use every day as I say my rosary. I've still got them. The little purse is very thin and it's nearly got a hole in it. I dearly loved Jane and her rosary is a daily reminder of so many happy pilgrimages that Jane and I had together, and of the great privilege I had in being her special friend.

Karin Harvey says, 'When I heard she had died I immediately remembered her hand with the statue of Our Lady in it, and that now, Jane would be with Our Lady in heaven.'

What of this extraordinary person? Sister Rose Mary believes, 'Of course she was saintly. She was like a new born baby: they never lose their first innocence. She was very close to God, very close to Our Lady. People don't canonise these good people really. They're so innocent, so beautiful but I would just say she was very near to God. She was a saint but not one of those that were going to be canonised because there are so many. In God's eyes, I'm sure she was a saint.' This faith in Jane's innate goodness is voiced by many, amongst whom is Cardinal Cormac, who continues to believe in this humble, illiterate girl on the stretcher with a statue of Our Lady in either hand.

He affirms, 'I think she is a saint. In other words, I cannot but believe that some of her acceptance of her suffering and disability and whatever recognition she had means that she is with God. Of that, I have no doubt.'

Fr Ian Doyle was with her in Lourdes in that last year and after attending her funeral bore witness to Jane's birth into the next life in a letter to a good friend, dated 23rd September 1982:

'Yesterday I attended the funeral Mass for Jane. It was a truly joyous occasion, all present knew with confidence that Jane was happy with God and with his Blessed Mother. There were many times in the ceremony that I felt very close to tears but I think that the most moving moment was when they carried out the body whilst we sang *As I kneel before you*. My thoughts were then totally with us at Lourdes at the Torchlight Procession. Remember the moments, those very intimate moments, that we witnessed with Jane. I never mentioned this before to you or anyone else, but it was Jane's complete faith in Our Lady that showed to me my lack of devotion and my great need to come more close to Mary. The moment which I am referring to is of Jane straining to sing the chorus 'Ave, Maria, gratia plena, Dominus tecum, benedicta tu.' I have told you of some of my close moments with sick people and particularly of those that were dying, but I felt a wholesomeness and completeness on that occasion with Jane, an occasion that I have rarely felt before. For this moment in Lourdes I pray, 'Holy, Holy, Holy, Lord, God of power and might heaven and earth are full of your glory hosanna in the highest.' I am sure that Jane was content as she watched us from on high pay our last respects to her and thank her for the great teaching she gave us. She is with God free from handicapped limbs. She is now complete and I am sure perfect in every way.

CHAPTER 10

'The Happy Pilgrim of Lourdes'

JEAN-PIERRE BÉLY

WITH THE PARTICIPATION OF
GENEVIÈVE BÉLY

The unexpected healing of Monsieur Bély has led to multiple medical investigations of a neurological and psychiatric nature, which have been submitted over the course of ten years to the Lourdes Medical Bureau and the International Medical Committee of Lourdes. We recognise that the fact of this sudden and unexpected healing escapes the normal and natural course of such a disease. In the name of the Church I recognise publicly the authentic character of the healing which Jean-Pierre Bély benefited from on 9th October 1987. This sudden and complete healing is a personal gift from God for this man, and an effective sign of Christ the Saviour, which was accomplished through the intercession of Our Lady of Lourdes.

> *Official declaration by the Church, 9th February 1999,*
> by Claude Dagens, Bishop of Angoulême

Beyond the witness that I bear, I am a man like any other.

> J-P. Bély, *Testimony (My healing, sign of love)*

A simple life

B orn on 24ᵗʰ August, 1936, Jean-Pierre Bély left school aged nearly fifteen with the minimum diploma required for any French student. He soon obtained a nursing diploma. He tried his vocation in the seminary, but left, realising this was not the path that God was calling him to. Instead he joined the Army, after which he began to work in the hospital of Girac in France as an anaesthesia and intensive-care nurse. It was there that he met the love of his life, Geneviève, who worked as a nurse in the blood transfusions department. 'He used to come and fetch blood,' she giggles. They married in 1968 and gave birth to a son with a learning disability and a daughter.

Jean-Pierre and his family lived in simplicity as traditional Catholics. Geneviève states, 'We had a bit of faith nonetheless,' in her characteristically unassuming way. She claims of her husband, 'He always had things which made him feel guilty. When he was working in the hospital, abortions were happening more and more: his work was to anaesthetise. He felt guilty about this act as much as the mother, but people said to him that his work was to anaesthetise, not to judge. It was the choice of the mother. Of course, he prayed so that she wouldn't have any regrets. He prayed a lot.'

'You'll have to make do with it'

In 1972, Jean-Pierre began to show signs of illness. His wife recalls, 'He lost consciousness. He had an episode of double vision. This left quite quickly during his recovery.' She recalls a gift from heaven even then: 'He left to finish his studies at Poitiers as an anaesthetist. He had been working in the operating theatre but he was not fully qualified. He had several episodes of illness, and I was concerned because I was alone with young children and said to myself that I would never get by. I became ill and very tired. I was sent to a cancer centre at Bordeaux. We were scared. The examinations took a long time, so in the end my husband said that he would stop his studies. The day he left Poitiers, in the evening, the house where he was living exploded due to a gas canister. His escape was already a form of miracle! There were two fatalities. My health came back without too many issues and we continued our little life with our children.'

In a few years, however, Jean-Pierre could no longer deny that his body was failing him. In October 1984, he became paralysed on his left side. Geneviève discloses, 'He could not get up. He was taken to the hospital. He was looked after. The Chief Doctor responsible for ophthalmology said, 'I cannot be sure but it resembles multiple sclerosis.' As my husband knew what that meant, it gave him a terrible shock. He was sent to Poitiers for more tests. They didn't tell him directly, but they said, 'You'll have to make do with it.' We installed a lift which went up to the first floor. Sometimes there were periods when he couldn't walk, and then he was better. He went on a special diet: only uncooked vegetables, fish and meat.

In 1985, he started to have a wheelchair which he found hard to accept. The car had been modified so that he could drive.' She speaks of his 'patience' and his 'humility', claiming, 'He did not want to cause any trouble to others.' This was accepted with difficulty by Geneviève: 'When you love someone, you want to do all you can to assuage his suffering.'

When illness reminds us that we are not invincible and leaves us with the uncomfortable feeling that we are not in control, how do we cope? '"If you have a burden, I will give you strength," says Jesus in the Gospel,' we are reminded by Geneviève. 'We lived from day to day. We didn't need to think about tomorrow.' Faith was crucial: 'Almost up to the end, he went to Mass. The Eucharist is to seek out the food which gives us trust and hope. It gave us strength to persevere.' Jean-Pierre wrote in his witness called *My healing, sign of love,* published by the Sanctuaries of Lourdes:

> The living of our faith within the family had been transformed for some years from traditional practice to a living and communicative faith, and during this time of trial, we experienced a feeling of total trust in the Lord. It was like children who find refuge in the arms of their father and mother. Every Sunday was a special time, a kind of oasis in the desert of my trials where it was good to drink at the Spring of Life.

Lourdes

Lourdes became an integral part of the life of the Bély family. They travelled there numerous times. Jean-Pierre went there when he was sick but always stayed with his family at the campsite. Geneviève recalls: 'It was always a haven of peace and of resources: building up strength. There are many who say that when you go to Lourdes you forget all your worries. In Lourdes, you feel that the sick are taken in charge. The helpers are full of tenderness. When he began to be sick, I said, "You could go to the Baths," but he didn't really want to. I used to like saying the rosary in front of the Grotto in the afternoon. Mary is there. I always feel her there.' For Madame Bély and her husband, Lourdes meant 'A haven of trust'. She asserts: 'There are moments of great happiness. And when you come back you have to get used to the real world again.'

'Get up and walk'

What made Jean-Pierre's trip to Lourdes in October 1987 so different from the previous ones? After initially refusing the offer to join the Pilgrimage of the Rosary to Lourdes, Jean-Pierre, aged fifty-one, agreed to travel to

Lourdes as a registered sick person for the first time. 'The idea became a profound desire which did not leave me,' he testifies. On 3rd October, the pilgrimage set off for Lourdes. Geneviève recalls with emotion: 'I took him to the station, my heart feeling tense, because it was going to be such a tiring journey for him. My son, who was eighteen years old, said "What if Dad comes back standing?"' Geneviève herself claims that she was not praying for a miracle, which could be easily assumed: 'He went to learn to accept his sickness, because it is not always easy. He did not always find it easy to eat or to wash. People go to Lourdes and always leave with renewed joy and peace.' She adds with tears, 'He wrote me a little letter, with very shaky writing:

> Today, Tuesday morning, I went to Mass at St Pius X but I was tired after the Mass. I went to lie down this afternoon. I will go to the procession on a stretcher because I am in too much pain. The nurses are perfect but do not replace the tender hand of Mummy! Big kisses to all of you.

What did happen from 3rd to 9th October 1987? Jean-Pierre wrote in detail in *My healing, sign of love* on the series of events, as if he were experiencing it once again:

> Our hearts were full of joy as we arrived at the Sanctuary and went to the Grotto of the Apparitions. It is there that we really find the heart of God. Are not the sick and handicapped children especially beloved by God? I remember this prayer which flowed out from my heart: 'Listen, O Lord, because you are all powerful, you can give me everything, so I ask you for everything. But as you know me better than I know myself, you will give me what you have that is best.' I did not particularly ask for healing, but what the Lord had that was best. From that moment I gave him 100% of my trust.

He recalls the soft feelings of being looked after: 'We are like children with our little mothers.'

On 7th October, the pain in Jean-Pierre's body was too severe for him to sit up. He was taken from his wheelchair to a stretcher: 'I felt like I was lying on a pile of pebbles.' At the Procession of the Blessed Sacrament, he was overwhelmed:

> Suddenly I was intrigued and surprised to see a young woman all dressed in white, coming in my direction. There were lots of women in white arriving at the Esplanade and I don't know why I noticed this woman more than the others. She came up to me and smiled. I did not know her and thought she was smiling at my neighbours. But they were looking elsewhere, so it was me that she was looking at. That smile, I will never

forget it. It is inscribed in my innermost depths. She smiled with great tenderness and was full of confidence. She continued to smile in this marvellous way as she said, 'Be confident. Do not be afraid. Mother Mary will put everything right!' I was troubled by these words which penetrated my inner being and upset me. What did she mean? Why me? It is now that I realise that Our Lady wanted to warn me by someone of something which I did not yet understand. What a mark of tenderness and kindness! I give myself over to the Virgin Mary and Our Lord. Even if I do not understand, it is the Lord's will which counts and not mine and I abandon myself to Him. The night was not good for me. All my being was still impregnated with the words which had been said to me by the woman in white.

Friday 9th October was the last day of the pilgrimage. For the sacrament of the Anointing, the following words were placed on him: *May the Lord in his goodness comfort you with grace of the Holy Spirit, release you from all sin, save you and lift you up. Amen.* He states,

We were four out of twenty-five sick in the ward to be chosen to be anointed. We arrived on the Esplanade which was bathed in light, like a spring morning. The sky was pure blue, and the sparkling sun was starting to spread its sweet warmth. Mother Mary spread her mantle of light over her dear children. I imagined her welcoming her children with outstretched arms. Pilgrims are coming from all directions. The celebration is starting. There is joy on heaven and in earth. The Lord is going to come. The Lord will comfort people in their misery. He will console the afflicted in their most intimate pains. He will give this strength, without which we cannot stand up. He is Tenderness and Love!

Jean-Pierre remembers the aftermath of the Anointing:

I see with much tenderness that the Lord forgives all my weaknesses as a poor sinner. What I perceive with great clarity is that when the Lord forgives, you must never come back on what is pardoned, as his forgiveness wipes out everything. The Lord took everything on himself, giving his life for mankind. Up to now I had not succeeded in recognising this sense of total forgiveness. In the sacrament of Reconciliation and Anointing of the sick I discovered an extraordinary liberating power, so much so that I would never want to deprive myself of such a grace.

I feel as though I am elsewhere, carried away in a dream. I feel well, very well...and yet according to those nearest to me, I was getting worse, even if I was not conscious of this. Back in the ward, I am on my bed, a little bit euphoric, happy; I feel elsewhere...

It was then I felt a sensation of cold, when it was warm outside, and this inner cold was quite disagreeable. Blankets and a hot water bottle are brought to me but the cold continues, more and more intense. I feel lethargic.

Then a sweet sort of warmth started from the tips of my toes, to my feet, my legs, my hips, my spinal column, and throughout my body, giving life to all the parts of my body paralysed by the sickness. The heat became all at once intense and difficult to bear. Suddenly I do not know how, I found myself on the edge of my bed, my legs dangling over the side. I am astonished and surprised to have made movements which I could not do before, when this very morning I had difficulty keeping the pilgrimage book open during the ceremony. I surprised myself in the act of stroking my hands, amazed to find feeling back in my skin and in my fingers.

I stay there, sitting up, trying to understand what has happened to me. I think back to the words which were said to me by the lady in white on Wednesday afternoon. Everything is difficult and it's like living a dream. And then this question comes to mind 'Why me, and not another person more handicapped than me?' Finally I decide to remain discreet, not daring to get up out of respect for the other sick who would not understand...

I am lost in these thoughts when my helpers come to fetch me for the closing Mass which will take place on the Esplanade. I tell them that I could go there in my wheelchair but they put me on the stretcher. There are strict instructions to observe and I comply with them. I let myself go along with this and trust in the Lord. I am astonished by the suppleness of my arms and wrists and no longer feel ill! I acclaim the Lord with my two arms raised up.

In the night, I am gently woken up. I felt someone touching me, which must be a helper wanting to cover me. I am completely awake and see no-one. Three o'clock sounds from the Basilica bells. Questioned afterwards, the night helper said that she did not remember coming to cover me in the night. I start to think of all the events of this pilgrimage, when an unexpected idea comes into my mind, like an order or an invitation: 'Get up and walk'. I think I am just having dreams, and also to get up in the night when I do not really want to... I am warm and no longer feel ill. I turn on my side, trying to chase this idea out of my mind. I close my eyes and try to get back to sleep. I can't avoid it! The call comes back, more insistent, more pressing than the first time. It makes me feel ill at ease. I turn over and over. The call is now very strong. Through this call, I hear an invitation to get up. It is insistent, yes, but with tenderness and respect for my freedom. Somehow, I feel free to respond or not. It is not words that I hear, but as if someone was speaking without saying any words. It's difficult to explain! 'Get up, it's time to walk!'

The night helper who heard me tossing and turning comes up and asks if I need something. I say that I need to get up, and I add...to go to the toilet. She gets ready to bring me my wheelchair, but I say that I want to go on foot, standing up. She replies that I will fall, and then she will as well. I insist, however, and she gives in. It is thus that I made my first steps, with no other support than her arm, tottering like a child who is learning to walk. I feel solid on my legs, although they have not functioned like this for a long time. It feels like living a dream completely awake. It seems unreal, and yet I am fully conscious of what is happening.

I say a whole rosary without falling asleep. Too many things were going on in my mind. I was not thinking of what I was saying. It is certain that each time I said a Hail Mary, I said 'Mother Mary, I love you!' like a child sunk inside the arms of his mother and who tells her how much he loves her. This rosary, said in the dark of night, probably for the first time in my life, was like a big thanksgiving for so many marvels and such tenderness. Morning arrived and I still had not slept, and I let my thoughts wander where they wanted.

Saturday 10th October. The entire ward is busily trying to prepare the way for the next set of pilgrims. Our priest shakes our hands and says a few words. I have an irresistible desire to tell him what has happened to me. I am scared of shocking everyone and, no, despite all I feel inside, it is not the time to talk about it...

We arrive at Lourdes station and the train is already there. Despite the objections of my helpers, I climb the few steps of the train by myself, without help, having taken under my arm the cushion of my wheelchair. I think that there also I was called to get up. Once in the carriage, a helper tells me that the places for the sick are at the other end of the train. I do not dare to walk up it by myself, in front of everyone. I ask the helper if she would mind helping me. She obviously has not understood because she took my cushion that is under my arm and sets off before me. No-one left to help me... I do not have the choice, all I have left to do is to follow her. I am very embarrassed as many people look at me and make comments like: 'That man, he was on a stretcher and now he is walking!'

The arrival in Angoulême was discreet. I go down the steps alone. My wheelchair awaited me at the foot of the steps of the train so I had to use it for the last time.

Reactions

Such an event wove a tapestry of unpredictable reactions and emotions in all who saw. As far as Jean-Pierre was concerned, 'What then happened with my wife and children cannot be said. It can only be lived. I can say that we did not have words to thank the Lord and Our Lady. Our whole beings were united in one thanksgiving prayer for such love, tenderness and kindness.' The blessed couple always said that it was 'a way of light' after that. Jean-Pierre does speak of the moment in which Geneviève discovers that he is a renewed man:

> It was only when we arrived at the house that she understood, when she asked me if I wanted my wheelchair. I replied that I no longer needed it. I got out of the car by myself and climbed unaided the sixteen steps which go up to the first floor, leaving to one side the lift which we had put in. As I climbed the stairs, I had a little heart pang. I was living this like a dream and my heart was full up when I realised what had happened.

He summarises his drastic physical improvement:

> My muscles, which had not functioned for a long time, were normal in a few weeks, without any rehabilitation, except the activities that I assigned myself afterwards. My fingers, which had many difficulties, started to function immediately, since I was able to write forty or so pages of a notebook, telling of all that I lived in Lourdes amongst my sick brothers. I was able to recount without any struggle to remember, reliving step by step all these marvellous events.

As he reflected on the future which lay ahead of him, he established in his head what his primary role was:

> My first duty is towards the family. It is the most important thing to preserve. It is the mission which the Creator gave me and everything revolves around this. Marriage is very special, listening to one another, constantly thinking about the other. It is with this personal investment that the family can grow, and flourish.

Geneviève recalls her thoughts on that singular night in October: 'It was a sign from God, a sign that He exists. No-one is forced to believe it. We are not exuberant people. I said, "Why not?" In the evening, we did a thanksgiving prayer, all four of us. We prayed and thanked God.' They were full of joy. The couple's two children reacted in different ways. 'My son did not say a lot for a few days,' Geneviève remembers. 'The third day, we saw him, head in his arms on his desk, crying and crying. "What is wrong?" we said. "I've just realised what has happened to you!"'

My daughter said, "Daddy, I love you like this," because when we were in the shops, she did not want to push the wheelchair.' Geneviève recalls that Jean-Pierre struggled at first with his cure and pondered, 'Why me?' but, through the examples of saints such as St Bernadette and St Thérèse, who were humble, he accepted. The family developed a strong devotion to 'Mother Mary' and, according to his wife, became immersed in total abandonment to God, whom they trusted as never before.

Above and beyond the family, the parish, the community and the medical team had to face the reality of Jean-Pierre's sudden cure. All were dumbfounded. Jean-Pierre records the medical point of view:

> As soon as I arrived back, I booked an appointment with the doctor. When he saw me, I think he must have wondered whether he was dealing with a double. Once the first effect of surprise had died down, I started to explain to him, with the eyes of faith, because without the enlightenment of faith, what I had lived would have no meaning. He listened to me, without interruption, then, visibly ill at ease, tried to find an explanation for this unbelievable situation. He explained to me that, sometimes, with a strong will to get better, a morale for all challenges, the "crowd phenomenon, the atmosphere in Lourdes...", all that could have triggered a shock... In actual fact, he did not find a plausible explanation. He just told me not to talk about it... But how could I not talk about it? Everyone could see me standing, when people were used to seeing me in a wheelchair or lying down the last weeks which preceded the pilgrimage. Hard to say that nothing had happened! I could not go back to my wheelchair! No, I wouldn't!

> I also booked an appointment with the specialist in neurology at the hospital. He had already heard from others about what had happened. I will never forget my entrance into the external consultations service. The doctor looked at me, stunned first of all, and then made me walk down the corridor. He said to me: 'I was told that you could walk, but I did not expect you to walk with such ease!'

> I told, once more, still with the eyes of faith, though I knew that the doctor did not share my convictions. Very respectfully, he listened, without interruption, taking many notes. I explained to him what my doctor had said to me and he replied that strength of will and crowd phenomena were not enough to lift up someone who had not walked for a long time, that a rehabilitation of several months would have been necessary. This phenomenon was inexplicable.

> He examined me in detail: completely normal reflexes. I remember that after each test, he said: "cleared, cleared...!" Everything had been cleared in a few hours, gone...

The doctor's conclusion was as follows: 'We are very surprised at the change that has led to spectacular improvement, from one day to the next, on 9th October 1987. Mr Bély has recovered a perfectly normal walk. The climbing of stairs is well-managed. There is no incontinence... I have no explanation as to the reason for this improvement.'

Geneviève tells of other extraordinary encounters: 'Another time at the hospital there was a physiotherapist who had helped him move his limbs every week, and who on seeing him said, "You've been to Lourdes!" There was another who said, "I have followed the wrong path. I will have to change my life." His old teacher saw him and said, "I'm telling you this but you mustn't talk about it. I believe now that someone is watching over us!"'

She reveals how the community reacted: 'He was able to get out his bike. One neighbour, when he saw, had tears in his eyes. Then the news got round: "Have you seen Monsieur Bély?" One man came by and said, "Have you seen Jean-Pierre? He climbed up a ladder!" Then, in the parish, on the following Sunday, there was a meeting of sick and disabled people. The curate said, "Where is Jean-Pierre? They're looking for a wheelchair." No-one had told him. I said, "He's here." Oh! It was a shock. It was a time for great thanksgiving.

Ten days later, the curate announced before the Mass, "Do you know in what state Jean-Pierre went to Lourdes? You will see that now he is standing!" People were moved, crying. A lady who always wore a lot of makeup was wiping her eyes. We prayed. It was difficult to sing! The emotion!'

She also speaks of Gilles, a man whose soul and being was affected by this transformation: 'He was someone who, when my husband was cured, came back to the parish to practise when he was never religious before. He said, "There is something!" He was faithful until last Sunday when he died. His wife said, "It's he who pushes me to go to Mass!"'

'A priest once said to him,' states Geneviève, "You who are the favourite of Our Lady," and he said, "No, I am not. She likes all of her children the same." Similarly, Geneviève recalls, 'Someone said, "Your husband is a saint!" I said, 'He's a man like any other. He has his weaknesses and his strengths!'

In the same way that fantasies were made about Jean-Pierre, fantasies were also made about 'the woman in white' who had told him that things would be put right. His wife recalls, 'Some said, "You saw Our Lady!" No, not Our Lady, she was just a normal girl in white, like a helper. He did not look to see if it was Our Lady or a saint.' Lourdes was a place to offer thanks above all. We went there four or five times per year.'

How did the family live through such an abrupt change in the person who, until his return from Lourdes, had been the weakest and most vulnerable family member? 'We lived it like anyone else,' is Geneviève's reply. Indeed, 'Very quickly, he entered into an active life. He did not think about his illness any more. He got involved in parish activities.'

One obstacle he did encounter, however, was the State's refusal to modify his status as one hundred percent disabled. He was not allowed to return to work. From then on, he called himself a 'healthy invalid.' Geneviève notes that the change in lifestyle brought with it some advantages: 'After his cure he had more time for his children.' His main intentions in prayer became 'above all peace in the world,' reveals his wife, 'and all sick people, so that they could have this trust in the Lord.' The inner healing improved Jean-Pierre's exchanges with others: 'He judged others less,' comments his wife, 'was more respectful of other people's lives, and always thankful. Sometimes, things would make me react, but he would say, "Let things sort themselves out."' Jean-Pierre proved that he was not invincible after his cure, but a healthy man as he should be, a child of God:

> I am like anyone, a victim of illness and accidents. It did not prevent me from jumping from a van and fracturing my left heel in three places... maybe it is to remind me that I have limits and that I mustn't forget them!

Visit to the Vatican

Jean-Pierre wrote in his testimony, which dates back to the time when John Paul II was Pope:

> At the beginning of the year 1989, I had the immense joy of meeting the Holy Father, our Pope John Paul II. This personal encounter touched me very much. I was able to share with him the wonders that the Lord had done for me, through the intercession of Mary.

Geneviève adds, 'When the Pope arrived in front of my husband, and they explained what had happened to my husband, the Pope called him, "The happy pilgrim of Lourdes" and he asked him to pray for him.' Soon after the visit, Bishop Claude Dagens of Angoulême, (Jean-Pierre's diocese), received a letter from the Vatican, which he then passed on to Jean-Pierre:

> The Pope has recognised the feelings of faith and love witnessed by the pilgrim and thanks in particular the prayers said for his intention.

He wishes this pilgrim from Lourdes to live in joy and thanksgiving and asks the Holy Spirit to fire up his heart to spread the good news of Christ through a generous missionary life in the paths of St Thérèse of the Child Jesus and St Bernadette. With affection, the Holy Father blesses him and his family.

Geneviève recalls her husband's reaction upon receiving the letter: 'He said to me, "How did he know that they were my favourite saints?"'

A miracle

This cure was soon to be recognised by the Church as a sign from God, a miracle. A miracle is by definition 'an extraordinary event, believed to be due to a benevolent divine intervention, to which is attributed a spiritual significance.' The process leading up to this conclusion was long and strenuous. The medical criteria for a cure are as follows:

...the illness has been authenticated and the diagnosis is correct; the prognosis of the disease must be clear cut, including those regarded as permanent or terminal in the near future; the cure is immediate, without convalescence, complete, definitive and lasting; and, the prescribed treatment could not have contributed to the cure or have been an aid to it.

On Thursday 6th October 1988, at his Bishop's request, Jean-Pierre came to declare his cure to the Medical Bureau of Lourdes. He wrote:

At the time, I was not very enthusiastic about entering in this long and difficult process. It's because a sign had been given, and that this sign does not belong to me, that I did not feel I had the right to keep it for myself. I had to tell, to go and tell... .

According to Geneviève, he was told not to bear witness to his cure as it had not been confirmed by the Church. The process lasted eleven years. Every year, he had to be seen at the Medical Bureau by between fifty and eighty doctors. On 17th June, 1992, Jean-Pierre was examined at the request of the International Medical Committee of Lourdes (CMIL). They concluded that 'such a cure is not just unusual but inexplicable'.

In November 1992, the Committee asked for a two-year delay to observe whether the cure was, as policy demands it, permanent. In Lourdes with the Rosary Pilgrimage in October 1998, Jean-Pierre was examined, for the last time, by one hundred doctors. He states,

I had started to become used to it and felt relatively at ease with them, despite quite embarrassing questions at times.

On 14th November 1998, after further detailed consultations and examinations, which proved at times very trying for Jean-Pierre, the members of the CMIL issued the following statement after a majority vote, written by Dr Patrick Theillier, Resident Doctor and Doctor-in-Charge of the Medical Bureau:

> It is possible to conclude, with a good margin of probability, that M. Bély suffered an organic infection of the multiple sclerosis type in a severe and advanced stage, of which the sudden cure during a pilgrimage to Lourdes corresponds with an unusual and inexplicable fact with regard to science. It is impossible for medical science to say anything more today. It is for the religious authorities, however, to make a pronouncement on the other dimensions of this cure.

In the Underground Basilica, at 10am on 11th February 1999, the World Day of the Sick and the anniversary of Our Lady's first apparition to Bernadette, Bishop Jacques Perrier of Lourdes and Tarbes officially recognised, in the name of the Church, the sixty-sixth miracle of Lourdes.

Geneviève recalls the furore in the aftermath: 'All the papers rang after the recognition of the miracle. After the bishop had a press conference, journalists from all over the world came.' Soon the Bélys had to go ex-directory. Newspapers in France and worldwide published articles about this extraordinary case, with titles from 'I hid my cure from my wife' to 'A sign from God' and 'Science surrenders to the inexplicable'. A Mass of thanksgiving was said in their own parish.

Jean-Pierre, however, never liked to think of his cure as a miracle, but as a sign from God or a healing. People listening to him talk would say amidst excitement and confusion, "It's a miracle! Why do you never talk of a miracle?" He considered, however, that the word 'miracle' was used in far too many contexts and that Jesus himself had never talked of a miracle, only signs. Do these words not echo those of Bernadette, who refused to call Our Lady by her name, and merely referred to her as a beautiful lady in white?

The sensational side of Jean-Pierre's cure which made headlines was ironically not the more powerful healing. It was his interior cleansing. Even with a healthy body, Jean-Pierre proved in his constant vulnerability to illness and accidents that we will always be limited. With God in one's heart, anything is possible. His wife claims: 'You have to explain to people that there are miracles that take place which are invisible, in the heart.' Jean-Pierre left the healing of his body behind him in a coffin, left to decay and crumble. He carried his interior healing with him into eternity.

'Go and tell'

When people ask me to say what happened in Lourdes, I do it with joy, but I never propose to witness in such and such a place. I am very keen to respect the freedom of each person. My witness is full of respect. You are free to believe it or not. Bernadette said, 'I am responsible for telling, but not for convincing.' I am not seeking to convince anybody but I simply desire to go and tell...*and I will go and tell...*!

And he did. His wife, who retired as a nurse in 1999 and who always accompanied him on his travels, says, 'We always wanted to bear witness. He often went to speak to secondary schools and colleges, twice in the morning, and sometimes two or three times in the afternoon and sometimes in the evening with parents or in parishes. It was very tiring. Each time he told the same story of his healing. I said, 'Do you want to slow down?' He said, 'No, I must continue to witness.' He didn't want to keep it for himself. He felt called to go and proclaim, tell the good news. That was the theme of the Pilgrimage the year he was cured.' They went as far as Austria and Belgium to bear witness to God's mercy and love. Sacrifice is the only proof of love. For Geneviève, their love for God which pushed them to share the story of Jean-Pierre's healing, was often a sacrifice of their life as a couple: 'Often, he was away and I didn't see him anymore! I said that when he was sick, I had him with me, but now that he is well, he escapes me!'

In his testimonies, Jean-Pierre always delivered a message of trust in God. His wife recalls, 'People would say, "Pray because my diabetic daughter is very ill," etc... He used to say, "I will pray and you pray with me, but I did not ask for my healing. Ask simply that this person can accept his or her state." It was the prayers of friends and the family, and it is everyone who is in Lourdes who prays for the healing of the sick. It was not he who asked for healing. It was the others. He referred often to the story of the paralytic at Capernaum. He didn't ask for healing. It was the others carrying him.'

Did the sick and disabled people listening to Jean-Pierre's testimony of his sudden healing find the story of this man's cure from a terrible disease difficult to bear? Geneviève reveals: 'There were able people who had said, "Does it not bother you to talk in front of very sick people?" In the North, in one of his testimonies, there was a man with multiple sclerosis who could hardly talk. He said, "Continue to testify. For us, you are a messenger of hope."'

God's workings on the human spirit

Once the miracle had been recognised, Jean-Pierre and those around him were able to reflect on the series of events with more clarity and understanding: In Jean-Pierre's testimony of 1999, Bishop Claude Dagens of Angoulême preceded Jean-Pierre's testimony with a few comments, written on 10th October 1999:

This testimony is profoundly revealing. It shows that God's action impacts both man as sinner and man as a sick person. In a miracle, we must not forget that there are two inseparable aspects: the forgiveness of sins and physical healing. If one wants to speak of a miracle, then let's do it in accordance with the spirit of the Gospel, remembering that a man who is forgiven and healed is called to witness to the great sign of contradiction of Jesus himself, the humiliated and glorified Saviour of whom we are the disciples. The story which is continuing in Lourdes is the history of salvation: a marvel in our eyes, especially when a sick person starts to walk again, but also the visible trace on earth of our living God, of Christ who comes to his own and waits always to be recognised by them. Luckily she is there, the Virgin Mary, to teach us to believe that nothing is impossible to God!

Jean-Pierre included some of his reflections in the testimony entitled, *My healing, sign of love*:

By the Sacrament of Anointing of the Sick, the Lord raised me up in my heart and in my body, and freely gave me an extraordinary strength to fight against all form of evil. The Lord gave me an amazing gift. He made me stand up again. He did not tell me to talk about it, he left me free in that regard. That explains my discretion at first. It is now that I feel that I have to go and tell but with great sensitivity, just as I received. It is not the spectacular aspects that I want to talk about, but everything that I received in the spiritual sense.

To children I say, 'Pray a lot with Our Lady, the Lord, with your parents, with all those you love!' To parents I say, 'Teach your children to pray with simple words, with their hearts.' To couples I say, 'Do not be afraid to take Mary for your mother! It is the Lord who gave her to us as mother at the foot of the cross. That is the surest guarantee of your bond as a couple and the way to defend yourself against the Evil one who tries unceasingly to infiltrate your lives to destroy them, but who will not be able to prevail. Think of that.'

In raising me up in my heart and in my body, the Lord asked me nothing in return, only to give Him much love and I will do everything to love my Lord and serve Him, with all the strength of my poor human nature, with all my weaknesses.

The Lord alone can heal us. He asks us to make ourselves very small before Him and to trust Him!

Ghosts revisited

In 1997, the faithful disciple, carer and love in Jean-Pierre's life contracted breast cancer. Geneviève was prescribed a chemotherapy treatment and lost her hair, as well as undergoing various operations. Although she recovered from it, she is moved in remembering her husband's loving attitude: 'He said, "We both fought together for me. In my turn, I can help you."' They had become indomitable and would not be conquered, particularly now that they had been given 'hearts of joy.'

In 2005, it was Jean-Pierre's turn. To everyone's shock and dismay, he contracted a cancer of the liver. Was he never to be permanently rid of illness? His wife observes that 'he suffered terribly in the last months.' It would have been excruciatingly painful for the family and for him if he had lost the gift of light given to him on 9th October 1987. Geneviève affirms, however, that his cure helped him to live through his last trials with great acceptance. By this time, his spirit far outweighed his body and mind. They seemed small and insignificant when he knew that all was a preparation for heaven, that if he offered up his suffering to God, God would take care of him.

During this period of uncertainty, Geneviève thought, 'If the Lord wants him to continue to witness He will have to do something.' Jean-Pierre did continue to witness, always with 'courage'. For example, he travelled to Lourdes in February 2005 with his wife to testify before a gathering of Hospitalité and sick and disabled people.

After regular visits from priests and reception of the Sacrament of the Sick at the beginning of October, which he declared was like 'a soft touch from the Holy Spirit' liberating him once more, he went on his beloved Rosary Pilgrimage to Lourdes in October 2005. His wife reflects that Lourdes was 'almost like a second home' by that time. The couple had filled in their inscription in August, when Jean-Pierre could still walk. Geneviève reveals, 'He was very sick when he went. The disease advanced very quickly. We thought it would be more sensible not to go. The doctor in the hospital saw that it gave him pleasure and gave him permission. In the end, he went as a sick person. From his bedroom he could see the Lourdes Basilica.' During his previous stay at the hospital, he was suffering from multiple sclerosis. Now, he was barely surviving with cancer. His wife recounts, 'The trip was very tiring for him. The first night, he had a fall from his bed and was transported to the Lourdes hospital. He didn't see the Grotto. He wanted to have a bath but he couldn't. People came to bring him Communion. He was only there for two to three days. From Lourdes, they took him back to the Girac hospital in an ambulance.'

Return to his healer

At home from Lourdes, Jean-Pierre was on a drip and hardly came back to the house.

Geneviève, who brought Holy Communion to her husband every day, recalls, 'He wanted to come back home for the last week, but he was too sick for me to keep him at home.' Finally, he came back to the place where so many emotions, prayers and love had been shared over the years.

The day after his return, during the night of 27th October 2005, Geneviève was by his side: 'It was a grace to be at his side. I think he only heard, because he was unconscious at the end. I saw that he was leaving and I said an Our Father and three Hail Marys. He wasn't afraid. The Lord takes people as they are. He trusted. At the last moment he was ready.'

Jean-Pierre and Geneviève, together at that moment and forever, married for thirty-seven years, said goodbye to each other as Jean-Pierre was taken to the Lord, his true healer. The one who had stood witnessing to all willing to hear had left. The one who had supported in the shadows and remained always faithful, would, as she had always done, follow on behind.

'Have trust'

Jean-Pierre Bély's funeral occurred on 31st October 2005 in the Cathedral of Angoulême. In his homily, Bishop Claude Dagens addressed the following message:

> He shone with God's goodness of which he had received a personal sign. He did not consider himself a hero. But with lots of modesty he was not afraid to say that you can hope for all from Our Lady, especially when we are afraid that we will be overcome by suffering. This faith in Christ, in the resurrection of Christ, dwelt in Jean-Pierre Bély until the end, and in particular in these last months. He knew that he had a cancer. But he stayed peaceful. In the month of June, when I went to see him in hospital, he spoke about another sick person who was just next to him, and who had a more serious disease than he did. And ten days ago during my last visit, we prayed together: I held his

hand, and I entrusted our diocese to him, and particularly our sick, so that they can exercise amongst us, as he did, a ministry of hope.

Dr Theillier, tells us: 'He lived a way of the cross. Like every believer it was a kind of martyrdom. His life was changed by his encounter with God.' For this doctor, there is a clear message in Jean-Pierre's healing and in the Lourdes experience: 'The word miracle is full of dangers. Yes, Lourdes is a place of healing above everything. A miracle is not contrary to the laws of nature, a very risky idea which developed some time ago. It is an action which works through the laws of nature, and goes further, we only know a tiny part of the laws of nature. The miracle is a small opening to the action of God today: he becomes a little more present and visible.'

François Vayne writes in the new edition of Jean-Pierre's testimony, published after Jean-Pierre's passing:

> 'Get up and walk': this call from Christ resounds today, each one of us can hear it, and answer it with the strength of faith, whatever the suffering, physical or mental...
>
> He knew how to receive others simply, get to the heart without detour or interpretation, radiating with a peace which was passed on from person to person, a sacred gift that we will tend for as long as possible as the best heritage that he left us.
>
> I was profoundly touched by this man's humility, always accompanied by his wife, a discreet and gentle woman. They lived in La Couronne, 'the crown', a name which could evoke both the crown of thorns of Christ and the crown of stars of the Virgin Mary, a unique mystery of suffering transformed into love which brings meaning to our journey on earth.
>
> Jean-Pierre and Geneviève were inseparable, bearers of a message of love which was completely beyond them. Since Jean-Pierre's cure, linked to the Sacrament of the Sick, their family life bathed in the light of the resurrection. They had placed God in the centre place and no longer belonged to each other, open to the liberating power of the Holy Spirit. One of their children, bearer of a handicap, chose a religious life, himself also a witness of the fraternal Kingdom which is already amongst us.

Indeed their son, who joined a monastery in 1995, made his solemn vows on 24th August, his father's birthday: 'That was another grace,' testifies his mother. 'He had said, "Dad, you know that it's not because you were healed in Lourdes that I entered the order." He was searching before his father was healed. When he entered, it was difficult for us but we knew he was there for the right reason. Since his profession, he is at ease. He used to have anxieties and he has lost that now. He has found his vocation.'

Since his death, Madame Bély testifies in her quiet way that she always feels her husband's presence and often relies on him to help her when she is faced with a challenge, like getting the computer to work or driving through heavy fog! She affirms that things are always put right. 'I have to keep living,' she tells us with a hint of her fighting spirit, trained in many battles. She has taken up some of his occupations, such as the page setup of a local newspaper. She also helps people who are in mourning like herself.

Above all else, she has taken up her husband's greatest message: 'Simply trust, even at the difficult moments. Always have trust. You must not say, "What will the future be?" You must not worry. You should leave things to the Lord.'

Acknowlegement

Thanks are due to M. Vayne and Mme Bély for permission to translate and use extracts from her husband's memoir, *Ma guérison, signe d'amour* (NDL Editions, n.d.).

CHAPTER 11

Lourdes:
Where Echoes Meet

I ADDRESS MY FINAL LOOK AT THE CROWNED STATUE OF OUR LADY. As I begin my walk out of the Domain, past the river and the well-used bridge and through the archway, aching pains stab at my heart, as I realise that this peaceful haven will soon be miles away and taken over by a more troubled world. There is no storm to destroy the heart in Lourdes, no wind to divert heavenly messages to some forgotten place. The completeness I have felt will soon be challenged. The encapsulating love will be tainted.

I am nearly at the top of the Domain, on the verge of taking a step through St Joseph's Gate into the town. What am I doing? Am I about to throw away the divine key? Whoever has heard of someone choosing to step out of the gates of paradise? Should I run back before it is too late? Something deep down is preventing me. I am not quite sure what it is. A quiet fire is burning in my soul, one which seeks to return and spread the good news from mountaintops and cry: *I believe in humanity! A seed of divine goodness lies within us all! Come and see!* This town is not mine to possess. It is a gift which has been laid in my heart, where divine echoes have met. In this place of sanctuary, God removed my hands from my ears and revealed the resounding echoes which call us to love. Now, as I collect my bags and make my way to the train, they have never been clearer.

Is it more miraculous that Jean-Pierre Bély was told in the depths of the night to get up and walk, or that bedridden Stuart Murrell has revealed that he feels strong enough after Communion to get up on his two feet? God's strongest gifts are often hidden from the public eye.

Lourdes became the greatest treasure of all for these nine people, who knew more than most of this little town's priceless value amidst the trials they faced. They guarded and nurtured this gift, as if it were an infant in need of care, and continue to testify to the unfailing power of healing.

Canon Seamus Hester recounts a story that occurred in Lourdes, in which society meets sickness, logic meets emotion and Man meets God.

'A parishioner of mine was very ill in hospital and it came to that crucial hour when the night staff were beginning to go off and reluctant to leave. It was very difficult because people were crying as this person was dying so I thought, "Let's start the rosary." I said the first decade and then I said to Dr Kevin Kelly, the Pilgrimage Chief Doctor, "Would you say the second decade of the mystery of the rosary?" I think he got to the second or the third Hail Mary, when he couldn't get through it. He just burst out crying. He suddenly began to realise that, as a doctor, he had never prayed as such with other people at the bedside of a dying person. He would come and do his medical bit and it would be appreciated but he never joined with the other members of the family in praying for the person.'

Another person who has been intimately exposed to the volcanic impact of sick and disabled people is John Sexton, the Pilgrimage photographer: 'It's been a great privilege for me to see Lourdes through the lens of a camera. I see things going on which are often deeply moving: a young teenage lad sitting at the side of a girl who is disabled in a wheelchair and she is dribbling and he is just very gently keeping an eye on her and wipes her mouth. Is that what he is doing each day when he is at home? And you discover, "No." He's not involved in any sort of care. He's not doing it because he's been told to do it. There is sort of a natural tendency and it is just a pure act of love.'

The visibly suffering are crucial to Lourdes, pulling divine strings to rescue people from illusion and lost lands. Their strong presence provides a contrast to society and reminds pilgrims of their essential humanity. 'They are representing the pain of the world,' believes Joy Keen, the mother of disabled Holly.

As Dr Theillier says, 'Here the presence of the visible sick liberates people to talk about suffering. The pilgrimage which has most progressed in the last twenty years is "Cancer and Hope". Twenty years ago, people did not talk about cancer. Now people accept to be seen with it. They speak with others. They live a very special time together. Even children come, and it has an extraordinary strength. They find the essential here. It is very mysterious. That is the strength of Lourdes: looking at sickness head on and overcoming it, finding out the hidden depths and meaning.'

Sophie Wellbelove believes, 'In Lourdes, if you're vulnerable, you're going to bring a lot more and get a lot more out of it because you're allowing yourself to be spoken to by God and you're allowing yourself to share with others part of yourself.'

There is something deep, something from within the physically needy, which is almost intangible. The pilgrim Chris Xerri states, 'I think these are the people showing the way to Jesus.' Dr Theillier testifies, 'I have known a person, Pierre Panis, who, for eighteen years, could only move an eye. He was immobile and needed two nurses all the time to look after him. The peace and serenity that he had could only come from heaven. It's not possible otherwise.'

Has Dr Theillier truly met sick and disabled people who belong to another world? 'Yes,' is his reply, 'from the inner world.' He adds, 'When the Virgin said to Bernadette, "I do not promise to make you happy in this world but in the next," it is not the future world, but it is the world of grace, and this world is in us, but we have hidden it with lots of layers. So the goal of the Virgin, helped by the symbol of the Spring, is to liberate this world, rediscover it, dig deep, find this real world. The great mystics live in this world. The great saints live in it. The healings remind us that this world is in us.'

What is the essence of Lourdes? Perhaps Sarah Clutton, who has been the Pilgrimage Co-ordinator for thirty-two years, could tell us from such a breadth of experience. She admits, however, 'There is something about Lourdes but I can't tell you what it is.' Are we destined never to grasp this holy place? Why is that we can describe to perfection a holiday on the beach but we just cannot reveal to others what is so special about Lourdes? It seems that our inability to capture this out of the ordinary sanctuary is the most powerful sign yet that God is at the heart of it, touching us beyond comprehension, bathing us in waters which are too deep for us to feel the ground.

Lourdes re-enacts God's coming to Man. Here, the ordinary becomes the sacred. 'Lourdes is an expression of the Incarnation,' believes Bishop Kieran Conry. Dr Theillier muses, 'We have too much tendency to see God as something exterior to us who is there at some moments and then disappears. But He is always in His creation. Lourdes is showing that God is still active: a continuation of the Gospel miracles.'

It is not about keeping one's feet on the ground and one's head in a divine, parallel universe. God finds us in Lourdes, in our smiles, our exchanges with others, our hugs, our pains. It is here that we realise that we are not called to be sub-human but asked to fulfil and live by our true humanity, which is one with Christ. It is a place for everyone. The reigning goodness is not the fruit of a selected gathering of 'good' people. It comes from God, who lifts up all who are there, regardless of their past and present and transfigures his processing people.

If a bereft child was hoping to feel the close touch of a mother once again on his cheek, then Lourdes, a place where the maternity of Our Lady is most profoundly experienced, could perhaps satisfy such a desire. Just as she comforted and advised Bernadette, so Mary continues to embrace her children today and lead them to God. Nick Brown recounts how he was a lost son guided by his mother: 'I was doing this big executive job flying all over the world, earning lots of money, eating in the top restaurants, making very big deals, chasing this career goal and I suddenly realised, "What am I doing?" The best time in my life each year is the week that I am helping other people in Lourdes. I thought, "I need to be doing something in the caring line." I've been one of those people saying that if you don't like what you are doing, you should do something else. And I wasn't listening to my own advice. I was at the Grotto one night about half way through the week and I knew instantly: I need to change, and I need to do this job. And I went back to the group next morning and said, "I am leaving my work" and told them what I was going to do. I was full of the joys of spring. I just knew instantly that that was what I was meant to do. It was my vocation. It took me a year to leave my job because of the interview process, and, for that year, I knew I was leaving and was so excited. I just love what I do now. Vocation doesn't have to be a religious vocation. There are lots of other vocations out there and mine was to work on the ambulances.'

Lourdes is 'the mother of God coming to us and saying to us we are loved but we have to do something about it,' believes Fr Dominic O'Hara. Fr Emmanuel Agius tells us, 'A parishioner of mine was in a wheelchair. Once he was in Lourdes, I said, "Dick, let's go to the Grotto and we'll pray for your recovery."

"No, no, no, no!" he said. "Don't interfere with her! She knows me quite well!"'

Dr Theillier believes, 'Our Lady wants to heal what is essential in us and what is essential today is to discover interior peace.' It is not by accident, he believes, that she appeared 'at the eve of a terrible century, the twentieth century,' when war led Man away from his true self and his relationship with God. Our Lady provided ammunition through Lourdes—

an oasis of spirituality in the violent deserts. Like any good mother, Mary leads us to the heart.

Cardinal Cormac believes, 'It's a living truth that while devotion to Our Lady is a very crucial part of the pilgrimage experience, she is pointing the whole time to her Son. In prayer, in the Eucharist, in everything we do, Lourdes is pointing to Him—with Mary having a special place.'

One pilgrim claims, 'It's like going to see my Mum.' She believes that Our Lady is precious to many mothers because they feel looked after and tended to. She recalls, 'When I was in the height of labour and in absolute pain, the midwife had told me to think of somewhere that was beautiful, calm and peaceful, and I thought of the Grotto. I just feel that I have been really looked after by Our Lady of Lourdes.'

Pilgrims learn that there can be no room for God in their lives where there is fear. Only in trust can He prevail. God is given His rightful place in people's suffering. 'Lourdes isn't "happy clappy", nor is it desperation,' states Fr Dominic O'Hara. Lourdes is that point where suffering and God meet. 'Our Lady allows you to weep,' reveals Maureen. 'She gives you the freedom to be at your most vulnerable and be accepted in that way.'

Fr Stephen Ortiger believes, 'Healing is to do with adjusting creatively to what has happened. It is the difference between a scar and a wound. A scar has been incorporated. It's very striking that Christ's wounds have not been airbrushed out. That is a code for getting hold of our past and incorporating it as a scar, not a bleeding wound.'

During the Sacrament of Anointing of the Sick, pilgrims place their hands in Christ's wounds. When Fr Ian Doyle stood up for the homily at this Mass in 2004, there was a hush, as there always is before a homily. Mild interest flickered in people's eyes as thoughts wandered to the sacrament which was yet to come. On the vast altar at the core of the immense Basilica, dotted with robed priests, Fr Ian spoke about a reality that we all fear and avoid. He told the eight hundred people, Bishop and child, sick and able, that from the age of ten until the age of twelve, he was sexually abused by a lodger in his parents' home. He recalled before all present that the counsellor who he talked to later on in life claimed that it was the worst story of child abuse that he had ever heard. He voiced that in his journey through priesthood he had found healing.

Ian had lowered his mask. The tangible scent of God in suffering gave way to the reality of Christ. Like Jesus on the cross with gaping wounds, Ian chose to be seen in nakedness. At that moment on the altar of St Pius X, he became the child who had been abused, the man who displayed his wounds and the priest who preached from the depths of his soul.

Although Lourdes is a town situated in the Pyrenean South, it is also a place in the heart. It stretches beyond all geographical boundaries. John Sexton speaks for many when he says, 'Lourdes is a very special place because heaven and earth have actually touched.'

If Lourdes is a piece of heaven, then its fruits can be found in anyone, anywhere. Cardinal Cormac suggests, 'Lourdes teaches people and enables people to live with a certain freedom which they don't feel in our culture. We're constrained in society in so many ways, in the culture of today, which don't fit into the deeper instincts of what is true and what is right. Young people long to be free, to be able to be freed. The famous poet Seamus Heaney once said to me: "It's Lourdes where you meet a risen people."' Pilgrims travel to Lourdes starving and return satisfied. It is a place which displays the ingredients for happiness and showers people with what they thought they did not need.

Nick Harvey says, "I feel very whole when I am out there. I feel very complete, very happy. It is the only place that I know which truly fulfils all my needs.' Dr Theillier adds, 'Lourdes is about the changing of hearts, which is a miracle that is not always easy to see, but is the essential of the experience. The essential is to accept the challenge of transformation and to open oneself to the sacred.'

Mike Carver simply marvels, '*Look* at what happens here. Humanity is at its best. Laughter and joy among some of the most awful suffering and circumstances. Friendship. Equality. Confidentiality. Loyalty. Selflessness. Christ with us.' Libby Sexton affirms, 'The only way I can describe my first time to Lourdes was that when I came home I felt that I'd been picked up by my feet and swung round in the air fifty times and stood back down again!' Following his trip to Lourdes, the young boy, Maks Tobiasiewicz, recalls, 'I saw myself looking at ordinary things and finding them extraordinary.' Shards of heavenly light were penetrating his life. The young Redshirt helper, Stuart Prior, reveals, "It's my favourite place on earth that I have been to so far. It's not really the south of France. It's a whole new world.'